SACRED PLACES

SACRED PLACES

SITES OF SPIRITUAL PILGRIMAGE FROM STONEHENGE TO SANTIAGO DE COMPOSTELA

PHILIP CARR-GOMM

Quercus

CONTENTS

Stonehenge, England

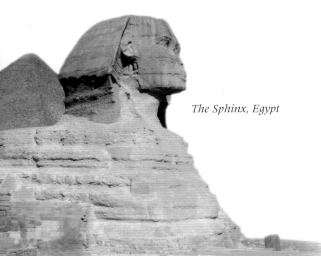

The Sphinx, Egypt

Previous page: Glastonbury Tor, England

Half Dome, Yosemite, USA

Temple carving, Angkor, Cambodia

INTRODUCTION

The Pure Land itself is near …
Truly, is anything missing now?
Nirvana is right here, before our eyes,
This very place is the Lotus Land,
This very body, the Buddha.

ZEN BUDDHIST MASTER HAKUIN'S *SONG OF ZAZEN* (C.1720)

I F YOU WALK TO THE END OF THE HOLLOWAY ROAD in the capital city of Wellington, New Zealand, you come to a pleasant area of grass and trees. Beyond this, a path beside a stream leads up into a small valley. The first time I followed this path, I found myself entranced by some intangible and magical quality that seemed present everywhere I walked. Then I came upon a clearing where crystals, feathers and prayer-ties hung from the branches. Other people clearly felt it was magical too.

Over time I learnt the story of this special spot. It used to be a dumping ground for old beds and fridges until the local community decided to clean it up and turn it into the Waimapihi Reserve. And now it has become a sacred place where people go to celebrate birthdays, to remember friends who have passed away, or just to walk in the woods and find peace in the middle of the city. What an inspiration – that a local community can succeed in turning one small spot on the Earth from a rubbish dump into a paradise!

Sacred Places are like doorways to another world, reminding us that life is more mysterious and wonderful than we can ever imagine. They evoke awe and reverence in us. For some, a sacred place will be connected with their religion – it will be a place of miracles, or where a key figure in their tradition was born, died or gained enlightenment. For others it will be, like the Waimaphi Reserve, a place in nature whose grandeur or beauty evokes a sense of wonder that stills the questing heart and mind with its powerful presence.

This book features sites that are considered sacred by the major world religions, and places of great antiquity that are seen as sacred by many, such as the Pyramids and Stonehenge. Places of great natural beauty and those connected with indigenous traditions have also been included, alongside some remarkable and lesser-known sites, such as Perperikon in Bulgaria and the Chauvet Cave in France.

A waterfall in the canyon at Yellowstone Park, Wyoming, USA. Awe-inspiring natural features such as this have long been revered as sacred places.

Most sacred sites are rooted in the past, but new sites are sometimes created and two have been included here, both coincidentally in Italy: The Tarot Garden in Tuscany and the Temples of Humankind in Valchiusella. Whether new or old, the sites have been arranged by continent, starting in that great crucible for humanity: Africa.

A pilgrimage to any sacred place can be a deeply fulfilling experience. But increasingly 'spiritual tourism', which includes New Age as well as conventional pilgrimage, is taking its toll on many of these sites, and on the environment in general. Encouraged by lower airfares, this kind of travel is growing exponentially – 70 million journeyed to the *Kumbh Mela* in India in 2000, 6 million to Jerusalem and 2 million to Mecca for the Hajj. The sacred mountains of China are now tourist attractions with cable cars ferrying visitors to heights once frequented only by sages and devout pilgrims.

Map of the world showing the location of the sacred sites covered in this book; the inset shows those sites that are located in Europe and the Middle East.

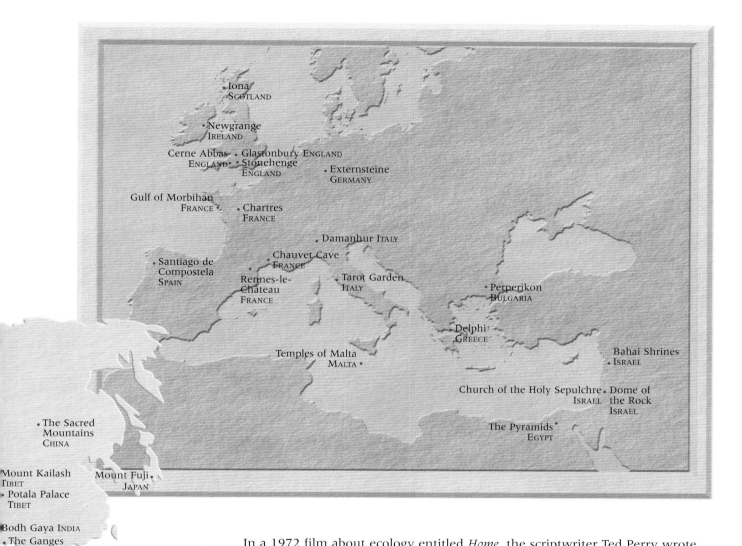

Iona
SCOTLAND

•Newgrange
IRELAND

Cerne Abbas • Glastonbury ENGLAND
ENGLAND• •Stonehenge
ENGLAND

•Externsteine
GERMANY

Gulf of Morbihan
FRANCE •

•Chartres
FRANCE

•Damanhur ITALY

Chauvet Cave
FRANCE

•Santiago de
Compostela
SPAIN

Rennes-le-
Château
FRANCE

•Tarot Garden
ITALY

•Perperikon
BULGARIA

•Delphi
GREECE

Temples of Malta
MALTA •

Bahai Shrines
• ISRAEL

Church of the Holy Sepulchre •Dome of
ISRAEL the Rock
ISRAEL

The Pyramids•
EGYPT

•The Sacred
Mountains
CHINA

Mount Kailash
TIBET
• Potala Palace
TIBET

Mount Fuji•
JAPAN

Bodh Gaya INDIA
•The Ganges
INDIA
• Luang Prabang
LAOS

• Angkor
CAMBODIA

•Uluru and Kata
Tjuta
AUSTRALIA

Tongariro and Taupo•
NEW ZEALAND

In a 1972 film about ecology entitled *Home*, the scriptwriter Ted Perry wrote the following prescient words about our stewardship of the planet that were later falsely attributed to the Native American leader Chief Seattle (c.1786–1866): *'Whatever befalls the Earth befalls the sons and daughters of the Earth. We did not weave the web of life; we are merely a strand in it. Whatever we do to the web, we do to ourselves.'*

We undoubtedly need sacred places to inspire us, and the economies of many of the local communities in these places depend upon visitors, but more than ever before we need to be aware of the inherent sacredness of all the planet. The idea of 'thinking globally and acting locally' can now be applied to sacred sites. Books, films and the internet can educate us about distant sites and help us visit them in our hearts and minds, and we can help to preserve them, and the environment, by visiting them only occasionally if we feel the need. And like the residents of Holloway Road in Wellington we can create new sacred places locally – inspired perhaps by the stories of those that already exist all over the world.

Philip Carr-Gomm

9

MOUNT KILIMANJARO

Ernest Hemingway immortalized the magnificent peaks of Africa's highest mountain in The Snows of Kilimanjaro, *but long before he wrote this story, the legend of King Menelik of Abyssinia – the son of King Solomon and the Queen of Sheba – haunted this mountain, which is known as 'The Roof of Africa' and 'The House of God'.*

IT IS SAID THAT THE KING SLEEPS WITHIN THE MOUNTAIN, surrounded by jewels and gold. Since no climbing skills are needed to reach its seven peaks, every year thousands of visitors come to trek up the slopes – many of them seeing their experience as both a spiritual pilgrimage and a personal challenge.

The mountain is considered sacred by the people who live in the region – including the Chagga and Masai – and often their dead are buried facing the mountain.

Gazing up at a mountain you feel humbled and uplifted at the same time. The possibility of achieving its peak tantalises you – it seems to tell you that if you could reach its summit you could realize all your dreams. Mount Kilimanjaro, the highest mountain in Africa, has had just this effect on countless travellers.

Located some 250 miles (400 km) south of the equator, on Tanzania's northern border with Kenya, the highest of Kilimanjaro's three volcanoes reaches a height of almost 6000 m (20,000 ft) and yet this summit can be reached by anyone who is reasonably fit and who can cope with the hazards of altitude sickness and scree slopes that are sometimes too icy to traverse. Between 10 and 20,000 people a year

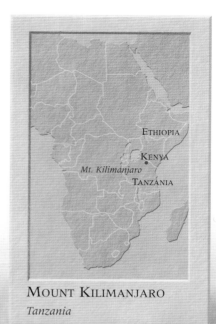

MOUNT KILIMANJARO
Tanzania

The mist-enshrouded summit of Mount Kilimanjaro: a place believed to be sacred by local inhabitants and inspiring awe in thousands of visitors each year.

Ernest Hemingway, shown here on a hunting trip, is credited with bringing this mystical mountain to the world's attention in The Snows of Kilimanjaro – *a story considered by many to be his finest work.*

attempt the climb, but only about 40 percent of these achieve the summit. For many the experience is a spiritual one, and climbing to the 'Roof of Africa' has made Kilimanjaro one of the world's major pilgrimage sites. Sadly global warming is starting to have an effect on the mountain's glaciers and snow cover – scientists estimate the plateau ice cap will be gone by 2040.

THE HOUSE OF GOD

As well as being Africa's tallest peak, Kilimanjaro is the world's largest free-standing mountain and it supports five different eco-zones: rainforest, heath, moorland, alpine desert and glaciers. As you trek up the mountain over a number of days you may see elephants and buffalo on the lower slopes, monkeys in the forest belt, and buzzards and mountain eagles as you climb higher. At about 4000 metres (13,000 ft) all fauna and flora disappear due to the cold, apart from some mosses and lichens. On the summit, three glaciers and the mountain's three volcanic peaks rest in silence above the vast plains of east Africa spread out before you over 3.5 miles (5.5 km) below.

While nobody is sure of the origin of the name Kilimanjaro, it is thought that it may mean 'Shining Mountain' in Swahili. The Masai regard it as a holy place and call its summit 'Ngaje Ngai', meaning 'The House of God'. But early inhabitants of the area apparently believed the mountain was guarded by evil spirits – or by 'Njaro' – a demon who caused frostbite and cold to any who dared come near.

The first mention of the mountain by a European was made by the Spanish geographer Fernandes de Encisco in 1519, who wrote: 'West of this port (Mombasa) is the Ethiopian Mount Olympus, which is very high, and further off are the mountains of the moon in which are the sources of the Nile. In all this country are much gold and wild animals'. But it took until 1848 for the so-called 'civilized' world to really take note of Kilimanjaro, when two German missionaries, Johannes Rebmann (1820–76) and Ludwig Krapf (1810–81), wrote of a snow-covered mountain in Africa that reached the sky. The scientific community initially reacted with disbelief – for how could there possibly be snow near the equator? By the end of 1884 the geographer Henry Hamilton Johnston (1858–1927) had trekked all around the perimeter of the mountain but did not attempt to climb higher, believing that nobody could survive there due to lack of oxygen. In 1889 the German explorer Hans Meyer (1858–1929) and Austrian mountain climber Ludwig Purtscheller (1849–1900) became the first to reach the summit along with their guide Johannes Kinyala Lauwo (1871–1996).

THE MOUNTAIN SNOWS

It took a short story – Ernest Hemingway's (1899–1961) *The Snows of Kilimanjaro* – for the mountain to become world famous, and to start to attract climbers and visitors in their thousands – many of whom saw it as a chance to make a pilgrimage to one of the world's most spectacular sites. Many consider the story to be Hemingway's finest. It was first published in *Esquire* magazine in 1936, and then appeared in a collection in 1938 before being turned into a feature film starring Gregory Peck (1916–2003) and Ava Gardner (1922–90) in 1952. *The Snows of Kilimanjaro* is almost certainly autobiographical – it is the story of a writer who is dying of gangrene near the mountain. Regretting his past, the mountain calls to him as a symbol of innocence and purity that rises above the world of misery and corruption. Just before he dies he has an ecstatic vision of the summit – he discovers the 'House of God' on the archetypal holy mountain.

KING SOLOMON'S RING

While Hemingway's story drew the attention of the world outside Africa to Kilimanjaro's snowy peaks, within Africa itself another story that is far more ancient worked its magic. Legend tells of Menelik, the first king of Abyssinia and the son of King Solomon and the Queen of Sheba. During his reign he had conquered a vast swathe of territory that included much of the lands we now call Somalia, Kenya and Tanzania. Returning home from one of his conquests with the spoils of war, he and his army came to the slopes of Kilimanjaro. They pitched camp on the desert-like stretch of land between the peaks of Kibo and Mawenzi. As night descended, Menelik gazed out at the stars shining over the snow-clad mountain and the wide plains below. He came to understand that his life was about to end – he was now an old man, and he knew what he had to do. The next morning he bid his army farewell and began to climb the mountain, accompanied only by a few of his warriors and slaves who carried his jewels and treasure. On reaching the crater of Kibo, one of Kilimanjaro's seven summits, Menelik bid his warriors farewell and entered the crater with his slaves and jewels – never to be seen again.

There he will sleep forever with the magical ring of his father King Solomon on his finger until one of his descendants climbs the mountain, finds the jewels and treasure and places the ring upon his own finger. At that moment, standing in the House of God, on the Roof of Africa, the new king will absorb the heroic spirit of Menelik and will possess the wisdom of Solomon. He will restore the land to its former glory. Kilimanjaro and the land to the north, east, west and south of it will once again be part of the great empire of Abyssinia.

TIMELINE

960 BC Obsidian tools, stone bowls and rings found on western slopes

2nd century AD The first written reference to Kilimanjaro, in Ptolemy's *Geographia*

1000–1500 The Kamba occupied the Mount Kilimanjaro area

1519 Spanish geographer Fernandes de Enciso writes of the mountain

1848 Johannes Rebmann and Ludwig Krapf make the existence of Kilimanjaro known in Europe

1936 Hemingway's *The Snows of Kilimanjaro* published in *Esquire* magazine

1952 *The Snows of Kilimanjaro* appears as a film

> **"*Wide as all the world, great, high, and unbelievably white in the sun.*"**

ERNEST HEMINGWAY, *THE SNOWS OF KILIMANJARO* (1936)

BANDIAGARA

The Cliffs of Bandiagara have been inhabited for over a millennium. Caves in the soft sandstone were once home to the Tellem; this pygmy tribe was eventually assimilated or pushed out by the Dogon people, whose ancient lifestyle continues even today, in villages along the breathtaking escarpment. For the Dogon, their rugged homeland is alive with the spirits of their ancestors.

THE FIRST INHABITANTS OF THE BANDIAGARA CLIFFS were the Tellem, a tribe of pygmies who excavated cave dwellings there in the 11th century – gaining access to the cliff-face by scrambling up strong vines. The area's current inhabitants are nearly half a million Dogon. Most are animists, practising a religion that honours the ancestors and involves feasting, dancing and the use of ritual masks. Elders and sages, known as Hogons, live outside the villages in the foot of the cliffs, and are supposed never to leave their houses. Only their wives are allowed to bring them food, and they are not permitted to bathe in water – instead, the sacred serpent Lébé is thought to visit them every night and lick them clean to purify them.

Some believe the Dogon were visited by extraterrestrials from Sirius who gave them detailed astronomical information. Others believe there are more down-to-earth explanations for the symbolism of their paintings and legends.

'THE PLACE OF THE CROCODILES'
If you were to travel to the highlands of west Mali, you would find – not far from that ancient and legendary city of Timbuktu – a great escarpment of sandstone cliffs rising to a height of 609 metres (2000 ft) and running for 125 miles (200 km) across the landscape, forming one of the most imposing landscapes in West Africa.

"Among many African peoples, ancestralism is part of the religious system of the people. The dead assume responsibility for those they have left behind. Crucially, they are in direct contact with all the higher spirit forces of the universe, and consequently with the Supreme Being Him/Her Self. They act as intermediaries, interveners and interpreters between the living, to whom they are still linked by blood, and the spirit forces whose world they share in their condition."

GHANAIAN WRITER KOFI AWOONOR

Previous page: A cliff village, nestled in the Bandiagara Escarpment in Mali. These cliffs have been inhabited for nearly 1000 years.

Masked dancers, taking part in the Sigui Ritual, a colourful and mysterious ceremony of the Dogon's animistic religion.

The Dogon are a people rich in mythology and religious practices. Mali itself is named after the hippopotamus, and its capital, Bambara, is the 'Place of the Crocodiles'. According to Dogon legend, their people originally came to the region from the northwest, crossing the wide River Niger on the backs of crocodiles, and for this reason they consider the creature sacred. In reality they were probably helped across by the tribe with whom they feel most connected – the Bozo – known locally as 'masters of the river'.

Whereas most of the Bozo, and most of the population of Mali, are Muslim, the majority of the Dogon (now numbering at least 450,000) continue to practise their ancient animistic religion.

They arrived at the cliffs in the 13th or 14th century. The Tellem had already been there for at least two centuries, and for another 200 years these two tribal

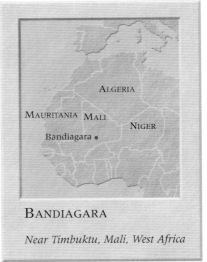

BANDIAGARA

Near Timbuktu, Mali, West Africa

groupings shared the region until the Tellem were either assimilated by the Dogon, driven away, or wiped out by another people – the Songhai. Whatever their fate, a number of Tellem granaries still remain among the 700 or so villages in the area.

THE SIGUI RITUAL AND THE SIRIUS MYSTERY

One of the most interesting rituals that takes place in the Bandiagara region is the ceremony of Sigui, in which a secret language is spoken by the men, who wear fabulous masks and dance in procession from village to village. The ceremony honours the first ancestor of the Dogon, and takes place every 65 years, taking several years to complete. The last one started in 1967 and ended in 1973. The next one will start in 2032.

In 1965 a book by the French anthropologist Marcel Griaule (1898–1956) appeared posthumously, detailing his conversations with a blind Dogon hunter. The information given to Griaule suggested that the Dogon possessed astronomical information that it was impossible for them to know – about Jupiter's four moons and Saturn's rings, and about the existence, density and rotational characteristics of the companion star of Sirius (Sirius B), which is invisible to the naked eye without a telescope.

This extraordinary information was picked up by the American author Robert Temple (b.1945), whose influential and controversial book *The Sirius Mystery* suggested that the Dogon could only have received this knowledge from extraterrestrials. Most scientists were unconvinced, agreeing with eminent astronomer Carl Sagan's (1934–96) assessment: 'There are too many loopholes, too many alternate explanations for such a myth to provide reliable evidence of past extraterrestrial contact.' Other anthropologists working among the Dogon have failed to find the same information told by the old hunter, despite spending years in the field and mastering the language – neither of which Griaule had done. Instead they suggest that the information may have come to the old hunter via Europeans, or even Griaule himself, who was a keen astronomer. Despite this, the art, customs and religion of the Dogon remain magnificent and mysterious, and Bandiagara remains an area of enormous power and enchantment.

TIMELINE

11th century Bandiagara inhabited by the Tellem

13/14th century The Dogon arrive from the northwest, either driving out the Tellem, or merging with them over the next 200 years

1770 The city of Bandiagara is founded by Nangabanu Tembély, a Dogon hunter, during a period when the jihads triggered by the resurgence of Islam resulted in the search for slaves as mercenaries. The Dogon then moved their villages to defensible positions along the walls of the escarpment

1864 Tidiani Tall chooses Bandiagara as capital of the Toucouleur empire

1965 French anthropologist claims Dogons knew detailed astronomical information

1975 Robert Temple's book *The Sirius Mystery* suggests the Dogon were visited by extraterrestrials from Sirius 5000 years ago

1989 Cliffs designated a World Heritage Site by UNESCO

> *" The breast is second only to God.*
> *A feeble effort will not fulfil the self.*
> *No one knows if a bird in flight has an egg*
> *in its stomach. "*

DOGON PROVERBS

THE SOURCE OF THE BLUE NILE

Ethiopia is one of the most evocative and exotic of African countries. Out of its highland mountains, the sacred source of the Blue Nile at Gishe Abbai flows into Lake Tana with its clear blue water and dozens of islands. There, monasteries preserve relics and hold fast to legends of the Ark of the Covenant, the history of the Queen of Sheba and the empire of Abyssinia. This rich heritage of the Ethiopian Orthodox Church offers inspiration and solace to a people whose lives have been devastated by war, drought, famine and political upheaval.

I<small>N THE IDYLLIC TOWN OF</small> B<small>AHIR</small> D<small>AR AT</small> the southern end of Lake Tana you can gaze north towards the ancient capital of Gondar, known as the 'Camelot of Africa', and imagine in the distance the city of Axum, where the Ethiopian Orthodox Church claims the biblical Ark of the Covenant (the sacred receptacle for the Ten Commandments) now rests. Although most Western historians are sceptical of this claim, an armed guard is posted outside the shrine in which the relic is housed in the church of Our Lady Mary of Zion.

A proverb in Amharic – the official language of Ethiopia, which has around 75 dialects – states 'Ye abbaien Inate Wuha Temat'. This means 'the mother of Abbai (the Blue Nile River) is dying of thirst'. Although the proverb might sound very simple, it has a deep resonance for Ethiopians, who live continuously under the shadow of drought and famine.

THE WHITE AND THE BLUE NILE

Sitting beside a river it is easy to become absorbed in contemplation. As the water flows past, we see before us a living example of both transience and permanence – the water changes continuously, though the river stays the same. Looking downstream, we can focus

Two fishermen in traditional papyrus-reed boats crossing the calm waters of Lake Tana just above Tis Isat Falls in Ethiopia.

on our goals, our destinations, our end. On the other hand, gazing upstream reminds us of our origins, our beginning and of our ultimate source beyond the world of time.

If you travel up the Nile, searching for its source like a spiritual seeker searching for the source of their own Being, you leave the safe and bustling world of the Mediterranean to travel past the ruins of Ancient Egypt and through the Nubian desert to arrive at Khartoum. There you are faced with a choice, as the river divides into two great tributaries. If you follow the river that flows southeast from Khartoum, the White Nile, you come to the Great Lake region of central Africa. To find the farthest source you would have to travel onward to the beginning of the Kagera river in Burundi. But it would be wiser to take the river that flows southwest from Khartoum, the mysterious Blue Nile, whose source lies in the remote highlands of Ethiopia.

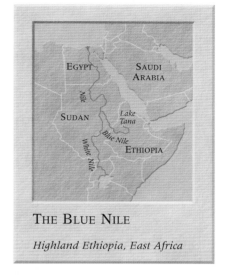

THE BLUE NILE

Highland Ethiopia, East Africa

The Blue Nile is the major contributor to the Nile of both water and fertile sediment, and following the river, if you can avoid its fierce crocodiles and the bandits who roam the area, you arrive at the spectacular Tis Isat Falls. Above the Falls you come to the origin of the Blue Nile itself: Lake Tana, the largest lake in Ethiopia, with intensely blue, clear water, and monasteries and churches situated on 20 of its 37 islands.

" I would love to live
Like a river flows,
Carried by the surprise
Of its own unfolding. "

IRISH POET JOHN O'DONOHUE,
BEANNACHT ('BLESSING')

THE TREASURES OF LAKE TANA

The monasteries on this tranquil lake, which were built between the 14th and 17th centuries, are filled with paintings and relics, including the mummified remains of emperors in glass cases. Monks on the holy island of Tana Qirqos believe that it was once a sanctuary for the Ark of the Covenant, and that the Virgin Mary rested here on her journey back from Egypt.

The region around Tana is home to the three principal cities of the ancient Abyssinian empire: Gondar, with its many castles, Lalibela, famous for its subterranean rock-hewn churches, and Axum, ancient capital, birthplace of the Queen of Sheba, and for some, the present-day home of the Ark of the Covenant. Farmland and grassland surround the lake, but also forest with wild coffee growing in the undergrowth. Vervet monkeys scamper around the canopy, hornbills and parrots screech in the air, papyrus grows in the water while acacia and huge figs grow by the shore.

At the southern end of the lake lies Bahir Dar. Emperor Haile Selassie (1892–1975) built his palace here, and its proximity to the lake and its broad palm-lined avenues make it the most pleasing city in Ethiopia.

North of the lake is the most sacred part of this region. At a height of nearly 1829 metres (6000 ft) the small spring of Gishe Abbai in the foothills of the Semien Mountains is believed by many to be the true source of the Blue Nile, and is revered as holy by Ethiopian Christians. Snow often falls on the mountains here, which are home to ibex, baboons and Ethiopian wolves, as well as many villages reached only by footpath, which once acted as important refuges for Ethiopian Jews.

The Tis Isat Falls (meaning 'smoking fire') near Bahir Dar plunge more than 45 m (150 ft) and form the second largest waterfall in Africa. However, by June every year they are virtually dry.

Monks arriving for morning mass at the Beta Giorgis (St George) church at Lalibela in highland Ethiopia. The 11 extraordinary rock-hewn churches here date from the 12th and 13th centuries.

Lake Tana may be the source not only of the Blue Nile but also of the tradition of coffee-drinking: a local legend tells of a goatherd named Kaldi who noticed that his goats became more active after chewing coffee cherries. He tried eating them himself, and recommended them to a passing monk who tried them too. Soon his monastery near Lake Tana was growing coffee, which the monks used to help them stay awake during their night vigils.

AN INTREPID EXPLORER

In the 1770s a Scottish explorer, James Bruce (1730–94), claimed that he had discovered the source of the Blue Nile, but his account seemed so implausible that he was ridiculed by Samuel Johnson (1709–84) and other influential contemporaries. Bruce had survived a shipwreck, a death sentence in Sudan, the perils of the Nubian desert and bandits, and had arrived at Gondar in February 1770. There he lived for two years, commanding the emperor's horse guard in battle, before returning home. As a freemason, Bruce may well have been on the trail of the Ark of the Covenant; his reputation was only redeemed a century later, when Europeans began to reach the region and heard accounts of Bruce's adventures there.

TIMELINE

1565 The first European description of the area at the Tis Isat Falls by John Bermudez

1768 James Bruce sets out to discover the source of the Nile

1770 Bruce reaches Lake Tana

1772 Bruce leaves Ethiopia

1790 Bruce publishes his *Travels to Discover the Source of the Nile* but is stigmatized as a liar

1970 Completion of the Aswan Dam ends the annual Nile floods

2001 The Nile Basin Initiative started

2004 Geologist Pasquale Scaturro and filmmaker Gordon Brown become the first people to navigate the entire Blue Nile

2005 Canadian Les Jickling and New Zealander Mark Tanner become the first to canoe the length of the Blue Nile from Lake Tana to the Mediterranean

THE NILE BASIN INITIATIVE

Today, while the region closest to the lake is fertile, northern Ethiopia is facing droughts and desertification on an alarming scale. Although the Blue Nile and other Ethiopian tributaries account for up to 90 percent of the Nile's total water supply, these resources have been almost totally neglected, partly because of a lack of irrigation systems and partly due to impediments in international law and competing demand from other countries (the river serves 300 million people, half the population of Africa). The Nile Basin Initiative, started in 2001, aims to help all the countries that depend on the river develop sustainable use of its resources for hydroelectric power, drinking water and irrigation.

Yet, for all its current ecological and political misery, Ethiopia remains an intensely sacred place. It is home to not only the source of the life-giving Blue Nile but also to an ancient denomination of Christianity that first took root in this region in around 330 AD, and which commands the fierce loyalty of its adherents. This devotion, along with the region's harsh mountainous terrain, helped preserve the unique culture of Ethiopia over the centuries, as the rest of North and East Africa came under the sway of Islam from the late 7th century onwards.

LAKE FUNDUDZI

Nestling in the lush and fertile terrain of Limpopo Province in northeastern South Africa is a lake and forest that even today has managed to resist the onslaught of tourism. The people of this region, the Venda, hold Lake Fundudzi and the surrounding forest of Thathe Vondo in such great reverence that visits may only be arranged by permit.

I N ONE OF SOUTH AFRICA'S LEAST VISITED AREAS, just below the arc of the great Limpopo River that marks the country's border with Botswana and Zimbabwe, lies Venda – homeland of the VhaVenda people (often known simply as the Venda). This is a land of high mountains and peaceful valleys, dense forest and an abundance of clear water. To the north is the magnificent site of Great Zimbabwe, while the northwest, beside the Limpopo, contains the ruins of Mapungubwe, capital of a thriving medieval kingdom. Meanwhile, to the south, the Soutpansberg Mountains guard the Venda's most precious secrets.

At the heart of the Venda region lies the sacred Lake Fundudzi (which means 'The Place of Learning') and the equally revered forest of Thathe Vondo. No-one is allowed to bathe or swim in this lake and access for visitors is strictly controlled and limited. If you are lucky enough to get anywhere near the lake, you will be asked by tribal guides not to look directly at it, but to honour the ancestors by facing away and bending down so that you can only see the lake upside down, through the gap between your legs, or by turning your back to the lake, looking at it over your left shoulder and advancing backwards, as is the custom for any of the numerous holy places in Southern Africa.

LAKE OF THE ANCESTORS AND THE HOLY FOREST

Lake Fundudzi's great sanctity derives from the Venda belief that it is the resting place of the *vhadzimu*, the gods, and the abode of water spirits and humans who after death become fish that

Lake Fundudzi in South Africa. The Tshiavha clan of the Venda are known as the vhatavhatsindi, *or 'guardians of the lake', and are responsible for preserving its sanctity.*

swim in the sacred waters. Some say that it is a 'zombie lake' where buried ancestors come alive at night and play drums beneath the water. And when the water is clear you can observe the inhabitants of a submerged village going about their daily business.

Offerings of sorghum beer are often made to the ancestors by a supplicant attached to a rope – so that he can be quickly pulled out should the lake spirits try to capture him.

Surrounding Lake Fundudzi is the Thathe Vondo forest. Although some of the land has been cleared for farmland and tea growing, the remaining forest is so thick it is almost impenetrable in many places. Within the forest is 'The Holy Forest' where the chiefs of the Thathe clan are buried. Few Venda people dare approach this area, which is believed to be filled with spirits. A white lion, spirit of Chief Nethathe, might be seen – or the lightning bird Ndadzi.

ZIMBABWE
BOTSWANA
Lake Fundudzi
Pretoria
SOUTH AFRICA

LAKE FUNDUDZI

Limpopo province, South Africa

TIMELINE

9th century The establishment of the first Venda kingdom of Mapungubwe

*c.*12th century The Venda probably settle in the Fundudzi region

13th century The stone city of Great Zimbabwe is built

19th century Europeans overrun the region

1979 The Republic of Venda recognized by the South African government

1990–4 Nelson Mandela released and South Africa's apartheid laws repealed

1994 The ANC wins elections, but Venda protest groups claim they are experiencing a new apartheid, as their sacred sites remain unprotected and their holy forests are exploited

You might also see *Zwidudwane*, creatures half-human and half-spirit, although just to see them means certain death. Offerings are sometimes left for them on a flat rock above the Phiphidi waterfall in the forest. At night the spirits can be heard taking the gifts down to the Guvhukuvhu pool at the foot of the waterfall. From the pool emerge the sounds of ghostly drumming and singing.

THE CROCODILE ROCK

The Venda also believe that a white crocodile once lived in Fundudzi. Crocodiles swallow stones to aid their digestion; perhaps in an attempt to possess the spirit of the albino crocodile and acquire its strength, Venda chiefs observe a tradition of swallowing a small white rock, which is passed down the generations in a highly unusual way. When a chief dies, his body is placed on a wooden platform and allowed to decompose. Once the flesh has fallen from the bones the white rock that he swallowed is retrieved and swallowed by the new chief. To prevent theft of the rock or it being swallowed by the wrong candidate, the body is guarded by women.

The lake today is still home to crocodiles and – according to Venda belief – a giant python god of fertility, who is honoured in the Domba Dance, which forms a major part of the initiation rites for young Venda women. In the centre of the village clearing a ritual fire is lit by the medicine man. The master of ceremonies then calls out 'The python uncoils!' and the 30 or more female initiates, wearing only brief loincloths, sing ritual songs and dance a conga imitating the movement of the python god. The ceremony is dedicated to the evening star Naledi – that is, Venus.

LEGENDS AND TRADITIONS

These eerie legends associated with specific locations in the landscape form part of the rich oral tradition of the Venda, which includes a wealth of proverbs, riddles and songs. Although most of the Venda have embraced Christianity (the Berlin Mission was established among them in 1872), traditional belief structures and healing practices are still very much alive within their communities. The use of indigenous roots, shrubs, plants and trees is also widespread, and over 120 different species have been proved by researchers to have medicinal properties.

As part of their tradition, many Venda believe that their ancestors built the city of Great Zimbabwe, which now lies within the state of the same name across the Limpopo, some 200 miles (320 km) to the north of Lake Fundudzi. The site was first occupied in the fourth century, but the city in the form we see it today was built from around 1200 onwards and reached its heyday in the 13th to 15th centuries. It was abandoned in around 1450, but continued to be used by local peoples for ritual purposes well into the 19th century. The impressive ruins of Great Zimbabwe bear witness to an ancient people with the technological skill to raise up vast blocks of granite and construct a complex of walls 3 metres

The ruins of the Great Enclosure at Great Zimbabwe. This imposing stone settlement is thought to have been the capital of a medieval empire created by the ancestors of the Shona.

(20 ft) thick, comprising enclosures, towers, monoliths and corridors. The city, which covers an area of 730 hectares (1800 acres) is the largest prehistoric stone structure in sub-Saharan Africa.

Many Southern African peoples claim to have created this site, which was once reputed to have been built by the fabled Christian ruler of Africa, Prester John, or the Queen of Sheba. The Shona, the dominant ethnic group in Zimbabwe, have the strongest claim, but other pretenders include the Lemba, who live in the Venda region. The Lemba have an oral tradition that they are of Jewish origin and migrated to Africa in the fifth century BC. Accordingly, they eat no pork or other pig-like animals (including the hippopotamus). Recent genetic research corroborates their belief, suggesting that they came originally from Senna in the Yemen. Yet there is nothing to support their, or the Venda's, claims regarding Great Zimbabwe.

What is certain is that the Venda came to Southern Africa from the Great Lakes region in the Rift Valley to the north; in their new home, they found themselves once more beside a lake, which over time has become the centre of their rich spiritual world.

> " *You may often think that deep in the darkness and density of the bush you are alone and unobserved, but that, Little Cousin, would be an illusion of the most dangerous kind. One is never alone. One is never unobserved.* "
>
> LAURENS VAN DER POST, *A FAR-OFF PLACE* (1974)

The Pyramids and the Sphinx

The pyramids and the Sphinx stand in the Egyptian desert, defying all attempts to fathom their mysteries. Some people imagine they have unlocked their secrets and discovered hidden passageways beneath the Sphinx or decoded the meaning of the pyramids' alignments or measurements. But the sense of mystery surrounding them remains intact – perhaps because the secrets they hold are spiritual rather than material.

VIRTUALLY EVERYTHING WE KNOW ABOUT THE PYRAMIDS IS DISPUTED. Conventional history and archaeology offers many answers, but alternative researchers have evolved intriguing theories that cannot always be dismissed out of hand.

Egyptologists believe the pyramids of Giza were built around 2500 BC as royal tombs to house the bodies of King Khufu (or Cheops, r. c.2589–2566 BC), his son and grandson in descending order of size. The small pyramids beside each housed the bodies of their wives. Originally each pyramid was smooth-sided and angled at exactly 52 degrees. They were aligned to the cardinal directions on the west bank of the Nile and sited on a rocky plateau facing the setting sun, which to the ancient Egyptians symbolized the realm of the dead.

The Sphinx was sculpted from a limestone outcrop near King Khufu's pyramid. The head was originally plastered and brightly painted. The nose was shot off in target practice by Turkish troops, and not by Napoleon's soldiers as is often recounted.

A Land of Mysteries

The pyramids and the Sphinx stand at the edge of the desert facing Giza (Gizeh) – a suburb of Cairo. The juxtaposition of suburb and Great Mystery is fitting; in one direction lies the known, the urban, the modern. In the other lies the unknown – the enigmatic face of the Sphinx luring you into the desert: perhaps to die, perhaps to be reborn.

Egypt is a land steeped in the sacred – from Alexandria in the north, where the Royal Library was reputedly the largest in the world, to the great rock temples of Abu Simbel in the south. But it is the pyramids at Giza that have found their way

The pyramids at Giza. The top of the largest pyramid, housing the tomb of Khufu, is still clad in limestone facing stones, which have otherwise been lost over time.

TIMELINE

2589–2504 BC 85-year period during which the pyramids were probably built

AD 1301 A massive earthquake loosens many of the casing stones, which are subsequently used to build mosques

1798 Napoleon Bonaparte visits the pyramids on his first Egyptian campaign

1880–82 The first precise survey of the pyramids is undertaken by Sir Flinders Petrie

1993 A robot camera discovers a door in a ventilation shaft

2002 The door is opened by a robot live on TV to reveal a further door behind it

into popular consciousness as emblematic of Egypt's mysteries – perhaps because of all Egypt's treasures it was the pyramids that were listed as one of the Seven Wonders of the World in the many lists and guide books that were produced in the Hellenic world from the 2nd century BC.

SCHOLARS AND HERETICS

Virtually every aspect of the pyramids and Sphinx is subject to dispute – from when they were built, to how they were built and to what purpose. Egyptologists believe they were probably built during a period of 85 years between 2589 and 2504 BC – around the same time that the great trilithons of Stonehenge were erected. But other researchers – some of whom are referred to as 'alternative Egyptologists' believe they are older. For example, the American psychic Edgar Cayce (1877–1945) claimed that the pyramids and Sphinx were 10,500 years old, while the Boston University geology professor Robert Schoch holds that they date to between 5000 and 7000 BC.

The alternative researchers dispute the conventional wisdom that these structures were built by the pharaohs of the Old Kingdom's Fourth Dynasty, which rose to prominence in the Nile Valley from about 3000 BC. Martin Gray, author of *Sacred Earth*, writes:

'The foolishness of the common assumption, that the Giza plateau pyramids were built and utilized by fourth Dynasty kings as funerary structures, cannot be overstated … The mathematical complexity, engineering requirements, and sheer size of the Gizeh plateau pyramids represent an enormous, seemingly impossible leap in abilities over the third dynasty buildings.'

Various alternative theories have been put forward to explain their origin: that they were built with the help of extraterrestrials, by refugees from Atlantis, by a civilization originating in Southeast Asia who took their knowledge of pyramid building with them into Egypt, China and Peru, and so on.

The reason that such exotic theories have evolved to explain the pyramids and the Sphinx lies in the remarkable nature of the structures. No-one can be sure how they were built – the pyramid is made of six million tons of stone – the weight of all of Europe's cathedrals combined. The Sphinx is made of massive 200-ton blocks which must have required enormous effort and sophisticated engineering to move. Alternative theorists doubt that Egyptian civilization had been in existence long enough to develop the technology needed for such a task.

CODES AND PYRAMIDOLOGY

In addition to the enigma of how they were constructed, it seems that information was encoded in the monuments. Originally the pyramids were encased with white marble facing stones, which are reputed (in some sources) to have been engraved with letters and symbols conveying the entire knowledge of antiquity. Over time these stones were removed and reworked to build the mosques and palaces of Cairo.

From the earliest times, some scholars have suggested that the dimensions of the largest pyramid of all, the Great Pyramid of Khufu, may encode significant information about the dimensions of the Earth. Agatharchides of Cnidus, a historian and geographer who lived in Alexandria in the 2nd century BC, claimed that the length of one side of the Great Pyramid's base was one-eighth of a minute of longitude and that the ratio of the pyramid's height to its base perimeter was the same as that of the Earth's radius to its circumference.

The modern era's interest in this subject was started by the French archaeologist Edme François Jomard (1777–1862), who accompanied Napoleon on his first campaign to Egypt in 1798. After his survey of the site, Jomard announced that its measurements indicated that the pyramid's builders must have had an accurate knowledge of the Earth and its solar system. 'Pyramidology', as this specialism of studying the mathematics and geometry of the Great Pyramid has become known, continues to give rise to speculation and now embraces theories regarding the shape's ability to preserve food, sharpen razor blades and enhance meditation.

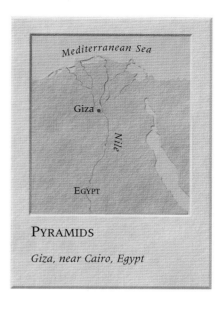

PYRAMIDS

Giza, near Cairo, Egypt

HIDDEN SHAFTS

The alignment of the pyramids has also supplied much material for speculation. *The Orion Mystery* (1994) by the British authors Robert Bauval and Adrian Gilbert argues that the pyramids were sited to replicate the pattern of the constellation of Orion on Earth and that the shafts in the pyramids, presumed to be for ventilation, actually pointed directly towards Orion, so as to project the soul of the dead pharaoh out towards the constellation. For ancient Egyptians, Orion represented the soul of Osiris, the god of death, rebirth and the afterlife.

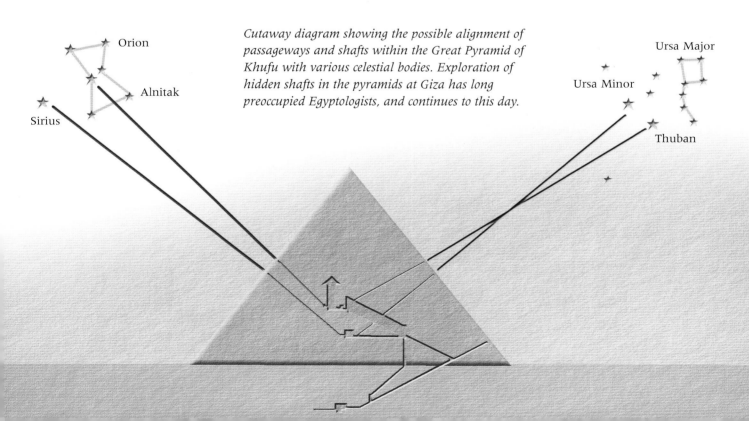

Cutaway diagram showing the possible alignment of passageways and shafts within the Great Pyramid of Khufu with various celestial bodies. Exploration of hidden shafts in the pyramids at Giza has long preoccupied Egyptologists, and continues to this day.

The Great Sphinx and the Pyramids of Giza, (1840) by the Scottish painter David Roberts (1796–1864). The popularity of Roberts' work reflected a growing interest in Egyptology in Europe from the early 19th century onward.

In 1993, while the Great Pyramid was closed for repair work, German robotics expert Rudolf Gantenbrink sent a robot with a camera crawling up the shafts. In one a door was found blocking the way 8 metres (27 ft) up the shaft. In 2002, on live television, a camera was inserted through a hole drilled in this door, only to discover another door.

Gantenbrink's website (www.cheops.org) explains why he believes the pyramid shafts cannot have been used for ventilation, or for star orientation, and suggests the best explanation is that they were designed as exits for the soul. On his website (www.robertbauval.co.uk), Bauval says:

> 'As for my hunch of what may be behind the doors in the shafts, my view is that we will probably find two serdabs … These are small sealed chambers often attached to royal tombs that contained a Ka-statue of the deceased and which was directed to the northern stars.'

The Ka was considered as an aspect of the spirit or soul.

THE SPHINX AND THE DREAM STELA

There has also been speculation about hidden chambers and passageways beneath the Sphinx. In the 1930s the American psychic Edgar Cayce popularized the idea by claiming that a 'Hall of Records' from Atlantis was hidden in a chamber whose entrance could be found between the paws of the Sphinx. At this spot stands an inscribed stone which is now called the 'Dream Stela', since it tells the story of the message King Thutmose IV (r. *c.*1401–1391 BC) received during a dream. At that time the Sphinx's body was buried in the sand. As he lay sleeping he was told to uncover the Sphinx, in return for which service he would be made king. A translation of the hieroglyphs on the Dream Stela runs:

> '… the royal son, Thothmos, having been arrived, while walking at midday and seating himself under the shadow of this mighty god, was overcome by slumber and slept at the very moment when Ra is at the summit (of heaven). He found that the Majesty of this august god spoke to him with his own mouth, as a father speaks to his son, saying: Look upon me, contemplate me, O my son Thothmos; I am thy father, Harmakhis-Khopri-Ra-Tum; I bestow upon thee the sovereignty over my domain, the supremacy over the living … Behold my actual condition that thou mayest protect all my perfect limbs. The sand of the desert whereon I am laid has covered me. Save me, causing all that is in my heart to be brought to fruition.'

The Dream Stela of the New Kingdom (18th Dynasty) King Thutmose IV between the paws of the Sphinx.

A passage has been found in the rump of the Sphinx, winding down under it before coming to a dead end about 4.5 metres (15 ft) below floor level. A 1926 photo shows what could be an entrance to another passage, now filled in, but this might be just a recess or grotto. Researchers are divided as to whether any further passageways or hidden chambers exist. A 1987 study by Waseda University in Japan reported evidence of a tunnel oriented north–south under the Sphinx, and two cavities about 3 metres (10 ft) below the surface near the two hind paws. In 1991 a US team found evidence suggesting a cavity beneath the front left paw and another running along the south flank. In 1992 an Egyptian team found no evidence, however, and further excavation at the site is opposed by the Egyptian Department of Antiquities, which cites the need to restore and conserve the monument.

> **❝** *May we come and go in and out of Heaven through the gates of starlight. As the houses of Earth fill with dancing and song, so filled are the houses of Heaven. I come, in truth. I sail a long river and row back again. It is a joy to breathe under the stars.* **❞**

HYMN TO OSIRIS, IN *AWAKENING OSIRIS – THE EGYPTIAN BOOK OF THE DEAD* (TRANS. NORMANDI ELLIS)

PIR-E-SABZ

Pir-e-Sabz in central Iran is one of the most revered shrines of the Zoroastrian religion. In Iran Zoroastrians now make up just one percent of the population. In India – where they are known as Parsis – there is a community of some 70,000, with other followers distributed around the globe. At its height, Zoroastrianism was the state religion of a great swathe of territory that extended beyond the limits of the Persian empire.

THE FOUNDER OF ZOROASTRIANISM was the prophet Zoroaster, also known as Zarathustra, who has taken on legendary status but was almost certainly a historical figure, living between around 628 and 551 BC in northern Iran. Zoroastrianism spread as far as China in the east and India in the south, and was the dominant religion of the vast Persian Empire, which included Afghanistan and parts of Turkey, Syria, Pakistan, Caucasia, Central Asia, Arabia, and at its height even Egypt, Jordan, Palestine and Lebanon for a brief time. The Magi, the Wise Men from the east present at the birth of Jesus, were traditionally regarded as having been Zoroastrians. Nowadays, there are estimated to be some 150–200,000 members of the faith worldwide.

A SEMINAL RELIGION

Zoroastrians often worship their one god Ahura Mazda (also known as Ohrmazd) through the medium of fire, which they believe represents his Holy Spirit and is symbolic of the truth. Although they are monotheists, they also believe in an active force of evil in the world – a powerful spirit by the name of Angra Mainyu, or Ahriman – and the religion emphasizes the necessity of moral choice and intention.

The strong dualistic tendency in the Zoroastrian religion is reinforced by a belief in an individual and a universal Last Judgment, and in a Heaven and Hell. These doctrines, along with the belief in the future resurrection of the body, and life everlasting for the reunited soul and body exerted a major influence on the Abrahamic religions of Judaism, Christianity and Islam. Zoroaster, Abraham and the pharaoh Akhenaten of Egypt were arguably the three most influential figures in the development of patriarchal monotheistic religion.

Being familiar with the theme of opposing forces, the Zoroastrian Persians enthusiastically embraced the game of chess, which arrived from India – with the first written reference to the game coming from Persia. In Europe,

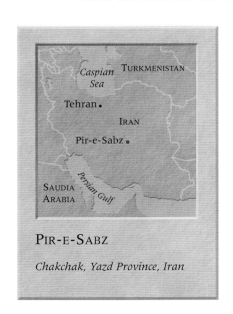

PIR-E-SABZ

Chakchak, Yazd Province, Iran

Zoroaster became known as a sage and miracle-worker, appearing as the wise and benevolent Sarastro who thwarts the evil Queen of the Night in Mozart's 1791 opera *Die Zauberflöte* ('The Magic Flute').

Whether one is a devout follower of Zoroastrianism or merely a traveller keen to experience the atmosphere of sites sacred to one of the world's oldest creeds, the undisputed cradle of the religion is the province of Yazd in central Iran, which is home to six major Zoroastrian shrines.

The remote village of Pir-e-Sabz (Chakchak) sits beneath a towering cliff-face in the desert region of central Iran.

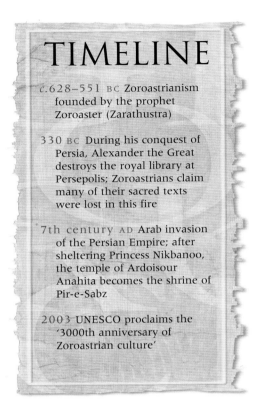

Many choose as their principal destination the remote mountain shrine of Pir-e-Sabz, also known as Chakchak, which lies 45 miles (72 km) from the city of Yazd. Here, according to legend, the conquering Arab army that overran the Persian (Sassanian) empire in the mid-7th century AD pursued Princess Nikbanoo, daughter of Emperor Yazdgird III (r. 632–51), across the desert. Arriving at the mountainside, she prayed to Ahura Mazda to protect her from the enemy. All of a sudden, the mountain opened, hiding her from the Arab soldiers who were in hot pursuit.

THE MOUNTAIN'S TEARS

The shrine itself is a cave that has been hollowed out of the mountainside at a point where a spring issues from a cliff. In imitation of the sound of the constantly dripping water, the site is also known as Chakchak ('drop drop' in Farsi, the language of Iran) and these drops are said to be the tears of grief shed by the mountain for the plight of the princess, and most likely for the fate of the people – many of whom were forced to convert to Islam or fled to India. A well-known contemporary letter, in which an Arabic commander offered Yazdgird III clemency if he agreed to embrace Islam, exhorts the Sassanian ruler: 'Stop your Fire Worship, command your nation to stop their Fire Worship which is false; join us by joining the truth'. Others claim that the drops are the tears of the princess herself, whose sister had fled in a different direction and who was captured and enslaved by the Arabs.

Before the site became a place of pilgrimage for Zoroastrians, the spring was revered by local people as the temple of 'Ardoisour Anahita' – the protector of water.

PILGRIMAGE TO THE HILLSIDE

Most pilgrims make their journey to the shrine around the time of the summer solstice, from 14 June onwards. Some stay here until 1 July or continue on to visit the other shrines in the region. The pilgrimage is referred to by the Muslim term, hajj. It is customary to wear white and to begin walking to the site from the moment it becomes visible from the road, taking shelter *en route* in pavilions constructed for this purpose.

If you travel there, walking beyond the hamlet that huddles on the hillside, you will soon begin to smell the fumes of aspand seeds being burnt as incense to ward off the 'evil eye'. These seeds contain the alkaloids harmine and harmaline, which some researchers believe accounts for the higher than normal incidence of Parkinson's disease among the Parsis who burn them frequently as devotional offerings.

Walking to the highest point you will see a great plane tree with a trunk over 1 metre (3.3 ft) in diameter. This is the cane of the princess, which miraculously became a tree when she was sheltered by the mountain. Intriguingly, a similar story is told about the legendary visit of Joseph of Arimathea to

Glastonbury in England. Arriving with his young nephew Jesus, he thrust his staff into the ground on Wearyall Hill, where it grew into a thorn tree (see pages 122–125).

A little further on, you come to another immense plane tree marking the entrance to this sacred place, which lies behind great bronze doors embossed with two austere figures who – like the tree – act as guardians and watchers.

With bare feet and a covered head you can enter the grotto whose walls are blackened by the smoke of the three fires which it is said have burned continuously for 700 years. The marble floor is wet and buckets catch the tears of the princess, who is still said to appear sometimes to the sick or downhearted to bring them healing and comfort.

THE TOWERS OF SILENCE

Returning to Yazd, you might stop to watch the sunset from the Towers of Silence – the old burial enclosures that now stand empty, since the government of the Islamic Republic of Iran decreed the custom of 'air burials' illegal. Zoroastrians had traditionally taken their dead to these towers to let the elements and birds strip them of their flesh. The bones were then swept into a pit in the centre of the enclosure, where they too eventually disintegrated. Zoroastrians believed that other forms of disposal polluted the earth, sea or air, but in Iran they now accept cremation or burial in the ground. The Parsis of India are faced with another problem, however. The vulture population there is declining to such an extent that they have been forced to focus solar panels on the corpses to aid their disintegration, and are considering building aviaries to house the 300 birds that are needed to ensure that all the corpses are consumed.

A Parsi man and woman from India pray at the eternal fire in the Zoroastrian temple at Pir-e-Sabz.

> **"** *It is every man's duty to have provided himself a sacred home to ease his soul therein; and none should squander away the hours of leisure, seeking life of dissipation, for that would lead him into the company and relationship of demons.* **"**

THE ZOROASTRIAN *DENKARD*, BOOK 6: *WISDOM OF THE SAGES*

THE CHURCH OF THE HOLY SEPULCHRE

Every Christian pilgrim to the Holy Land is intent on visiting certain sites: the Church of the Nativity of Christ in Bethlehem, the Via Dolorosa – the route that Christ took on his way to the crucifixion – and the Church of the Holy Sepulchre, which most Christians believe is built over the sites of the crucifixion, burial and resurrection.

CHRISTIAN WORSHIP AT THE SITE, which now lies within the Old City of Jerusalem, was first recorded in AD 66. Over the following centuries the fate of the site paralleled that of the city itself, which was invaded and conquered many times: by Romans who destroyed the church and built a temple to Venus over it, by Persians, by the Crusaders, by the Egyptian ruler Salah ad-Din (Saladin; *c*.1138–93) and by the Ottoman empire. In modern times the site was in territory controlled by Jordan up to 1967, and is now in Israel.

The Church of the Holy Sepulchre is actually three interconnected churches covering the area of the supposed site of the rock of Calvary (Golgotha) where Jesus was crucified and the site of the cave-tomb in which his body was subsequently placed by his disciples. Custodianship of the site is in the hands of no fewer than six different Christian denominations, who maintain an uneasy peace with each other: the Orthodox Greek, Armenian, Coptic, Syrian and Ethiopian churches along with the Catholic Franciscans each control certain parts of the church and hold services at different times.

CHRISTIANITY'S HOLIEST SITE

Because of its strong association with the Passion of Christ, an early tradition in the Christian Church identifies the Church of the Holy Sepulchre in Jerusalem as the centre of the world. A similar Judaic tradition locates the *axis mundi* at the Foundation Stone nearby on the rock of Temple Mount.

A number of authorities are reasonably confident in the authenticity of the site. Israeli scholar Dan Bahat, former City Archaeologist of Jerusalem, states: 'We may not be absolutely certain that the site of the Holy Sepulchre Church is the site of Jesus' burial, but we have no other site that can lay a claim nearly as weighty, and

A worshipper lighting candles at the Edicule of the Holy Sepulchre (Christ's tomb). Large numbers of Christians flock here annually to perform their devotions.

we really have no reason to reject the authenticity of the site.' Likewise, the *Oxford Archaeological Guide to the Holy Land* asks: 'Is this the place where Christ died and was buried?' and answers: 'Very probably, yes.'

ALTERNATIVE BURIAL SITES

Although the authenticity of the site of the Church of the Holy Sepulchre seems extremely well attested, there are still those who believe that Jesus was buried elsewhere. For instance, local legend in Shingo, Japan, maintains that Jesus' brother took his place on the cross, allowing him to flee across Siberia and Alaska to arrive finally in the Aomori district, where he became a rice farmer, married, and raised a family, dying in the village of Shingo, where a shrine now attracts many visitors. A similar story recounts how Jesus fled to Kashmir, where his tomb can be found in the Khanyar district of Srinagar. Yet another theory recounts how Jesus married Mary Magdalene and escaped to France, and that he is buried in the region of Rennes-le-Château in the Pyrenees (see pages 102–107).

Two further locations have been put forward, which lie closer to the Church of the Holy Sepulchre. In the 19th century a tomb was discovered on the side of a rocky escarpment near Calvary, which became known as the Garden Tomb. Although now considered unlikely to be authentic, the site is still visited by many pilgrims, and is often favoured by Protestants. Additionally, in 1980 a tomb, now known as the Talpiot Tomb, was discovered 3 miles (5 km) south of the old city of Jerusalem and some believe this may be the authentic site, though again most scholars disagree.

A 6th-century mosaic map from the Church of St George in Madaba, Jordan, shows the city of Jerusalem with the Church of the Holy Sepulchre at its heart. By this stage, the church was already a major site of pilgrimage.

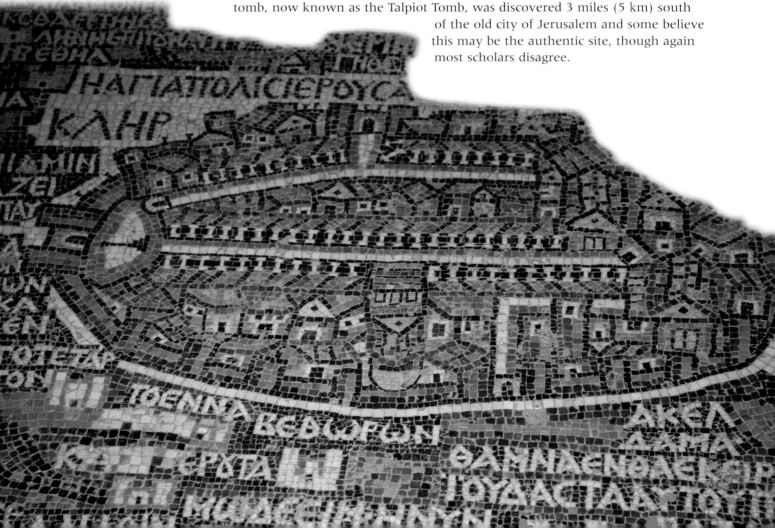

The French knight Godfrey of Bouillon (c.1060–1100), one of the leaders of the First Crusade, is shown in this later engraving giving thanks for his capture of the Church of the Holy Sepulchre.

THE ORIGINS OF THE CHURCH

The place where the Church of the Holy Sepulchre now stands was known to have once been a quarry outside the city walls, with tombs spanning the first centuries BC and AD cut into the vertical west wall and left untouched by the quarrymen. According to the historians Eusebius of Caesarea and Socrates Scholasticus, the Christian community in Jerusalem held services at the site of Jesus' tomb until AD 66, but by 135 the site had been covered with earth and a temple to Venus erected there by the emperor Hadrian (r. 117–38).

In 312 Emperor Constantine (r. 306–37) converted to Christianity. He and his mother Helena set about searching for relics and building churches to commemorate the life of Jesus. Both the Church of the Nativity at Bethlehem, commemorating his birth, and the Church of the Holy Sepulchre – reputedly a church of 'wondrous beauty' that commemorated the end of Jesus' earthly life – were completed in 333.

THE MIRACLE OF THE HOLY FIRE

Before work could begin on the church, however, Hadrian's Temple of Venus had to be destroyed and the original site uncovered. Once the building was completed, within a few decades the church became famous for a miracle that is believed to recur every Easter Saturday to this day. In 385, Etheria, a noblewoman from Spain, undertook a pilgrimage to Palestine and wrote of her experience of a ceremony at the Holy Sepulchre in the church, in which an 'infinite light' spontaneously arose from the small chapel enclosing the tomb, filling the entire church with light.

Today great crowds of pilgrims gather inside and outside the church on Easter Saturday to witness the miracle. The Greek Orthodox patriarch then enacts a ceremony which has been performed in unbroken succession for nearly 15 centuries. In 1106 the Russian abbot Daniel recounted how the patriarch enters the Sepulchre chapel alone with two candles. The patriarch kneels in front of the stone on which Christ was laid after his death and says certain prayers, at which point the

TIMELINE

AD 66 Christians begin venerating the site as the tomb of Jesus

325–6 Emperor Constantine orders the site to be uncovered and a church built there

333 Completion of the Church of the Holy Sepulchre

385 The first reports of the Miracle of the Holy Fire

614 Persian forces invade Jerusalem, damage the church and capture relics of the Cross

630 Emperor Heraclius captures Jerusalem and restores the relics to the rebuilt church

1009 Church is destroyed by Caliph Al-Hakim bi-Amr Allah

1099 The rebuilt sites are captured by the knights of the First Crusade

1149 Crusaders finish rebuilding church in the Romanesque style

1187 Jerusalem falls to the resurgent Muslims under Saladin

1229 Emperor Frederick II regains the city and the church by treaty

1244 The city and church are captured by the Khwarezmians

1555 Franciscan friars carry out renovations on the church

1808 Fire damages the church, causing the dome of the rotunda to collapse (rebuilt 1809)

1840 Another fire breaks out. Dozens of pilgrims are trampled to death trying to escape

1927 An earthquake damages the buildings

1959 Extensive renovations are carried out to the church

miracle occurs. Light emanates from the core of the stone – a blue, unearthly light which, after some time, kindles unlit oil lamps as well as the patriarch's two candles. The Patriarch then emerges with the 'Holy Fire' and candles are lit from his flame. Enraptured, some find the fire does not burn them and they 'wash' their hands or even faces in the flames.

THE MAD CALIPH WHO BANNED GRAPE EATING

A more conventional kind of flame damaged the church in 614, when the Persians invaded Jerusalem and captured relics of the cross that Constantine's mother Helena had discovered. Twenty-six years later the Byzantine emperor Heraclius (r. 610–41) walked barefoot as a pilgrim into Jerusalem, having defeated the Persians. He restored the relic of the 'True Cross' to the church, which survived another four centuries before being completely destroyed by Caliph Al-Hakim bi-Amr Allah (r. 996–1021), famous for a series of insane and often brutal decrees, including banning people from eating grapes and watercress and playing chess. He also ordered the killing of all dogs in Egypt, and prohibited women from leaving their houses, ordering shoemakers not to make any women's shoes.

The Sacred Fire of Jerusalem (1898), by the French painter Eugène Alexis Girardet, depicts the miracle of spontaneous fire that is said to occur in the Church every Easter.

The mad caliph's destruction of the church provided one of the motives for the Crusades, even though the caliph's successor had permitted the rebuilding of small chapels on the site. The First Crusaders, who succeeded in capturing Jerusalem, rebuilt the church, but after 50 years the church and the city of Jerusalem fell to Muslim forces once more, under the Egyptian ruler Saladin.

At the end of the Third Crusade in 1192 Saladin allowed worship in the church and gave the responsibility for opening and closing the main entrance to the church to two Muslim families. Over 800 years later, these two families still fulfil their roles. Every morning and evening two armed Israeli soldiers accompany a member of the Joudeh family, who brings the door's great key to a member of the Nuseibeh family, who unlocks or locks the door.

DEVOTION AND AGGRESSION

In the centuries that followed, Jerusalem's history remained troubled as it fell under different dispensations. The political stability of the church was equally uncertain and continues to be so today. Control over it was shared, and sometimes oscillated, between the Greek Orthodox, Armenian Orthodox and Roman Catholic churches, with violent clashes or bribery occurring as factions vied for supremacy. Meanwhile the church continued to be renovated and repaired after various disasters struck, including a fire and subsequent collapse of the rotunda in 1808 and an earthquake in 1927. During the 19th century, three further denominations became involved in its custodianship: the Coptic, Ethiopian and Syriac Orthodox churches.

In a bizarre and sorry example of the way religious beliefs sometimes fail to temper the urge to violence, 11 people were hospitalized in 2002 when a fight broke out after the Coptic monk who is stationed on the roof of the church to symbolize Coptic claims to the site moved his chair from its agreed spot into the shade, which was interpreted as a hostile act. Two years later another altercation occurred when a Franciscan chapel door was left open, which was interpreted as a sign of disrespect by Orthodox Christian worshippers.

CHURCH OF THE HOLY SEPULCHRE

Jerusalem, Israel

As with the nearby Temple Mount, the Church of the Holy Sepulchre acts as a focus of intense devotion and smouldering aggression. The American writer Mark Twain commented that Jerusalem was a place 'polluted by religion'. The contemporary expert on sacred sites, Martin Gray, is more restrained in his remarks on the church:

'One of the most venerated buildings on the earth, the Church of the Holy Sepulchre is also one of the most confusing and poorly maintained; this resulting from the constant squabbling amongst the Franciscan, Greek, Armenian, Coptic, Syrian, and Ethiopian religious orders who jointly watch over the site. The doctrinal diversity of its keepers certainly lends the sanctuary some of its fascination and colour, but it also keeps the building in shambles and under perpetual reconstruction.'

❝*On his arrival, the celestial fire descended suddenly, and the assistants were deeply moved ... the Saracens ... said that the fire which they had seen to come down was produced by fraudulent means. Salah ad-Din, wishing to expose the imposter, caused the lamp, which the fire from Heaven had lighted, to be extinguished, but the lamp relit immediately. He caused it to be extinguished a second time and a third time, but it relit as of itself. Thereupon, the Sultan, confounded, cried out in prophetic transport: 'Yes, soon shall I die, or I shall lose Jerusalem.*❞

ENGLISH CHRONICLER GAUTIER VINISAUF (1192)

DOME OF THE ROCK
AND TEMPLE MOUNT

On the rock of the highest hill in Old Jerusalem, it is said that God fashioned both the Earth and Adam, the first man. And it was here, according to legend, that Abraham offered his son up in sacrifice to God. In the 10th century BC King Solomon built his famed temple here, with the Ark of the Covenant being housed in its Holy of Holies. In 586 BC the Babylonians destroyed the temple, but 70 years later a second temple was constructed, which lasted until it was destroyed in the First Jewish–Roman War in AD 70.

IN AD 622 THE PROPHET MUHAMMAD, FOUNDER OF ISLAM, was taken in vision from Mecca to the rock on top of the hill. There he ascended to Allah and was given instruction before returning to Mecca. Just 69 years later one of the most beautiful mosques in the world was built to enshrine the rock, and the site became a goal of Islamic pilgrimage until 1099 when the Crusaders stormed Jerusalem and turned the Dome into the Temple of Our Lord. Less than a century later, the great commander Salah ad-Din (Saladin) reclaimed the site for Islam.

During the Six-Day War in 1967, the Israelis captured the old city and the Temple Mount, but the Mount continues to be administered by an Islamic authority, and welcomes Muslim pilgrims and countless tourists of other faiths, although some areas are restricted and non-Muslim prayers are not allowed.

THE *AXIS MUNDI*

Imagine arriving in Jerusalem, and making your way to a shining dome of gold on a hilltop encircled by a high fortress-like wall. This is the Dome of the Rock, which stands within one of Islam's holiest shrines, and which for Orthodox Jews is the centre of the world. The idea of an *axis mundi* – a mystical centre of the world where Heaven and Earth meet – occurs in almost every culture on Earth. Many mythologies depict it as a tree or pillar: for the Saxons it was represented by Irminsul, the World Pillar, and for the Norse by the great ash tree Yggdrasil. But in many cultures and religions a specific place – often a mountain or hill – is venerated: Mount Kailash in Tibet (see pages 242–245) is viewed as the centre of the world by Buddhists, Hindus and Jains, while the Black Hills in Dakota are revered in this way by the Sioux.

The Dome of the Rock on Temple Mount (Arabic: Al-Haram As-Sharif; Hebrew: Har HaBayit). This exquisite mosque was begun in AD 685 and completed in 691.

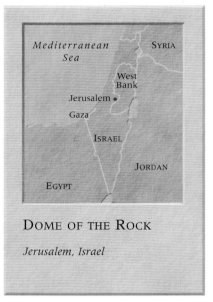

DOME OF THE ROCK

Jerusalem, Israel

In Judaism, the rock on the Temple Mount is believed to be the foundation stone of the world. The hill upon which the rock is found used to be the highest point in Old Jerusalem, and for Jews it is the most holy place in the world – to such an extent that Orthodox Jews are forbidden from entering the area. The price of transgression is 'Divinely hastened death'. Not all rabbis agree, though, and some consider it permissible provided a *mikvah*, a ritual bath, is taken before ascending if seminal or menstrual emissions have recently occurred.

KING SOLOMON'S TEMPLE AND THE FARTHEST MOSQUE

Today, as you approach the hill, and depending upon your direction, you will see the great walls that once protected Solomon's Temple, the Wailing Wall on the western side, above them the golden Dome of the Rock soaring into the air, and glimpses of the gardens and Masjid Al-Aqsa ('the Farthest Mosque').

Since at least the Early Bronze Age, a settlement has existed beside this hill, which Orthodox Jews believe is the Mount Moriah of the Old Testament. Here the world came into existence, with the rock at the summit of the hill being the first formed. Beside it God gathered the earth he needed to create Adam. Later Adam, Cain, Abel and Noah offered sacrifices to God on the rock. Here too Abraham prepared to sacrifice his son Isaac, and Jacob dreamt of angels ascending and descending on a ladder that reached up to Heaven.

In about 1000 BC the town beside the Mount, called Urusalim, was captured by David, and became the Jewish kingdom's capital. The portable shrine containing the two stone Tablets of the Law that Moses had received on Mount Sinai, known as the Ark of the Covenant, was installed in Urusalim, and David chose the Mount as the site of his future temple. His son Solomon built the first temple there, which survived for over three centuries before being destroyed by the Babylonians. Seventy years later work was begun on a second temple.

JESUS, MUHAMMAD AND THE NOBLE SANCTUARY

The site enters Christian history when we read of Jesus chasing the money-changers from the courtyard of this second temple. He is also said to have foretold its destruction, which occurred in AD 70 when the Romans crushed a Jewish revolt and set fire to the temple, possibly accidentally.

Later, in the 7th century AD, it was from here that according to Islamic tradition Muhammad was taken up into Heaven by the angel Gabriel. The Prophet was awoken one night while he lay sleeping in Mecca. Gabriel presented him with a strange creature like a horse called

❝ The world was not created until God took a stone called Even haShetiya and threw it into the depths where it was fixed from above till below, and from it the world expanded. It is the centre point of the world and on this spot stood the Holy of Holies. ❞

FROM THE JEWISH KABBALISTIC WORK, THE *ZOHAR*

al-Buraq ('Lightning') with wings, a woman's face and a peacock's tail. Muhammad mounted al-Buraq and rode through the skies to Jerusalem to land at the rock of the Temple Mount. There he met Abraham, Moses, Jesus and other prophets and prayed with them. A ladder made of golden light then appeared out of the sky, and Muhammad climbed this ladder through the seven heavens to come at last before Allah, who gave instructions for him and his followers. By dawn he had returned to Mecca with the aid of Gabriel and al-Buraq. This night journey of Muhammad turned the rock into the third of a trio of holy sites: the other two being Mecca, where the Prophet was born, and Medina, where he died.

Within a remarkably short space of time, 69 years, one of the most beautiful shrines of the Islamic world was built to enclose the rock by the Caliph Abd al-Malik (r. 685–705). The entire site of Temple Mount came to be known as 'The Noble Sanctuary' or the Al-Aqsa Mosque, which also refers specifically to the congregational mosque that was built on the southern side of the Mount. Large enough to accommodate 5000 worshippers, it was this building that the Knights Templar commandeered as their headquarters in *c*.1119. Since it lay on the site of the Temple of Solomon they named their order 'Poor Knights of

This painting (1864), by the Romantic artist Francesco Hayez (1791–1882), dramatically conveys the destruction of the Second Temple in AD 70. It was destroyed on the same day as the First Temple in 586 BC, events jointly commemorated in Judaism by Tisha b'Av, the most solemn fast day of the Jewish calendar.

> ❝ *Everywhere about the Mosque of Omar are portions of pillars, curiously wrought altars, and fragments of elegantly carved marble – precious remains of Solomon's Temple. These have been dug from all depths in the soil and rubbish of Mount Moriah, and the Moslems have always shown a disposition to preserve them with the utmost care.* ❞

MARK TWAIN, *THE INNOCENTS ABROAD* (1869)

As the closest permissible prayer location to the holiest site in Judaism – the Foundation Stone and Well of Souls within the Dome of the Rock – the Western (or Wailing) Wall is where Jews from around the world come to mourn the destruction of the Second Temple.

Christ and the Temple of Solomon', or 'Templars'. Many later Templar churches, such as the Temple Church in London, were modelled on the Dome.

They were able to do this because the city of Jerusalem had been captured by the invading Crusaders in 1099, who had massacred the population. The Dome of the Rock was converted into 'The Temple of Our Lord'. Steps were cut into the rock and an altar was placed upon it. Christian pilgrims began chipping off pieces of the rock as souvenirs, and so a protective marble covering was placed over it. The Crusaders also cut an entrance into one of the most mysterious and sacred features of this entire site – the Well of Souls.

THE ABYSS OF CHAOS AND RIVERS OF PARADISE

A hole gives access to a natural cave about the size of a small room. Here, long before the Dome was erected, it was said that the cave existed above the Abyss of Chaos (the dark void of space from which the first gods appeared), and that

the voices of the dead could be heard along with the sounds of the Rivers of Paradise. Researchers have suggested that the cave might have created a natural resonance so that someone lowering their head into the top of the cave would have experienced a similar effect to listening to the sounds of the sea in a sea-shell. Others have suggested that the Ark of the Covenant may have been hidden here when the temple was first destroyed, since legends state that the Ark was hidden beneath the temple. An Islamic tradition has developed which states that the Last Judgement will occur at the rock, and that the Well of Souls is the gathering place for souls waiting and praying for that event.

Christian control of the site lasted for less than a hundred years. In 1187 the sultan of Egypt, Saladin (r. 1174–93), recaptured Jerusalem and the Dome and Temple Mount were restored to Muslim rule. The marble covering was removed from the rock and a wooden railing was placed around it for protection. Over the centuries many repairs and improvements have been carried out – the most recent being the recovering of the Dome thanks to the generosity of King Hussein of Jordan (1935–99) who sold his house in London to pay for the US$8 million worth of gold required.

THE WAILING WALL AND THE ENTRANCE TO HEAVEN

Between 1948 and 1967 the West Bank and East Jerusalem were ruled by Jordan, but after the Six-Day War this territory fell under Israeli control. Although some Israelis wanted the Dome relocated to Mecca, and the Temple restored, the commander of Israeli forces, General Moshe Dayan (1915–81), decided to 'keep the peace' by allowing Islamic control of the site to continue.

Today no Christian or Jewish worship is allowed on the Temple Mount and Jews instead confine their religious activities to praying in front of the Wailing Wall, which is located on the western side of the old temple wall, and which devout Jews believe is located directly beneath the entrance to Heaven. Beside the wall a divider separates the men's and women's sections and written prayers are often inserted on small pieces of paper in gaps between the rocks.

The whole complex of the Temple Mount, and in particular the rock itself, is sacred to the three Abrahamic religions that between them claim the majority of the religious on Earth. In addition, Islam, Christianity, Judaism, Zoroastrianism and the Bahai faiths all believe in a Messianic age to come, in which peace and brotherhood will reign. For Christians and Jews this will come about through the restoration of the Temple and the Second Coming. In a supreme irony of human history – or perhaps in reflection of a deep truth about existence and human nature – the place that many consider the most sacred on Earth mirrors both the highest aspirations of humanity and some of its deepest wounds.

TIMELINE

3000 BC Remains of an Early Bronze Age settlement found beside the Mount

1010–970 BC David establishes Jewish kingdom centred in Jerusalem

970–931 BC His son, Solomon becomes king and builds the first Temple on the Mount c.950 BC

586 BC Babylonians destroy the Temple and the Ark of the Covenant goes missing or is destroyed

516 BC The Second Temple is built

19 BC Herod the Great tears down the temple to rebuild it. His new temple is still referred to as 'The Second Temple'

AD 70 The Temple is destroyed by fire when the Romans attempt to crush a Jewish rebellion

622 Muhammad is taken to Allah from the rock in a vision making the site sacred to Islam

691 The Dome of the Rock is built to enshrine the rock

1035 The Dome is rebuilt after destruction by an earthquake

1099 The Crusaders storm Jerusalem and take control of the Mount

1162 Saladin, ruler of Egypt, re-takes Jerusalem

1967 Israelis annexe Jerusalem and the West Bank, but leave control of the Mount in the hands of an Islamic council

MECCA

Every year for over 1400 years pilgrims have made their way to the holy city of Mecca to fulfil one of the key injunctions of Islam – to undertake a pilgrimage to the 'House of Allah' at least once in their lifetime. Today more than two and a half million people travel to Mecca each year to make this pilgrimage at the time of Hajj during the last month of the Islamic year, which currently falls in November of the Gregorian calendar. This forms the largest annual gathering of human beings for one purpose on Earth.

THE HAJJ OCCURS ACROSS A LANDSCAPE THAT INCLUDES A GREAT MOSQUE housing a sacred well, a mysterious black stone, two small hills, and the nearby plains and Mount of Arafat. Pilgrims walk in vast crowds under the blazing sun of Saudi Arabia to perform a series of ritual acts that commemorate the journey of Abraham and his wife Hagar as they travelled in this region, following God's command to sacrifice their son Ishmael. As the pilgrims perform their devotions, they are also following in the footsteps of the Prophet Muhammad (c.570–632), who was born in Mecca and who delivered his last sermon on Mount Arafat.

Only a true Muslim should make the journey to Mecca. As you approach the holy city, overhead signs announce 'Only Muslims are allowed beyond this point'. The idea that a 'Forbidden City' exists in the modern era intrigues many people and occasionally non-Muslims attempt to enter, but they risk being detained by the religious police. Saudi authorities maintain that this restriction helps preserve the religious atmosphere and experience for genuine pilgrims, while also safeguarding the already overburdened resources of the city.

Sir Richard Burton (1821–90), the explorer and translator of *The Arabian Nights* and the *Kama Sutra*, was the most famous infiltrator of the holy city, but he recognized that his motive was hardly noble: 'There at last it lay, the bourn of my long and weary pilgrimage, realizing the plans and hopes of many and many a year ... I may truly say that, of all the worshippers who clung weeping to the curtain, or who pressed their beating

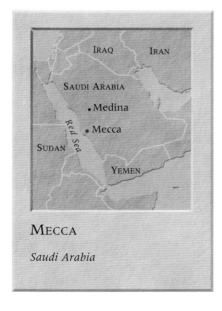

MECCA

Saudi Arabia

Muslims making their seven circuits of the Kaaba. The pilgrims' identical dress reflects the fact that they will all stand equal before God on the Day of Judgement.

TIMELINE

hearts to the stone, none felt for the moment a deeper emotion than did the *Hajji* [pilgrim] from the far north . . . . But, to confess humbling truth, theirs was the high feeling of religious enthusiasm, mine was the ecstasy of gratified pride.'

THE MOTHER OF CITIES

Mecca, known to Muslims as Umm al-Qura, 'The Mother of Cities', lies 45 miles (72 km) east of the Red Sea coast and the port of Jeddah in the kingdom of Saudi Arabia. The city of nearly 1.3 million people lies in the sandy valley of Abraham, hemmed in by the barren slopes of the Sirat Mountains.

Originally Mecca was an oasis town on the caravan network that connected the Mediterranean with Arabia, Africa and Asia. There, long before the days of Islam, nomadic peoples settled around the ZamZam spring, finding or bringing with them a black stone which may have fallen to Earth as a meteorite. The stone was treated as a sacred object, and around both stone and spring a place of worship developed with – according to legend – representations of 360 deities including Awf, the great bird, Hubal the Nabatean god, and three celestial goddesses Manat, al-Uzza and al-Lat. Later, statues of Mary and Jesus joined the pantheon, and then the polytheistic nature of worship changed as one god came to be seen as supreme – Allah the Creator – who was worshipped throughout southern Syria and northern Arabia.

AGE OF THE PROPHET

In *c.* AD 570 the Prophet Muhammad was born in the city. At the age of 25 he married a widow, Khadijah, 15 years his senior and managed her caravans. He began visiting a cave in the nearby hills, at Hira, to meditate and one night when he was aged

A famous incident from the life of Muhammad was his 'night flight' on the winged beast al-Buraq, seen here on a 16th-century manuscript.

40, known as the Night of Power, he received a revelation from the Angel Gabriel (Jibril). These revelations continued for 23 years, and were later collected to form the Qur'an – the holy book of Islam.

Muhammad's revelations angered the religious establishment in Mecca and after 11 years he was forced to leave the city for the town of Yathrib, which was later renamed Medina, or 'City of the Prophet'. Eight years later Muhammad returned to Mecca with an army of 10,000. Meeting little resistance, they destroyed the representations of the many gods at the shrine beside the spring, and dedicated it solely to Allah. Two years later the Prophet died, but within a hundred years Islam had become the dominant religion from Spain in the west to India in the east. Today Islam is the second largest religion in the world, with 1.3 billion followers – 21 percent of the world population. (Christianity takes first place with 33 percent, or 2.1 billion adherents.)

Followers of Islam are known as Muslims, meaning 'those who submit to God'. They are expected to make a pilgrimage to Mecca at least once in their life, provided they have the means and are well enough to undertake the journey. This pilgrimage, known as the Hajj, forms one of the Five Pillars of Islam, which defines the duties of a Muslim. The other four pillars are the profession of faith, the requirement to pray five times a day, to fast during Ramadan, and to pay a charitable alms-giving tax once every full lunar year.

The Hajj (sometimes called the Greater Pilgrimage) must be undertaken during the month of Dhu al-hijjah, which means 'Lord of the Pilgrimage'. This month marks the end of the Islamic year. Since the Islamic calendar is lunar, each year is 11 or 12 days shorter than in the West, and so the time of Hajj slowly migrates backwards through the commonly used Gregorian calendar – 26 November marking the beginning of Hajj in 2009, 15 November in 2010 and so on.

Medieval pilgrims on their way to Mecca, from the Maqamat *('the Assemblies'), a manuscript from c.1100 by the scholar al-Hariri of Basra.*

THE LESSER PILGRIMAGE

An alternative to the Hajj, is the Umrah, the Lesser Pilgrimage, which may be undertaken at any time. It is considered commendable to undertake an Umrah, but a full Hajj at least once in a lifetime is still the ultimate goal. To qualify for the Hajj, you must first have undertaken an Umrah, so many visitors combine both pilgrimages in one journey.

Both the Hajj and the Umrah involve performing various ritual acts across the sacred landscape in and around Mecca. On arrival, men and women alike must enter into a state of ritual purity known as ihram ('consecration'). Pilgrims put on the ihram dress of two seamless white sheets either on leaving their country, on arriving in Saudi Arabia, or in mosques at the boundary of the city.

Once in ihram pilgrims may not engage in sexual activity, cut their nails or hair, or kill animals – except poisonous ones such as scorpions and snakes. The Umrah is undertaken first. Taking a day, pilgrims perform the tawaf, the Rite of

    The first sanctuary appointed for mankind was that at Bakkah (Mecca), a blessed place, a guidance for the peoples.

THE QUR'AN, SURA 3:96

Turning, in which they process seven times anticlockwise around the great black cubical shrine of the Kaaba, reciting a set of seven prayers, and ideally kissing the Black Stone set in the southeastern corner of the shrine. In practice, so many pilgrims perform the ritual that a ritual gesture towards it usually has to suffice.

The Black Stone is set in the Kaaba – which is covered with a black silk cloth embroidered with sayings from the Prophet in gold thread. This cloth is renewed every year. Beneath it is an empty room clad in marble inset with sayings from the Qur'an. The marble and the Black Stone are regularly washed with rosewater and water from the Zamzam well.

Once the pilgrims have completed the circuit of seven tawafs, they perform two sets of prayers while kneeling and bowing before the shrine, and then set off on a brisk walk or jog between two small hills, which are now connected by a walkway from the mosque courtyard. This circuit must be repeated seven times in memory of the legend which recounts how Abraham's wife Hagar ran desperately between the two hills in search of water for themselves and their son Ishmael. While Judaism, Christianity and Islam are all Abrahamic religions, they differ in their belief over which son of Abraham was due to be sacrificed. Islam believes it was Hagar's child Ishmael, while Judaism and Christianity believe it was Isaac, born of Abraham's first wife Sarah.

Hajji gathering at the door of the Kaaba. The black cloth covering the Kaaba and embroidered with verses from the Qur'an is called a kiswah. At the end of the Hajj, it is cut up into small pieces and distributed to pilgrims from different Muslim countries.

The pilgrim may now continue to perform the Greater Pilgrimage of the Hajj or choose instead to visit the mosque and tomb of the Prophet and the tomb of his daughter Fatima in the city of Medina.

THE GREATER PILGRIMAGE

Pilgrims begin the Hajj itself in Mecca – along with over two million others at the same time. This extraordinary event can now only occur with an impressive amount of logistics – 20,000 water trucks around the city distribute 50 million bags of cooled water and ice packs while the world's largest abattoir, with enough space for 500,000 sheep and cattle, provides meat for hungry pilgrims.

After dawn prayers on the first day of the Hajj pilgrims walk to Mina, 5 miles (8 km) away, where they set up camp and pray. More than 1200 buses transport pilgrims unwilling or unable to walk. Some 44,000 air-conditioned and fireproof tents, provided at a cost of US$640 million, help to accommodate the vast numbers of pilgrims who must spend the next two nights in the desert. The next day, after dawn prayers, they join the millions of other pilgrims who now travel the 12 miles (19 km) to Mount Arafat chanting 'Bayak! Labayak!' (I am here! I am ready!). This day is known as The Day of Standing and pilgrims are encouraged to spend the day in prayer and supplication – reading the Qur'an and asking Allah's forgiveness for their sins, as did the Prophet in this very place. Gathering on Mount Arafat, the Mount of Mercy, they listen to a sermon – just as the first followers of Muhammad heard his last sermon here.

After sunset they leave for Muzdalifah, between Arafat and Mina, where pebbles are gathered for stoning the Devil, and camp overnight at Mina.

STONING THE DEVIL

The third and final day of the Hajj – the Day of Sacrifice – begins with a ritual stoning of the Devil, represented by three pillars in Mina; in 2004 the Saudi authorities erected three large walls and a bridge to increase safety at this overcrowded and dangerous site. The stoning re-enacts Abraham's stoning of the Devil, when he tempted him not to sacrifice his son. In spiritual terms the stoning repudiates the 'internal despot' with its base desires and wishes.

After the stoning, an animal is sacrificed as a reminder of Abraham's willingness to obey God and sacrifice his son Ishmael. It is most often impractical for pilgrims to slaughter an animal at this point, but a sacrifice voucher can be bought in Mecca before the Hajj begins. With this an animal is slaughtered in an individual's name on this Day of Sacrifice without the pilgrim having to be physically present. After eating the sacrificial meal, and hearing a sermon, the pilgrimage ends with a final circuit around the Kaaba in Mecca before pilgrims change out of their ihram clothes. Women and men both trim a little hair or men shave their heads to mark their completion of the Hajj.

Muslim pilgrims assemble for prayer on the Jabal al-Rahmah ('Mount of Mercy') on the Day of Standing during the Hajj in 2001.

THE BAHÁ'Í SHRINES AT ACRE AND HAIFA

Bahá'ís believe that their religion has been given to the world by a prophet, Bahá'u'lláh (1817–92), who is the latest in a series of great spiritual teachers that includes Abraham, Moses, Zoroaster, the Buddha and Jesus. His burial site in Acre, Israel, is their holiest shrine. Each day Bahá'ís around the world turn to face the shrine as they say their prayers, and a pilgrimage there marks the high point of a Bahá'í's spiritual life.

SOUTH OF ACRE THE HOLY MOUNTAIN OF BIBLICAL LEGEND – MOUNT CARMEL – stretches towards Haifa, and on its western slopes the city is now graced with the terraced gardens and stately buildings of the world headquarters of the Bahá'í movement. Here the remains of the prophet known as the Bab (1819–50) are housed in a domed shrine in the centre of the gardens. The Bab, meaning 'The Gate', is seen as the precursor to Bahá'u'lláh, in the same way that some believe John the Baptist preceded Jesus.

So great is the demand by the Bahá'í faithful to come and pay homage to their religion's founders that they must wait for up to five years to make a pilgrimage to the shrines at Haifa and Acre. Nine-day pilgrimages are organized, which include lectures, prayer and meditation at each of the shrines including that of Abdu'l Bahá (1844–1921), Bahá'u'lláh's son, who led the movement after his death.

The Bahá'í faith originated in Persia in the 19th century. It now claims over 5 million adherents worldwide. The two great shrines of this movement are to be found beside the city of Acre and within the city of Haifa, both of which lie a short distance from each other in northern Israel, close to its border with Lebanon. Nine miles (14 km) to the southwest of Acre, the slopes of 'the holiest of all mountains',

The beautifully laid-out gardens at the Bahá'í headquarters on Mount Carmel, Israel. On the far left is the Universal House of Justice, seat of the Bahá'í governing council.

Mount Carmel, rise and then sweep south for 16 miles (25 km). On its heights a profusion of aromatic plants and wild flowers shelter roebuck and wild cats. On its western side the range slopes downwards towards the sea and the busy port of Haifa – now Israel's third largest city.

TWO RELIGIOUS MOVEMENTS

The 4th-century AD philosopher Iamblichus wrote that Mount Carmel was 'the most holy of all mountains and forbidden of access to many'. It was the spiritual stronghold of the northern Essenes and home, many believe, to the Prophet Elijah whose cave, altar and spring were found in 1958. In the 19th century the region around Mount Carmel became the spiritual home of two unusual movements. In 1868 two German Lutherans, Christian Hoffmann (1815–85) and G. D. Hardegg (1812–79), founded a religious community they called 'The German Temple' on the slopes of Mount Carmel. They were hoping to build a 'living temple to God' in the Holy Land, and started commercial farming in the area, establishing the 'Jaffa' orange brand. By 1910 they had created thriving communities in half a dozen places, including Jerusalem.

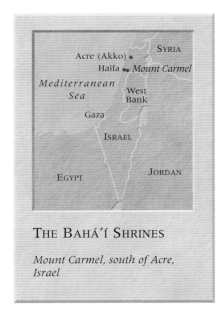

THE BAHÁ'Í SHRINES

Mount Carmel, south of Acre, Israel

In the same year that Hoffmann and Hardegg came to Haifa, the spiritual leader of the Bahá'í's, known as Bahá'u'llá, together with a group of his followers, was imprisoned in a penal colony in Acre. The prison, and the house nearby in which Bahá'u'llá died and beside which he is buried, are now pilgrimage sites for devout Bahá'ís who come from all over the world to pray and meditate there. Later, a shrine for the remains of the Bab, and the world headquarters of the Bahá'ís were located in nearby Haifa.

TIMELINE

1817 Bahá'u'llá is born

1819 The Bab is born

1844 The Bab announces he is the Mahdi – the prophesied redeemer of Islam

1850 The Bab is shot in Tabriz

1852 Angry Babis fail in their attempt to assassinate the shah; thousands are executed

1863 Bahá'u'llá openly declares himself the Promised One

1868 Bahá'u'lláh and followers are sent to a penal colony in Akko, Palestine (now Acre, Israel)

1892 Death of Bahá'u'llá

1909 Remains of the Bab placed in the Shrine of the Bab in Haifa

1912 Abdu'l-Bahá tours the USA and lays the foundation stone of the first Bahá'í House of Worship in Wilmette, Illinois

1920 Abdu'l-Bahá is knighted by the British in recognition of his humanitarian work in the war

1921 Abdu'l-Bahá dies in Haifa. His brother Mírzá Muhammad 'Alí forcefully occupies the shrine of his father when his claim to leadership is disputed. He is defeated in a legal battle

1937 Mírzá Muhammad dies, shunned by the Bahá'í community

1953 The shrine of the Bab in Haifa is completed

1963 First Bahá'í World Congress takes place in London

1979 Iran's Islamic Revolution sees persecution of Bahá'ís, with over 200 killed by 2006

2001 The terraces on the Mount Carmel site are completed

THE BAB AND THE ORIGINS OF THE BAHÁ'Í FAITH

The roots of the Bahá'í faith lie in the Abrahamic religion of Islam. Many Muslims believe that a prophet, a redeemer of Islam, will one day arise and usher in an era of peace and justice. In 1844 a 25-year-old man from Shiraz in Persia (now Iran) calling himself the Bab declared himself to be the awaited prophet, and began to assemble a group of followers around him. His claim outraged the established clergy and he was tried, sentenced to death and executed by firing squad in 1850. His body was thrown outside the city walls to be eaten by dogs, but his followers managed to rescue his remains, which are now buried in the Bahá'í shrine in Haifa. In the years following his death over 20,000 of his followers were slaughtered in a series of massacres.

The Bab claimed that a future prophet – 'The Promised One' – would arise, who would be far greater than him, and in the years following his death 25 men claimed the role. One above all succeeded in convincing others that he was indeed the predicted prophet: Bahá'u'llá. Most followers of the Bab came to accept his claim and formed the core of his movement, although today there are still those, known as Babis or Bayanis who continue to follow only the Bab, or Subh-i-Azal (1831–1912), who claimed to be the true heir to the Bab movement.

THE PROMISED ONE

In 1853, while imprisoned for his beliefs in Tehran, Bahá'u'llá was visited by a 'Maid of Heaven', who informed him that he was the Promised One foretold by the Bab. Ten years later he revealed this to his family and close followers while in a public park, which Bahá'ís later named the Garden of Ridvan, outside Baghdad. They stayed in the garden for 12 days, and commemoration of this event has become the most important festival of the year for Bahá'ís. The celebration of Ridvan lasts from 21 April to 2 May.

After leaving the Garden of Ridvan, Bahá'u'llá made a more public declaration by announcing the news of his status in letters to the kings and rulers of the world, including Emperor Napoleon III of France (1808–73). The leader of the Bábí community, Subh-i-Azal, was furious and a period of severe conflict arose which led to numerous accusations, murders and the poisoning of Bahá'u'llá.

The authorities finally decided to separate the rival communities by exiling them to distant regions of the Ottoman empire. Subh-i-Azal and his followers were sent to Famagusta in Cyprus, Bahá'u'llá and his followers to Acre in Palestine. Unfortunately seven followers of Subh-i-Azal ended up in Acre and were killed by over-zealous devotees of Bahá'u'lláh, who was swift to condemn their behaviour. Bahá'u'lláh was eventually allowed to live in a house in Acre, even though he remained officially a prisoner to the end of his life. His burial site beside the house has become the 'Qiblah' – the sacred direction in which all Bahá'ís must turn daily in prayer, wherever they are in the world.

PILGRIMAGES TO MOUNT CARMEL

During his time in Acre, Bahá'u'lláh visted Haifa and Mount Carmel four times. Land above the German Temple community was purchased for a world headquarters of the movement and in 1909 the remains of the Bab were buried there in a shrine, completed in 1950, that has become a landmark in the city. Today the immaculate terraced gardens attract thousands of visitors each year. Although the gardens are open daily to the public, Bahá'ís who wish to make a pilgrimage to the holy shrines of their faith must register their desire with the 'Department of Pilgrimage', and provide them with their Bahá'í identification number. They then have to go on a waiting list and wait between three and five years before receiving notification of dates available for visits. Pilgrimages offer the opportunity for Bahá'ís to meet fellow pilgrims and undertake a series of guided visits with lectures and opportunities for prayer and meditation. There is now an extensive film on the internet video site Youtube giving a good insight into the experience, which moves most pilgrims deeply.

Abdu'l-Bahá, leader of the movement from 1892 to 1921. His lecture tours to the West helped spread the Bahá'í faith far beyond its Middle Eastern roots.

Bahá'ís believe that all revealed religions come from the same source, and are therefore essentially one religion expressed in different ways to suit the cultures and times in which they arise. Abraham, Krishna, Zoroaster, Moses, Buddha, Jesus and Muhammad are seen as divine messengers, with the Bab and Bahá'u'lláh being the most recent. They believe that Bahá'u'lláh represents the fulfilment of a long process of progressive revelation by these prophets, with the aim of this revelation being the ultimate unity of all humanity.

Bahá'ís commit to daily prayer and a life dedicated to the service of humanity. Cremation is prohibited, they are expected not to drink alcohol or gamble, and are committed to the independent investigation of truth in a way that embraces a study of science as well as religion.

" I bear witness, O my God, that Thou has created me to know Thee and to worship Thee. I testify, at this moment, to my powerlessness and to Thy might, to my poverty and to Thy wealth. There is none other God but Thee, the Help in Peril, the Self-Subsisting. "

THE SHORT FORM OF OBLIGATORY PRAYER THAT EVERY BAHÁ'Í SHOULD SAY EACH DAY BETWEEN NOON AND SUNSET WHILE FACING IN THE DIRECTION OF THE BURIAL SHRINE OF BAHÁ'U'LLÁ

THE TEMPLES OF MALTA

Situated in the middle of the Mediterranean, the islands of Malta are the guardians of some of the world's most ancient mysteries. The temple of Ggantija – the world's oldest building – stands on Malta's western island of Gozo, while on the main island of Malta, the vast subterranean Hal Saflieni Hypogeum has the distinction of being the world's only surviving prehistoric underground temple.

THESE TEMPLES BOTH DATE FROM AROUND 5500 YEARS AGO – a thousand years before the Pyramids – by a culture that vanished in around 2500 BC, leaving behind only a few clues to help later generations explore their mysteries. Most scholars believe the temples were built by colonizers from Sicily during the Neolithic age, who were forced to leave after three thousand years due to the depletion of resources or climate change.

Female figures discovered at the sites – including the famous 'Venus of Malta' and the 'Sleeping Lady' – have led to speculation that the temples were the devotional sites of a goddess-based culture. Today they have become important places of pilgrimage for those exploring the Goddess mysteries.

Like the seven stars of the Pleiades in the night sky, the seven islands that make up the Republic of Malta lie in the middle of the southern Mediterranean, just below the island of Sicily, looking west to Tunisia and south towards Libya.

TEMPLES OF MALTA

Malta and Gozo, Mediterranean

Malta's wild rugged landscape has witnessed a turbulent history of conquest by a series of invaders that have included the Phoenicians, the Romans, the Arabs, the Normans, the Turks of the Ottoman empire, the French under Napoleon and the British. In 1522 the military order of the Knights of the Hospital of St John of Jerusalem was driven out of its headquarters on Rhodes by the Ottomans and made its home in Malta. Eight years later the Holy Roman Emperor Charles V (r. 1519–56) gave the islands to the Order, which henceforth became known as the 'Knights of Malta'. In the Second World War the islands' strategic position within the shipping lanes of the Mediterranean and importance as a British naval base

Closed to visitors for restoration work between 1992 and 2000, the Hypogeum at Hal Saflieni is a unique structure. Seen here is the middle chamber of the temple.

made them the target of heavy bombardment by the Axis forces of Nazi Germany and Fascist Italy. Today Malta, an EU member since 2004, is struggling to cope with waves of illegal immigration from Africa.

ORIGINS LOST IN TIME

No-one knows when the first humans arrived on Malta. Most historians believe that the islands were colonized during the Neolithic period across the sea from Sicily. But some scholars believe that colonization occurred earlier – during the Paleolithic period, when, due to the Ice Age, sea levels were much lower and the islands we see today were simply the high points of a landscape that is now under water.

Whether the first humans here were Paleolithic or Neolithic remains a subject of debate, but what we do know is that the sacred structures that can be identified today represent the surviving visible remains of a sophisticated culture that was capable of erecting buildings so massive that local folklore maintains that they were built by giants.

Threshold of the southern entrance to the Ggantija megalithic temple on the Maltese island of Gozo.

On Malta's western island of Gozo, where in Greek mythology the nymph Calypso held Odysseus imprisoned for seven years, the temple complex of Ggantija is the oldest free-standing building in the world – erected over five thousand years ago, between 3600 and 3300 BC. Ggantija is Maltese for 'giant', and one local legend recounts how a great giantess Sansuna, who lived on a diet of broad beans and water, constructed the temples in a single day carrying the great stones on her head while she carried her baby under her arm. The shapes of mother and daughter are reflected in the sizes of the two temples that stand side by side.

THE GGANTIJA TEMPLE COMPLEX

Some 2300 feet (700 m) away from the stone circle of Xaghra, built above sacred caves, a boundary wall of megaliths, some of which exceed 5 metres (16 ft) in length and weigh over 50 tons, surrounds the complex and protects the two temples, which are constructed from rough, coralline limestone blocks. The earliest of the temples is built to a pattern like a clover leaf, reminiscent of the plump body shapes of figurines unearthed elsewhere on the island, with broad rounded areas connected by narrow 'waists' or corridors. In the larger temple there are altars, libation holes and relief carvings of spiral designs. The walls are made of corbelled stone, curving inwards towards the top, possibly in an attempt to create a domed roof. However, there are no signs of collapsed stone roofs, leading archaeologists to conclude that these were probably created with animal hides stretched over poles (indeed, post-holes for these poles have been discovered). There is some evidence that the altars were used for animal sacrifice, but beyond this we can only guess at the nature of the rites that were performed here.

MNAJDRA AND HAGAR QIM

On the southern coast of the main island of Malta, just a few hundred metres from the entrancing, but tourist-infested Blue Grotto, stand two of the most spectacular Maltese prehistoric temple complexes – Hagar Qim and Mnajdra. On a rocky plateau overlooking the sea, the temples are so close to each other they were probably part of one complex which was built a little later than Ggantija – between 3150 and 2500 BC.

The three temples of Mnajdra are remarkable for their stone 'furniture' of benches and tables, doorways and windows that are cut out of solid rock, and their stones with spiral and drill hole decorations. The lowest temple seems to have been deliberately orientated to the equinoctial sun which passes through the main doorway and lights up the major axis, while the solstice suns illuminate the edges of the megaliths to either side of the doorway.

Similar alignments have been noted at Hagar Qim which is notable for its massive blocks of stone, the largest of which is 7 metres by 3 metres (22 ft x 10 ft) and weighs approximately 20 tons. The finely worked entrance façade of the temple leads to six large oval rooms connected by a broad interior passage. An open-air shrine is set into the outer wall, and a small, three-apse structure near the temple may have housed the temple's priestesses or priests.

TIMELINE

3600–3200 BC Ggantija and upper level of Hal Saflieni Hypogeum created

3300–3000 BC Middle level of Hypogeum created

3000–2400 BC Lowest level of Hypogeum created

2500 BC Prehistoric Maltese civilization disappears

700 BC Phoenicians inhabit the island

480 BC Malta becomes a colony of Carthage

255 BC Malta plundered by the Roman navy in First Punic War

218–201 BC Second Punic War: Malta and Gozo are absorbed into Roman Republic

AD 870 Arabs overrun Malta

1090 Normans conquer Malta

1530 The Holy Roman Emperor leases Malta to the Hospitallers in exchange for one bird – a Maltese Falcon (now extinct) – each year

1824 Charles de Brochdorff paints watercolours of some of the sites, providing valuable reference material for later restoration work

1827 Colonel John Otto Bayer clears the site around Ggantija

1902 Building work unearths the Hypogeum of Hal-Saflieni

1908 Hypogeum first opened to the public

1980 Hypogeum is made a UNESCO World Heritage Site

2000 Hypogeum reopened to public after 1992 closure, but with strict limitation of visitor numbers

THE VENUS OF MALTA

It was here that a number of statuettes were found, including the famous 'Venus of Malta', which have made the prehistoric island temples a pilgrimage destination for contemporary Goddess worshippers. The archaeologist Marija Gimbutas (1921–94) cited them as examples of a matristic culture that existed prior to the arrival of patriarchal Indo-European peoples in Europe: 'I call it [this proposed culture] matristic, not matriarchal, because matriarchal always arouses ideas of dominance and is compared with the patriarchy. But it was a balanced society, it was not that women were really so powerful that they usurped everything that was masculine.'

Gimbutas developed an interdisciplinary approach that she termed 'archaeomythology', combining conventional archaeology with a study of linguistics, mythology and comparative religions. Her approach attracted many admirers, including the American mythographer Joseph Campbell (1904–87), and many critics, and it provided a major stimulus to the Goddess movement, which developed out of a convergence of feminism with the resurgence of interest in paganism and alternative spirituality that occurred in the 1970s.

Critics of the theory that the Maltese temples are specifically dedicated to goddesses or the Goddess point out that many of the figurines discovered are of indeterminate sex, and that the carved phalluses also found suggest that the temples may have been dedicated to fertility in general rather than one gender of deity in particular.

THE HYPOGEUM

The most remarkable of all the sacred sites in Malta is the Hal Saflieni Hypogeum. It was accidentally discovered by a builder in 1902, when he burst through its roof while digging the foundations for a housing development.

The Hypogeum is an enormous subterranean temple dated to between about 3600 and 2500 BC, which exists on three levels. The highest level was probably the first to be built by extending natural caves. The second level is made up of a roughly circular main chamber that was painted in red ochre, which leads to various small side chambers. One of these, 'the Oracle Room', produces a powerful echo for a male voice, but strangely not for a female one. Its ceiling is elaborately painted in ochre with spirals and blobs. From here you can enter another spacious circular hall that is decorated with geometrical patterns and the carving of a human hand. Another chamber is known as the 'Snake Pit', since it may have been used for keeping snakes.

The deepest level, 11 metres (35 ft) below street level, contains 11 chambers, but no artefacts have been found there to offer any clue as to their use. 7000 skeletons were found in the two upper levels, dating back to 3600 BC, which has led scholars to speculate that the site was used as a necropolis.

In the rubble that lay on the floor when archaeologists first entered the Snake Pit, there was a small figurine – just 5 inches long – that has become known as the Sleeping Lady. Perhaps she offers a clue as to the purpose of this mysterious underground 'city'. Perhaps she is a priestess exploring the Underworld of Dreams – acting out a practice that is found all over the world: incubating a dream in the hope of receiving divine guidance.

The Hal Saflieni Hypogeum is one of the most mysterious and evocative of all sacred sites in the world. It connects us to the womb of the Earth and of the Great Mother. It is a place of the Dream of Humanity in its very earliest days. To protect its stone which is sensitive to human breath, only 80 visitors a day are now allowed inside, but each of us can visit it, and the other ancient sites on these small islands, in our dreams.

The small terracotta statue with a tiny head and outsized limbs, known as the Sleeping Lady, was found in the 'Snake Pit' on the second level of the Hal Saflieni Hypogeum.

“ All during our lives, in any and every place we live or visit, the sacramental landscape unrolls before us. It is our text. It is public and private, social and wild, political and aesthetic. To see – that is, to discover – is not an act of interpretation, of transfixing with preconceived ideas what is before us; rather, it is an act of surrender. ”

AMERICAN WRITER GRETEL EHRLICH, *ISLANDS, THE UNIVERSE, HOME* (1992)

THE ORACLE OF DELPHI

The holiest place in ancient Greece was the shrine at Delphi, on the slopes of Mount Parnassus. Nestling between shining cliffs and facing the Gulf of Corinth, the Greeks believed that this was the location of the omphalos, *the centre of the world. Generations of people, especially ancient leaders, came to Delphi to have their future foretold by the Pythia, the priestess who presided over the shrine.*

THE SITE PROBABLY BEGAN LIFE AS A BRONZE AGE GODDESS SANCTUARY beside a natural spring in the rock, but later it became a sanctuary of Apollo and a site of pilgrimage for nearly a thousand years, before falling into decay in the Christian era, and being closed down in the 4th century by the Roman emperor Theodosius (r. 379–95). Kings and common people, representatives of states and of business enterprises came to hear Apollo's advice, given to them in hexameter verse by priests who would interpret the utterings of the Pythia – prophetesses whom some say were intoxicated by fumes arising from a chasm beneath them.

Greece was the birthplace of much of our modern culture; dance and drama, sport and poetry, architecture, literature, philosophy and politics all originated here. And at the very heart of Greek civilization stood Delphi, situated some 90 miles (140 km) northwest of Athens, just north of the Gulf of Corinth, on Mount Parnassus, which the ancient Greeks believed was the home of the god Apollo. Here in the dry primal landscape of this mountainous region the visitor's senses are assailed – in the bright summer sun, bees and cicadas fill the air with their sounds, buzzards and vultures soar above the cliffs, olive trees sway in the breeze, while every so often Zeus hurls his thunderbolts in an electrical storm.

It was Zeus who made Delphi the centre of the world. He released two eagles from opposite ends of the Earth and where they met marked the *omphalos* or navel of the world. A conical stone carved with strange lattice-work was erected to mark the spot. A replica now stands there, but the original can still be seen in the Delphi museum.

THE CHASM AND THE PYTHON

The eminent historian of religions, Mircea Eliade (1907–86), points out that sacred places draw humans to them, rather than humans choosing the spots themselves, and so, according to legend, it was to Delphi that the Earth goddess Gaia attracted the early inhabitants of this region to worship at her shrine.

The Tholos, *one of the buildings at the sanctuary of Apollo at Delphi. In ancient times, the Delphic oracle was widely consulted for favourable augury or warnings.*

You enter Greece as one might enter a dark crystal; the form of things becomes irregular, refracted … Other countries may offer you discoveries in the manner of lore or landscape; Greece offers you something harder – the discovery of yourself.

LAWRENCE DURRELL, *THE GREEK ISLANDS* (1978)

To explain the origins of the oracle, one legend recounts how a herdsman, Koretas, came upon a chasm on the mountainside from which strange fumes issued. He noticed that his goats were behaving oddly, before himself falling into a trance-like state in which he had visions of the future. Soon others began to experience similar visions, and a timber-built oracle house dedicated to Gaia arose by the chasm where sibyls (Greek for prophetesses) would utter oracles while entranced. The first sibyl, Herophile, was said to have predicted the tragedy of the Trojan War. A giant serpent, the Python, guarded the shrine, which was called Pytho in its honour. When Apollo, god of music and poetry and leader of the Muses, discovered the shrine he killed the Python that was threatening his mother and installed his own priestess, known as the Pythia.

From these legendary origins arose the most famous of all the oracles in the classical world. For nearly 1000 years visitors would travel from far and wide to consult the priestesses on matters that troubled them. They would arrive either by ship in the harbour below at Kirrha or by land across the Plain of Thessaly. Accounts of the way the oracle worked vary, but we can still piece together a picture of how a pilgrim would have experienced a visit to this shrine.

A PILGRIM ARRIVES AT DAWN

Imagine you are the traveller who has arrived at dawn to visit the oracle at the height of its fame, in the 7th century BC; as you climb through olive groves towards the sanctuary, the sea falls away behind you. You catch your breath as the sacred city of the oracle comes into view ahead of you, with its white buildings and terracotta roofs held within the embrace of the Shining Ones, the Phaedriades – soaring cliffs that glow with an incandescent light in the early morning sun. You stop at the Castalian spring to bathe ritually; perhaps it is there that you are asked to pay a fee towards the administration of the sanctuary – such payments were later to spark three 'Sacred Wars' over the ownership and administration of the site.

The spring, tumbling out of the side of the cliff was said to have been created when the winged-horse Pegasus struck the ground with his hooves, and archaeological finds suggest that a Bronze Age goddess cult was centred here.

Continuing from the spring, you find yourself entering a sanctuary that boasts numerous elegant buildings surrounded by gardens filled with statues and small temple-like structures known as 'treasuries', which house precious offerings donated by kings and city states as tributes to Apollo. There are so many statues here that when Nero decided to steal some, he was only able to take 500, leaving 3000 remaining. In the 6th century BC King Croesus donated a golden lion that weighed a quarter of a ton and was displayed on a pyramid of white gold.

As you walk along the Sacred Way through the gardens, the temple of Apollo and a great statue of the god dominates the scene, but behind it you can see the amphitheatre used for performances, and beyond it the stadium, used every four years for the Pythian Games. You encounter a wall of great polygonal blocks covered in inscriptions from grateful pilgrims – many from slaves celebrating their freedom.

Some writers say that just before entering the temple a goat was sprinkled with water to see if it shivered. If it did, this was a good omen for a successful oracle. Imagine that the goat has shivered vigorously for you. You then buy a sacred cake and place it as an offering on the altar outside the temple, before entering and being led to the adyton – the inner sanctuary.

REACHING THE INNER SANCTUARY

Here, in the glow of torches you sense the Pythia seated on a tripod – but you cannot see her. She is hidden from view behind a curtain, attended by a priest who conveys your question to her. Some believe that her tripod was positioned over the fissure in the ground that the shepherd Koretas had first discovered. Archaeologists have found no trace of such a chasm, and believe the idea of intoxicating fumes comes from a misunderstanding of the Greek terms *pneuma* meaning 'breath' or 'soul', and *atmos entheos*, an atmosphere that causes 'enthusiasm'. Recently some scientists have suggested that earthquakes may have erased any evidence of the fissure. Geologists have found a previously undetected fault line that runs directly beneath the temple, which is built on deposits of bitumen-rich limestone, and they suggest that seismic activity on the faults may have heated up these deposits, releasing light hydrocarbon gases. Water from a spring northwest of the temple has been found to contain methane and traces of ethylene. Ethene, a sweet-smelling gas, although fatal in large quantities, produces a floating sensation and euphoria in small doses. Intriguingly, one of the temple's priests, the writer Plutarch (*c.* AD 46–120) described the fumes as smelling like perfume.

This circular painting (tondo) from a drinking vessel of c.440–430 BC is the only surviving contemporary image of the Delphic Pythia. It depicts Aegeus, a mythical ruler of Athens, consulting the priestess, who is sitting on a tripod and is screened from the king by a curtain.

THE ORACLE SPEAKS

However the Pythia obtains her prophecies, she utters them to her priest, who converts her message into verse before conveying it to you. Perhaps you understand it at once or perhaps it gives an enigmatic answer to your question. Either way, if you are wise you will take a while to ponder on Apollo's message to you. Croesus asked the Pythia if he should march on Persia. The oracle said 'If Croesus crosses the river Aly a mighty empire will fall'. It never occurred to the king that it might be his empire that would fall – but this is precisely what happened.

As you leave the sanctuary, the Phaedriades are shining with an incandescent light once more – but this time in reflection of the fiery light of the sunset. Your mind is now clear, your heart is free. You will make a votive offering to Apollo at your own shrine as soon as you reach home.

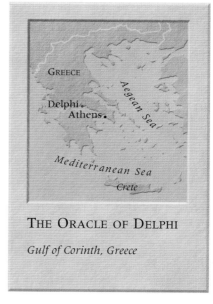

THE ORACLE OF DELPHI

Gulf of Corinth, Greece

PERPERIKON

In southern Bulgaria, close to the border with Greece, the ruins of an ancient city stand perched high on a hill. Called 'the mountain of ghosts' by the old villagers, Perperikon may well be the site of the fabled Oracle of Dionysus that was visited by Alexander the Great. At this oracle a prophetess predicted Alexander's conquest of Asia as wine was hurled on to a sacred fire.

PERPERIKON IS SITUATED IN THE TERRITORY OF ANCIENT THRACE. Here, megalithic and later sites abound and are still coming to light. For example, in 2007, in the dense forest at the southern foot of the mountain, archaeologists unearthed the remains of a Thracian palace, including scores of buildings and water-storage systems. In the valley below, the gold-bearing Perpereshka river and one of the largest gold mines in antiquity provided the source of Perperikon's material wealth; the gold that was mined in this region was smelted to produce spectacular treasures, including masks, goblets and jewellery, some of which have turned up in archaeological excavations. Meanwhile the source of the area's spiritual richness may well lie 12 miles (19 km) downstream, where a womb-like cave shows evidence of early cult practice.

Together, the holy mountain and the sacred cave provided a perfect setting for the growth of myths concerning Dionysus, and later Orpheus – the god of poetry and music who descended to the Underworld to rescue his wife Eurydice.

IN SEARCH OF DIONYSUS

Seeking out the most likely location for the legendary Holy Mount of Dionysus takes you to the Rhodopes – a range of high hills and mountains that stretches for over 137 miles (220 km) through Macedonia, Greece and Bulgaria in the heart of the Balkans. Driving southeast from the Bulgarian capital Sofia you cross the great central plain before climbing into the foothills of the Rhodopes. This is a land of rock and sun – of deep gorges, vineyards and tobacco plantations.

Perched on a hillside in the eastern Rhodopes mountains, the remains of the ancient Thracian city of Perperikon command a fine view over the valley below.

As you make your way towards the border with Greece, the winding road climbs ever higher before descending again as you enter a valley formed by the River Perpereshka. And then, suddenly, there it is standing ahead of you – the ancient city of Perperikon perched on a peak 427 metres (1400 ft) high.

With its ruined buildings and paved avenues, Perperikon is so spectacular that it has been called the 'Machu Picchu of Europe'. Despite this, mass tourism has not yet spoiled this impressive site: there are few hotels nearby, and even in these days of cheap air travel the long drive from Sofia on poor winding roads acts as an effective deterrent. For this reason it is perfectly possible that you will find yourself alone or in the company of just a few visitors as you explore the city.

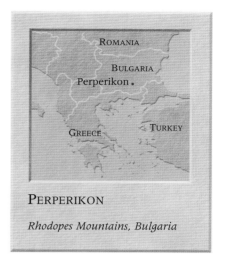

PERPERIKON

Rhodopes Mountains, Bulgaria

A CITY OF SACRIFICE TO THE GODS

The earliest traces of human occupation of Perperikon come from the Neolithic era, 7000–8000 years ago. Fragments of pottery from this time have been found in crevices in the rocks. By the late Bronze Age, between 3800 and 3200 years ago, when further south the Minoan and Mycenaean civilizations were at their peak, Perperikon had become a major place of worship and habitation for the proto-Thracians.

During this time a huge hall was carved into the rock and a great avenue was developed out of a natural cleft in the hillside making it look like a pathway for giants. Thrones were carved out of the bare stone, and a drainage network of troughs, basins and spillways was created. In the centre of the huge hall, which was probably roofless, a round altar almost 2 metres (6 ft) in diameter and 2.75 metres (9 ft) from the ground was carved out of the rock. In addition to this one great altar, the remains of smaller clay altars and various niches cut into the rocks suggest there were numerous altars here.

Archaeologists offer two theories to explain their use and the existence of the troughs and basins. One theory suggests that the site was used for ritual sacrifice, since we know that the ancient Thracians sacrificed bulls, horses, rams and sometimes humans. The fact that the drainage system includes the altars supports this idea, but it also supports the suggestion made by other scholars that the sacrifices were of grapes rather than animals. Drawing on classical accounts and parallels from the Caucasus, the idea has been advanced that the site was used for the making of sacred wine, which would have been prepared and drunk in special rituals.

THE ORACLE OF DIONYSUS

Classical scholars wrote about a mysterious Oracle of Dionysus where wine was offered to the god, and it now seems likely that this oracle was located at Perperikon.

In the early 2nd century AD, the Roman biographer Suetonius (c.75–130) described a visit to the Oracle of Dionysus on a holy mountain by the father of the first Roman emperor, Augustus. There, in the inspiring setting of the temple, Augustus' proud father heard the prophecy of his son's rise to power.

The Greek historian Herodotus (c.484–425 BC) wrote that a tribe of Thracians, known as the Satrians, 'possess the Oracle of Dionysus; which Oracle is on their most lofty mountains … which are covered with forest of all kinds and snow'. Herodotus gave no further indications of the temple's exact location. His contemporary, the playwright Euripides (c.480–406 BC) was a little more precise: 'some say that the Oracle of Dionysus is in

Pangaea [the Rhodopes] and others say it
is in Hemus [the Balkan range north
of the Rhodopes]'.

Dionysus was a principal
god of the Thracians and
there were many temples
dedicated to him
throughout the region,
but the work of one
Roman writer has helped
scholars pinpoint the most
likely location. The historian
Cassius Dio (c.160–230)
described how Marcus Licinius
Crassus (c.115–53 BC), a general in
Augustus' service, in 29–28 BC, seized
the temple from the Bessi and gave it
to the Odrysae, a rival Thracian tribe.
According to the latest research, Perperikon lies
exactly on the boundary between these two tribes,
making it highly likely that the city was indeed the
location of the famed oracle on the 'Holy Mount of Dionysus'.

An example of the spectacular gold artefacts found by archaeologists digging in the territory of ancient Thrace is this 5th-century BC mask, discovered in 2004.

Herodotus said that on this mount 'it is a prophetess who utters the oracles, as
at Delphi'. Facing the great altar dish which stands to this day at the site, you
can imagine the wine being cast into the flames as two of the most momentous
predictions of all time were declared by the seer: to Alexander the Great that
he would conquer the world, and to Augustus' father that his son would
establish the Roman empire.

Time has reduced the cry of the seer, the sounds of fighting, of the clash of
swords, to silence. Here is a place where the rise and fall of civilizations can be
contemplated in peace as you gaze south towards Greece, towards the plains
and hills below these ancient ruins.

*66 When Octavian, father of Augustus, at the head of his army, came upon
the Holy Mount of Dionysus, he consulted the oracle about his son, and the
prophets said to him that his son was to rule the world, for as the wine was
spilt onto the altar, the smoke rose up above the top of the shrine and even
unto the heavens, as had happened when Alexander the Great himself had
sacrificed upon that same altar. 99*

ROMAN HISTORIAN AND BIOGRAPHER SUETONIUS

THE TAROT GARDEN

The cradle of the Renaissance was Tuscany, with its great cities of Florence and Siena. Michelangelo, Leonardo Da Vinci and Dante Alighieri all came from this region. Less well known is the fact that the Tarot derives from this same milieu; in homage to this deck of mysterious cards, which is used both for games and for divination, the 20th-century French artist Niki de St Phalle created an extraordinary symbolic sculpture garden near the Tuscan coast.

IF YOU DRIVE TOWARDS THE TUSCAN TOWN OF CAPALBIO along the winding roads through the gently rolling hills, vineyards, olive groves and cypress trees that characterize this region, you eventually come to a curious garden that might at first strike you as a joke. In reality you will find yourself entering a magical world that was most certainly created to make you laugh, but also to help you contact those deeper feelings and ideas that the Swiss psychiatrist Carl Jung (1875–1961) called the archetypes.

The *Giardino dei Tarocchi* is the creation of the artist, sculptor and film-maker Niki de St Phalle (1930–2002), who designed and helped to build its towering sculptures, which illustrate certain key cards from the Tarot deck. St Phalle was a cosmopolitan figure, born in Paris and raised in New York, and it was fortuitous that she chose northern Italy as the location for her garden, since it was from there that the Tarot made its first appearance in European culture in the 15th century. In 1442 the earliest recorded mention of these mysterious cards comes from Ferrara, which lies just a short distance away to the northeast.

St Phalle had long been intrigued by the expressive possibilities of monumental sculpture; one of her best-known works, first exhibited in Stockholm in 1966, is a 27-metre (88 ft) long woman, whose interior space can be explored by entering through the vagina. Inspired by this work, one of the first Tarot figures she made was of the 'Empress' – a giant goddess figure that she lived in while the garden took shape around her. This task, a true labour of love, took fully 20 years, from 1978 to 1998.

TAROT GARDEN

Capalbio, Tuscany, Italy

The High Priestess *and (behind)* The Magician, *two of the sculptures in the Tarot Garden. The artist's aim was to create a joyful space where people could meditate.*

MEDITATIVE GARDENS

St Phalle's creation has a number of antecedents in both garden and art history. First and foremost, it can be seen as the most exuberant example of a long-established genre of sacred place: the meditative garden. Perhaps the most familiar manifestation of this is the Japanese Zen garden – composed mainly of rocks and raked gravel, perhaps with bamboo or a water feature. It is designed to be observed, not walked through or touched. The same is true of the cloistered gardens traditionally attached to monasteries and convents. Although the cloisters themselves are designed for walking, the gardens remain out of reach – paradises to be glimpsed but not entered. But in other forms of sacred garden, engaging with the natural world with all the senses is encouraged, and recent years have seen a renaissance in the creation of such places: Chalice Well in England, Findhorn in Scotland, the Esalen Institute in California and the Omega Center in upstate New York, to give just a few examples, have all created meditative gardens that can be walked through and sat in, and whose trees and flowers can be touched and smelt. Books and workshops on creating sacred gardens now proliferate, as more and more people are drawn to creating 'paradises on Earth' – havens of tranquillity and microcosms of the wider world of nature.

The Tarot Garden draws on several additional inspirations – notably the tradition of the Renaissance narrative garden and the sculpture park. As a young artist, Niki de St Phalle greatly admired the work of the visionary Spanish architect Antoni Gaudí (1852–1926). She was especially captivated by the outlandish mosaic sculptures, portraying lizards, sea serpents and other organic forms, which he created for his Park Güell in Barcelona (1910–14). St Phalle was also influenced by the Bosco Sacro (Sacred Grove) laid out near the central Italian town of Bomarzo by the 16th-century hunchback sculptor Duke Vicino Orsini (1523–83). In complete contrast to the formal designs of the age, Vicino created a garden scattered with sculptures and engravings bizarre enough to attract the attention of the 20th-century surrealist artists Jean Cocteau (1889–1963) and Salvador Dalí (1904–89). Dalí, a friend of St Phalle, was also fascinated by the Tarot, and produced his own set of cards. One final source of inspiration for St Phalle, especially in her use of boldly coloured tilework, was her close contemporary, the Austrian artist Friedensreich Hundertwasser (1928–2000).

UNLOCKING THE SOUL'S SECRETS

The idea of the narrative garden is essentially Bardic – the garden tells a story, and the Tarot Garden is no exception. But here that story concerns nothing less than the journey of the soul. Each of St Phalle's 22 sculptures represents one of the Major Arcana; their name derives from the fact that, when the Tarot is used in divination, these trump cards are believed to reveal 'greater secrets' – in other words, the deeper currents that guide our lives. Here, these flat card images spring to life in the third dimension and stand, colourful and glittering, before our eyes.

St Phalle's sculpture of the Hierophant *in the Tarot Garden. In the Tarot deck, this figure represents a spiritual guide who forms a bridge between humanity and the gods.*

A walk through the garden begins with the Fool, the first card of the series, and ends with the same figure dancing, this time entitled 'The World'. By each sculpture the artist provides an opaque 'explanation': 'The World is the card of the splendour of interior life. It is the last card of the Major Arcana, and the spiritual exercise of the game. Within this card lies the mystery of the WORLD. It is the answer to the Sphinx.'

A charitable foundation now curates St Phalle's personal collection of over 1000 sculptures and 5000 graphic works of art. But her masterpiece remains the Tarot Garden. Using the cards' magic symbolism as its starting point, it playfully holds up a mirror to our soul and invites us to explore our innermost longings.

" *Life is like a card game, and we are born not knowing the rules, but each of us must continue playing the game we are dealt.* "

NIKI DE ST PHALLE

THE TEMPLES OF HUMANKIND

In the Piedmont region of northern Italy, not far from the border with France and Switzerland and an hour's drive north of Turin, Valchiusella is home to one of the most unusual sacred places ever built. There, an alliance of alternative communities called the Damanhur Federation has created a series of breathtaking temples dedicated not to a pantheon of gods or a single deity but to the inherent divinity in humankind.

T HE TEMPLES AT VALCHIUSELLA ARE A KALEIDOSCOPIC CLUSTER of cavernous rooms, glittering with mirrors, crystals and mosaics like the treasure in a dragon's den. Created over a period of 14 years from 1978 onwards, their dazzling beauty has prompted some to call them the eighth wonder of the world. Whatever its artistic and cultural merit, this new sacred place is the latest in a long tradition of underground edifices created for a variety of reasons both spiritual and secular.

INNER WORLDS

Humans have been burrowing into hillsides and mountains for millennia. Examples, ancient and modern, can be found all over the world. Perhaps the most famous underground buildings are the Ellora Caves in central India (see pages 222–225), begun in the sixth century AD. In the Jordanian desert, the beautiful 2000-year-old rock temples of Petra, the 'rose red city half as old as time,' were carved out of red sandstone. And in Staffordshire, England, the Kinver Edge rock houses, hewn out of a similar form of red sandstone, were inhabited until the 1950s. These troglodyte dwellings inspired local scholar J.R.R. Tolkien (1892–1973) with the idea of hobbit holes for his masterpieces of fantasy fiction, *The Hobbit* (1937) and the trilogy *The Lord of the Rings* (1954–5).

More recently, underground complexes have arisen out of fear for what the future might hold. For example, in the state of Colorado in the western United States, Cheyenne

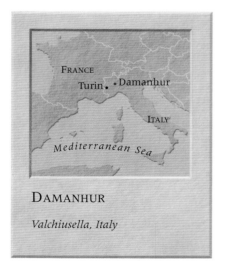

DAMANHUR

Valchiusella, Italy

The Hall of Mirrors at Damanhur, with the largest Tiffany cupola in the world, is dedicated to the air, sky, and light. Four small rooms lead off the hall, each one containing an altar to one of the four classical elements: earth, air, fire and water.

TIMELINE

1950 Damanhur's founder, Oberto Airaudi, born in Balangero, near Turin

1975 Airaudi founds the Horus Centre in Turin, to teach and conduct research into healing, spirituality and the paranormal; this group forms the nucleus of the Damanhur Federation

1978 Excavation of the temples begins

1992 The secret temples are discovered and made public

1998 The temples are opened to visitors

2005 The Damanhur Federation receives a United Nations award for excellence as a model of sustainability

Mountain houses a command centre of the North American Aerospace Defense Command (NORAD). Behind 25-ton steel blast doors and almost a mile into the granite mountain, a 1.8-hectare (4.5-acre) area contains over a dozen buildings three storeys high. This facility was constructed in the early 1960s as a centre for directing combat operations in the event of an intercontinental ballistic missile strike against the USA. Likewise, the largest collection of genealogical records in the world are stored by the Mormon Church in the Granite Mountain Record Vault, a network of chambers protected from a nuclear blast by great steel doors in the Wasatch Mountains near Salt Lake City, Utah.

THE DAMANHUR FEDERATION AND THE GENESIS OF THE TEMPLE PROJECT

By contrast, the Valchiusella temples were built to express the Damanhur Federation's hope for the future, to celebrate humanity's divine nature and creative power, and to create a sacred space that connects lines of energy across the Earth. These dragon lines or 'ley lines' as some people understand them, are called 'synchronic lines' by the temple builders.

The Damanhur Federation is the brainchild of the Italian philosopher and healer Oberto Airaudi (b.1950). In 1975 Airaudi founded a spiritual research group known as the Horus Centre in Turin; shortly thereafter, he called the new organization Damanhur, after a city dedicated to the god Horus 100 miles (160 km) northwest of Cairo. Airaudi's fascination with this falcon-headed ancient Egyptian deity also manifested itself in his change of name to Falco – now all members of the federation adopt the names of animals, plants or mythological creatures. Falco shuns all attempts to label him as a guru and stresses that the movement he helped to start is not a religion.

The inspiration for the temple project came to Falco one evening in 1978 while he was sitting around an open fire with a group of friends. A shooting star that appeared in the sky moved Falco to suggest building a temple inside the hill that some of them were already living beside. Since there were no laws regulating underground buildings of that kind in their region and no authority could grant them a building permit, the group embarked on their grand excavations in secret. They dug mostly by hand, with the aid of only a few jack-hammers.

"Instead of delving into one's painful past to heal one's inner being, the idea at Damanhur is that by nurturing that which is of beauty in each person, all will flourish."

AMERICAN NEW-AGE AUTHOR RANDY PEYSER

THE BLUE TEMPLE AND THE HALLS OF WATER AND THE EARTH

As they began digging into the hillside, they realized it was having a powerful effect on them – it felt as if they were delving into themselves to discover their inner riches. Although they had no experience of building they were filled with enthusiasm, and combined digging with periods of meditation and ritual.

The first part of the temple complex to be completed was the Blue Temple, a cavern-like space lavishly decorated with paintings. On the floor of this cave is a complex mosaic depicting the Star image of the Tarot deck, an archetype of beauty and practical idealism. A section of the floor here can be moved to reveal a hidden stairway.

The second room to be built was the Hall of Water, a tall circular chamber, designed as a chalice, with a great domed stained glass ceiling that is lit from above to create an eerie underwater effect. Seven steps lead to a stained-glass window depicting the moon, and gold-leafed images of dragons snake around the walls, symbolizing the flow of synchronic lines in the chamber, while a glowing sphere can be seen in a cavernous alcove.

The Hall of Water is dedicated to water and the feminine principle in nature. Inscribed on the walls here are texts in 12 ancient alphabets.

As the years went by, the temple complex steadily expanded. Beneath the Hall of Water is the Hall of the Earth, dedicated to the male principle and the memory of past lives. The soaring pillars and Tiffany glass windows are complemented by paintings that tell the history of the universe, from its creation to the role of humanity in reawakening to its inner divinity.

Stairways and corridors lead to further halls. Damanhurians believe that in the Hall of Spheres four important synchronic lines converge, and they say that 'from here it is possible to contact all points of the planet and transmit and receive messages, ideas and dreams to help create harmony and evolution for humanity and the planet'. The Hall of Mirrors, dedicated to the spiritual role of light, incorporates the largest Tiffany cupola in the world.

A crisis hit the Damanhurians in 1992, when a disgruntled former member disclosed their activities to the Italian authorities. The police arrived at the temples with explosives, threatening to blow the place up unless every corner of the complex was shown to them. They emerged stunned by the beauty of the subterranean world they had experienced. The local judge who had ordered the raid vowed to protect the site and work on the temples was allowed to proceed.

Since then, Damanhur has gone from strength to strength, growing into a confederation of 30 small communities of around 20 people each, all sharing the same vision. Members participate in a range of initiatives both practical and spiritual. They produce their own food and wine, are engaged in reforestation programmes and are moving towards self-sufficiency in energy. In addition they run meditation and healing schools, and guide visitors around the temples. They have their own schools and publish a daily newspaper. Over 60 businesses, owned by community members, as well as other local businesses, honour the Damanhur currency, the Credit. In 2005 the federation was presented with an award by the United Nations as a model of excellence for sustainable communities.

AMBITIOUS PLANS

Emerging from the Temples of Humankind, you might be tempted to think that nothing more extraordinary or ambitious could ever be created here. But you would be wrong. It appears that the work at Damanhur has only just begun, and that the temples will ultimately comprise just 10 percent of the entire finished complex.

In 2003 the federation bought a disused factory in the valley that had once belonged to the typewriter and computer firm Olivetti and transformed it into an arts and research centre, which includes conference facilities, an organic food store and restaurant, and a healing centre. There are also plans to reclaim a forest area and large abandoned quarry next to the temples to create a 'modern cathedral dedicated to art and human creativity'. The largest glass dome in the world will cover the new complex, which will be linked to the Temples of Humankind by an electric train and to the villages below by cable car. Inside the dome will be health spas as well as places for art and research, a library of sacred texts and a theatre that will seat 1000 people.

The Temples of Humankind are an inspiration because they show us what is possible. There is something powerful in the way that they are hidden within the Earth. Nothing is what it appears to be. We enter a mountain thinking that it is a mountain but a world of light and crystals suddenly unfolds before us. Mountains have been revered for millennia as God's domain. Caves have been venerated for millennia as the realm of the goddess. Here in the cavernous Temples of Humankind goddess and god are united, and the result is fertility and an abundance of hope and dreams.

"Every one of us gasped when we first entered the Labyrinth, which led to the various sacred rooms: the Hall of Water, of the Earth, of the Spheres, of the Metals. What makes these more than just museum pieces, though, is that the sacred science upon which Damanhur is founded … is embedded inside the walls!"

AMERICAN MUSICIAN STEVE HALPERN, *DAMANHUR AND THE TEMPLE OF MANKIND*

EL CAMINO DE SANTIAGO (THE WAY OF ST JAMES)

Every year thousands of pilgrims make their way along a network of routes across Europe that converge on the cathedral of Santiago de Compostela in Galicia, northwest Spain, where relics attributed to Jesus' apostle James lie buried beneath the high altar. In medieval times this pilgrimage, often known simply as 'El Camino' – 'The Road' – was considered as beneficial as a pilgrimage to Jerusalem or Rome.

IN THE PRE-CHRISTIAN ERA, A ROUTE THAT LED OVER THE PYRENEES and across northern Spain to Cape Finisterre was used for trade and religious purposes by the Celts and Romans. As one of the most westerly points of Europe, and named from the Latin 'Finisterrae', which means 'Land's End', the cape faces the region traditionally associated with the realm of the Dead: the land of the setting sun that lies across the sea and beyond the horizon.

That same route, and others that feed into it, is now known as the Way of St James and has become one of the most important and most popular Christian pilgrimage routes. The origin of the Way of St James lies in the legend that Jesus' disciple James travelled to western Spain after the crucifixion to preach the gospel and that his earthly remains lie buried in Santiago de Compostela, just 37 miles (60 km) inland from the cape.

James and his brother John were fishermen, who left their boats and nets to follow Jesus. They became some of his closest disciples, and because of their fiery tempers and evangelical zeal were known as the 'Sons of Thunder'. In the sixth century a tradition began to develop that James had travelled to 'Hispania' to convert the Hispanic peoples, just as his brother John had evangelized Asia Minor, and that he was buried in an unspecified location in Spain. Most historians reject the idea that James could have preached in Spain, since the writings of the early Church state that he did not leave Jerusalem after the crucifixion, and the Acts of the Apostles recount that he became the first Christian martyr when he was beheaded by king Herod Agrippa in AD 44.

Even so, by the eighth century the legend was well established, and at the beginning of the following century, in 814, a marble sarcophagus was allegedly discovered by the monk Pelayo, who, echoing the story of the Nativity, was guided to its location by a star. For this reason, the place came to be known as 'Compostela' (Campus de la Stella) – the Field of Stars. From this the legend evolved that the Milky Way represents the Way of St James in the heavens, formed from the dust rising from the feet of countless pilgrims.

THE FIRST PILGRIM

Teodomir, the local bishop, immediately declared that the newly discovered tomb was that of St James. King Alfonso II of Asturias (r. 791–842) and his court visited the site and ordered the building of a wooden church around the tomb. Over the next 30 years a literary tradition arose, recounting how James' remains came to be there, despite the biblical references to his death in Jerusalem. By these accounts, James had returned to Jerusalem after preaching in Spain, and was then executed. His body was transported, or miraculously transferred, to Spain for burial 'contra mare Britannicum' – 'close to the British sea'.

SANTIAGO DE
COMPOSTELA

Galicia, Spain

The cathedral of Santiago de Compostela is the reputed burial place of St James, one of Jesus' closest disciples.

This statue of 'St James the Pilgrim' by the 18th-century sculptor José Gambino adorns the cathedral in Santiago. Another statue by the same artist, 'St James the Moor Slayer' has been the subject of much controversy. In 2004, a proposal to move it from the cathedral to a museum to avoid offending Muslims was abandoned after a public outcry.

Some suggest that King Alfonso himself was the first pilgrim to the site, and over the coming years the story of St James and his relics became politically useful for rallying Christians in the region against the Islamic invaders who had succeeded in conquering much of Spain. Protected by mountains, Galicia had remained unconquered and as the movement to eject the invaders from the rest of the country gathered strength through the ninth century, St James was often invoked as Spain's patron and protector. Victories were attributed to his aid and at the Battle of Clavijo in 844, he was said to have appeared on a white horse leading the charge against the enemy.

An Alternative to Jerusalem

The church and tomb at Compostela quickly became a site of pilgrimage, both locally and for pilgrims from France. By the time the first recorded foreign pilgrim, Gotescalc, bishop of Le Puy in central France, made his way across the Pyrenees in 947, just over a century after the tomb's discovery, the pilgrimage was already well established, and by the following century the traffic to Santiago de Compostela was substantial.

In 1100 the diplomat Diego Gelmírez (*c.*1069 – *c.*1149) was made bishop of Compostela, and over the next 40 years vigorously promoted the cause of the pilgrimage, as well as of the cathedral, whose construction in granite had begun in 1075. By 1120 he had become an archbishop and papal legate and in

1122 the last stone of the cathedral was laid, although decoration and building continued for many years thereafter. By this time the Way of St James had begun to rival the major Christian pilgrimage to Jerusalem, which was far more dangerous and sometimes impossible to accomplish when cut off by the Saracens. Although the rigours of crossing the Pyrenees and the arid lands of Castile made the journey to Santiago de Compostela seem as arduous as the way to the Holy Land for many, by the 12th century it was reported that 1000 pilgrims arrived in Santiago each day.

From Britain, Ireland and northern Europe many took the journey partly by boat, while others walked or rode by horse or donkey along one of four traditional routes through France. Pilgrims would gather first at assembly points in Paris, Vézelay, le Puy-en-Velay or Arles before setting off in groups for safety and camaraderie. In northern Spain, the four routes merged into the Camino Francés, which passed through Burgos and León before arriving at Santiago de Compostela.

THE PILGRIMS' GUIDE

The popularity of 'El Camino' was considerably enhanced by the publication in 1140 of one of history's first guidebooks – *The Pilgrims' Guide*. This was the fifth volume in a series about St James and the pilgrimage entitled the *Codex Calixtinus*. The guide's 11 chapters gave details of the four routes across France that eventually join together to become the Camino Francés, and described much of the terrain and rivers that the pilgrim would encounter along the way.

The pilgrims' symbol was the scallop shell, which recalls James' connection with fishing and the sea, and which some people suggest may allude to an earlier fertility cult of Venus.

All along these routes shrines were built, often with the relics of saints, which *The Pilgrims' Guide* compares to pearls on a string. In addition to the prosperity that the pilgrimage brought to the regions it passed through, it also acted as an important cultural stimulus. Laurie Dennett, formerly chairperson of the Confraternity of St. James – a charity founded in 1983 to bring together those interested in the pilgrimage – gives a vivid description of its cultural impact on the area in medieval times:

> *'With the pilgrims to Santiago, and often as pilgrims themselves, there came French stonemasons, German artisans, Tuscan merchants, Flemish noblemen, English and Burgundian crusaders. The more educated among them brought, as part of their intellectual baggage, Provençal lyric poetry, Slav legends, Carolingian and Scholastic philosophy, new building techniques, and endless music. On the Camino Francés all these influences intermingled and returned to their lands of origin, along with Arab aesthetics and science, medicine and culinary arts.'*

INDULGENCES

By the mid-13th century, taking the Way of St James had, like the pilgrimages to Jerusalem and Rome, become a way of gaining a remission from sins known as a 'plenary indulgence'. Since a plenary indulgence granted by the Catholic Church is seen as annulling the punishment due for all the transgressions a person has committed up to the time of its granting, this became the dominant motivation for many pilgrims.

TIMELINE

814 Purported discovery of tomb of St James

947 The first recorded foreign pilgrim to Santiago – Bishop Le Puy from France

1100 Diego Gelmírez becomes bishop of Compostela. Over 40 years he lavishes funds on the cathedral and energetically promotes his see

c.1140 The first guide book listing four routes – *The Pilgrims' Guide* – is published

12th–15th centuries The pilgrimage is at the height of its popularity

16th century The Protestant Reformation, plagues and political unrest in Europe contribute to the Way's decline

1589 Sir Francis Drake leads a raid on La Coruña. The relics are hidden for safe-keeping and are then lost

1879 Remains are excavated that are believed to be the relics

1884 Pope Leo XIII authenticates the relics, which are placed under the high altar

1948 A major three-volume study of the pilgrimage is published

1971 First modern pocket guidebook for pilgrims

1982–7 Major efforts undertaken to restore the Way. The Camino Francés is waymarked along its entire length

1987 The Way is declared the first European Cultural Route by the Council of Europe

1993 The Way is designated a UNESCO World Heritage Site

Indulgences are still granted by the church, and are detailed in a document entitled the *Enchiridion*. In modern times it has become easier to obtain a plenary indulgence: since 2002 believers can obtain them every Easter on 'Divine Mercy Sunday' at any Catholic church, provided three conditions are fulfilled: confession, communion and a prayer for the intentions of the pope. Pilgrims to Santiago de Compostela can also obtain such an indulgence if they fulfil the conditions in the cathedral on three other days – the feast days of St James on 23 May, 25 July and 30 December.

THE DECLINE AND RENAISSANCE OF EL CAMINO

During the 14th and 15th centuries the Black Death decimated the population of Europe and affected the numbers of pilgrims making the journey to Santiago. The Protestant Reformation in the 16th century precipitated a further decline in the fortunes and popularity of the Way.

In 1589 Sir Francis Drake (*c.*1540 – *c.*1596) attacked the coastal city of La Coruña, just 40 miles (64 km) from Santiago. Fearing for the safety of the relics, the archbishop opened the tomb and hid them. For 300 years their location was unknown, and once this fact became general knowledge much of the inspiration for making the long pilgrimage vanished.

In 1879 the relics were found while the cathedral was being redecorated, and after being authenticated by the pope in 1884 were replaced under the high altar. War in Europe prevented a revival of interest, but soon after the end of the Second World War pilgrims once again started to follow the Way to Santiago. A major study of the Camino was published in 1948 and a number of organizations were formed to foster interest in its development.

A key figure in the renaissance of the Way was a Galician priest, Elias Valiña Sampedro (1929–89), who produced the first pocket guide book for pilgrims in modern times in 1971. Just as *The Pilgrims' Guide* of 1140 had encouraged and guided countless pilgrims centuries before, Sampedro's *Caminos a Compostela* – Roads to Compostela – had a similar effect, enhanced in 1982 when he organized the waymarking of the Camino Francés. He did this by obtaining surplus paint from the highway authority which was used to paint yellow arrows pointing to Compostela on trees, rocks and buildings along the entire length of the route.

POPULARIZATION OF THE PILGRIMAGE

In 1987 two events occurred to introduce the Way to a wider audience: the Council of Europe declared the Way the first

European Cultural Route and the Brazilian author Paulo Coelho's (b.1947) book *The Pilgrimage* was published. In this he described his own pilgrimage taken the year before. In subsequent books and interviews Coelho continues to refer to the Way as a powerful influence in his life, as does the American actress Shirley Maclaine (b.1934) whose account of her pilgrimage *The Camino*, was published in 2000.

In 2003 the British art critic and lapsed Catholic Brian Sewell (b.1931) made a moving and witty television series, 'The Naked Pilgrim', which followed his own pilgrimage to Santiago. Despite his scepticism, he was frequently moved to tears during his journey, which he finished, in the traditional way, by travelling to Cape Finisterre and making a bonfire of the clothes he wore on the journey. He then walked naked into the sea, echoing images of the earliest Christian baptism. Sewell conveyed the idea that in essence a pilgrimage is a journey that involves freeing oneself of attachments of every kind until one stands 'naked before God'.

> **"** *If the journey meant anything, it meant that the last steps into Santiago were the first steps of another journey.* **"**
>
> LAURIE DENNETT, *A HUG FOR THE APOSTLE* (1987)

By the end of the 20th century, the Way was being walked by growing numbers of people – not only Catholics, but also those who were interested in pilgrimage as a spiritual or cultural experience. This way-marker displays the modern symbol of the Camino, a stylized scallop shell.

THE CHAUVET CAVE

A journey to the roots of the human creative urge takes us to southern France, where – some scholars claim – the oldest rock art in the world is to be found in a cave in the high cliffs above the Ardèche River. Here, in 1994, three cavers stumbled upon a treasure trove of Paleolithic art that had remained undisturbed for perhaps 27,000 years, thanks to a rock fall that had sealed the entrance to the cave.

IN SOUTHERN FRANCE, ROUGHLY MIDWAY BETWEEN LYONS AND MARSEILLES, the Ardèche River, a tributary of the Rhône, winds its way through the largest canyon in Europe, where limestone cliffs rise to 300 metres (984 ft). If you were to join the many holidaymakers who visit this region and kayak down the river, you would find yourself moving swiftly towards the Pont d'Arc – a great natural bridge of rock that spans the river and seems to have been shaped by some prehistoric giant.

It is near this bridge that an astonishing find was made in 1994. A week before Christmas, Jean-Marie Chauvet took his two friends, Éliette Brunel Deschamps and Christian Hillaire, up on to the cliffs near the Pont d'Arc to investigate a phenomenon that had piqued his curiosity on a previous visit. He had noticed a faint current of air coming from an opening in the back of a small cave. He and his friends began digging and soon created a passageway that revealed a shaft descending into darkness. Climbing down a ladder they found themselves in a cave system 500 metres (1640 ft) long that had remained undisturbed for many millennia.

Here were spectacular images of animals painted in profusion on the walls of the cave; bones lay on the ground, and a bear's skull rested on a stone as if placed on an altar. They announced their discovery to the authorities and ten days later showed the cave to Dr Jean Clottes, scientific advisor to the French Ministry of Culture and a specialist in decorated caves.

Tests were carried out to ensure that the site was authentic, and six months later, when the results of Carbon-14 dating were released, the official news broke that the Chauvet Cave contained works of art between 30,000 and 32,000 years old.

FRANCE

Chauvet Cave
Marseilles

CHAUVET CAVE

Ardèche, southern France

Images of big cats (left) and rhinoceroses in the Chauvet Cave. Of their creators, Dr Jean Clottes, leader of the preservation team, has said: 'To these people's way of thinking, those animal spirits were in the walls'.

"I believe that the discovery of the art in the Chauvet Cave is as important as mankind travelling into space and walking on the moon. Art is the pinnacle of human civilization. The Florentine Sperone Speroni, 16th-century Renaissance writer, defined the key to civilization as 'the creation of wealth and the patronage of the arts'. Art is the culmination of mankind's achievements and the oldest evidence of its existence is in the Chauvet Cave."

JOHN ROBINSON, ARTIST AND CO-FOUNDER OF THE BRADSHAW FOUNDATION

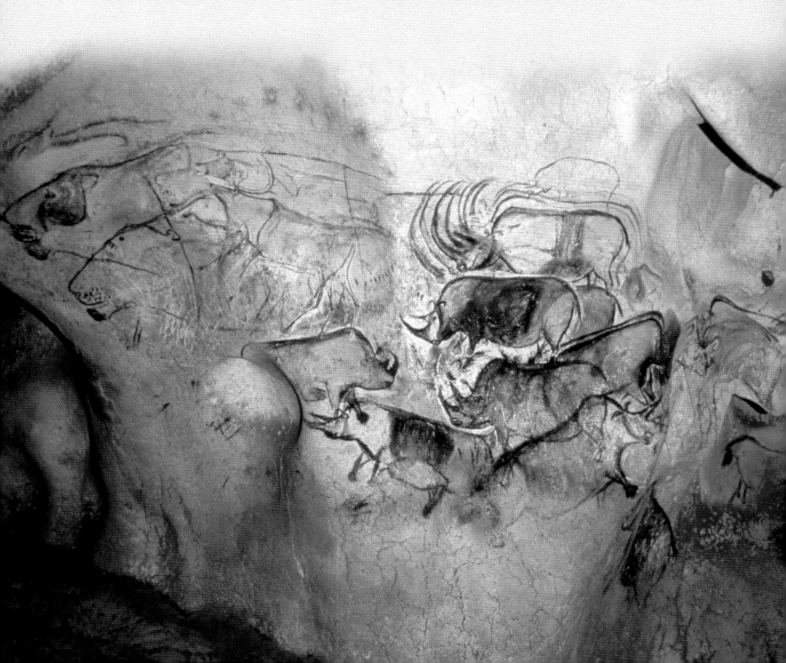

THE OLDEST WORKS OF ART IN THE WORLD?

France is especially rich in prehistoric rock art; no fewer than 160 caves containing such images have been found here. Perhaps the most famous are the Lascaux Caves in the Dordogne. Discovered in 1940, these caverns have been dated to around 17,000 years ago, and contain more than 2000 paintings. Many are faint and hardly discernible, but those that can be identified include many geometric shapes and 900 images of animals, including 364 of horses. Other animals depicted at Lascaux include bison, deer, bulls, mammoths, ibexes, aurochs (a prehistoric species of ox) and felines. There is also a single image of a human being.

The paintings in the far older Chauvet Cave portray a quite different world of prehistoric fauna, with many of the animals extinct even by the time of the Lascaux paintings. Cave bears (far larger than modern grizzlies), and ancient species of panther, rhinoceros, megaceros deer, musk oxen and lion roamed the landscape when the Chauvet Cave was inhabited. Hundreds of images depict over 13 species of animal, and there is one 'Goddess' icon (now known as the 'Chauvet Venus') which depicts a vulva, hips and legs. A study of these pictures has greatly increased our knowledge of the very earliest period of human artistic development.

The cave paintings of Chauvet are claimed by some scholars to be the oldest known works of art on the planet, and looking at them we see a skilled use of perspective, shading and composition. These are not the rudimentary scrawls of 'primitives' but the work of a people who were fully capable of depicting their world both naturalistically and with some degree of abstraction, shading and blending the colours they used. The images also show evidence of sophisticated artistic techniques such as perspective, which were once wrongly thought to be a Renaissance invention. The Chauvet artists remembered the sight of creatures in the wild and reproduced them with artistic flair in the interior of a cave by the light of torches. Mysteriously, they decided not to depict themselves. Instead they did what rock artists the world over have done – enigmatically showing us just the silhouette of their hands, and their children's hands, by blowing paint through a bone over the palms and fingers pressed against the cave wall.

Many fossilized bear skeletons and paw prints were found throughout the cave – it seems that it was used by hibernating bears for millennia before its first human Palaeolithic visitors turned it into a vibrant studio and art gallery that was in use for perhaps 5000 years. When the first human visitors arrived, they found the skulls and bones of its earlier inhabitants and the marks of their scratching on the walls. Whether the cave was used solely for art or whether a magical or religious impulse was also at work here we will probably never know. Because several of the images are of game animals, it is possible that creation of the pictures was a ritualized activity designed to ensure a successful hunt. The combination of animal images with abstract lines and dots has also caused experts to speculate that the paintings may have had some shamanistic function.

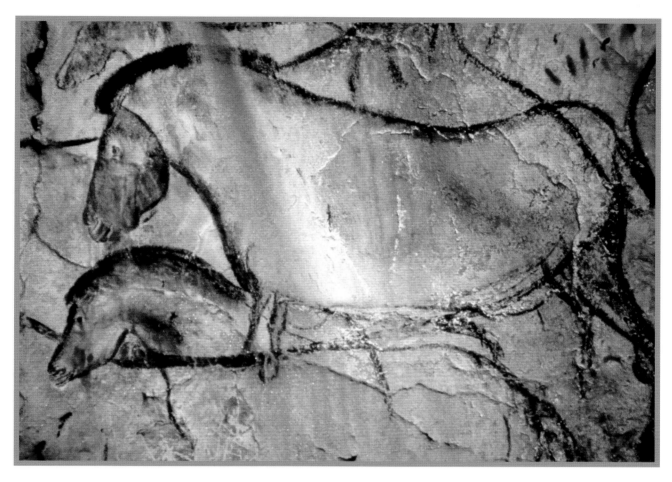

PRESERVING THE PAST

Because less than 20 years of public access had caused irreparable damage to the Lascaux paintings, the Chauvet Cave was quickly declared a national monument, and guarded by the police until the entrance could be sealed to protect the site from all but qualified researchers. In 1983 an exact replica of the two main caves at Lascaux was opened just a short distance away from the original. Perhaps, one day, the Chauvet Cave will also have its own facsimile, allowing visitors to imbibe the atmosphere without endangering the priceless archaeology.

In the meanwhile, we can only dream of revisiting our earliest origins. As the eminent Romanian historian of religion, Mircea Eliade (1907–86) pointed out, these primal spaces were almost certainly key sites of early religious activity, in particular for contact with the spirit world: 'It is in caves that aspirants have their dreams and meet their helping spirits'.

Images of horses at the Chauvet Cave. Iron oxide and calcite deposits overlaying the images allowed researchers to date such images as this and establish their great antiquity.

" *This may be the childhood of art, but it is not the art of children.* "

CHRISTOPHER CHIPPINDALE, ROCK-ART SPECIALIST

THE GULF OF MORBIHAN

Ritual sites often exist in the wider context of a sacred environment that may stretch for miles around, and include a number of different places of pilgrimage or worship. The Gulf of Morbihan in Brittany is one such location. Its 500-plus sites represent one of the greatest achievements of the megalithic culture of the Neolithic period – the New Stone Age that began around 9000 years ago.

THREE OF THE MOST STRIKING SITES AT MORBIHAN are the chambered passage-grave of Gavrinis, which now stands on its own island and boasts entrancing carvings on most of the stones that line its walls; the beautifully carved Table des Marchands, which lies beside the Great Broken Menhir that once formed part of an alignment of 19 stones; and the famous massed rows of stones at nearby Carnac, which continue to baffle researchers.

Although these monuments guard their secrets closely, one clear feature emerges from the alignments of the standing stones and the tumuli: it seems that the people who built them incorporated observations of the heavens into their constructions. The light of the sun, moon and stars was used to position massive stones and create sites that may have served as observatories alongside their ritual or funerary function.

In creating tombs within mounds of earth, there is the inescapable feeling that our ancestors were also creating temples to life rather than death. Emerging from Gavrinis at dawn on the winter solstice, or from the Table des Marchands on the summer solstice, who could fail to feel reborn?

LAND OF MYTHS AND MEGALITHS

The whole of Brittany is filled with megalithic remains, which stand as silent witnesses to its mythical past peopled by Druids, King Arthur and the wizard Merlin, whose legends migrated from Great Britain to the Little Britain of Brittany with the Norman conquest. Not far south from the forest of Broceliande, the focus of these legends, lies 'Ar Mor Bihan' – Breton for 'the little sea'.

Legends state that there were once 365 islands in this great natural harbour, but today only 40 or so can be seen at low tide. Twenty-five of these are inhabited. A short trip on one of the tourist boats that ply the Gulf of Morbihan brings the visitor to one of the most remarkable chambered tombs in the world.

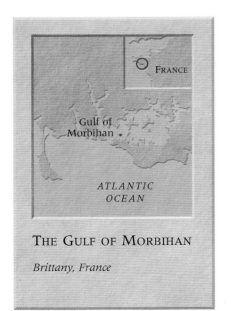

FRANCE

Gulf of
Morbihan

*ATLANTIC
OCEAN*

THE GULF OF MORBIHAN

Brittany, France

Step off the boat onto the island of Gavrinis, and you find yourself face to face with the ancestors. The great mound that stands not far from the jetty draws the visitor into its heart with an attraction that is primal, almost magnetic.

A GREAT COASTAL PLAIN

Some 7000 years ago the whole area provided the perfect environment for human settlement. Since the polar ice-caps were larger than today, the sea level was 7 to 8 metres (26–28 ft) lower than it is now and the Gulf was a great coastal plain, ideal for cultivation, which contained a much smaller and shallow inland sea that would have been ideal for fishing.

It was only as sea levels rose that Gavrinis became marooned and formed an island. The effect of this dramatic change in the landscape can be clearly seen on the island adjacent, where half of a stone circle lies above the high tide on the shore while its other half is submerged in the water.

The cairn of Gavrinis is remarkable because many of the stones, 23 in all, that line the tomb and its entrance passage are ornately carved with great swirls and shapes that have intrigued scholars for over 150 years. Among the patterns they have identified highly schematized human figures, snakes, arrows and axes. Viewed by the torchlight provided by the guide, the swirling lines are reminiscent of giant fingerprints; some researchers believe that these shapes, along with many others found in megalithic temple-tombs, act as 'entoptic phenomena' – images designed to induce trances or altered states of consciousness.

The entrance to the tomb is oriented towards the winter solstice sunrise, just like its counterpart in Ireland, Newgrange, which was built at about the same time, and whose kerbstone is similarly engraved with swirling spiral shapes.

The long passage leading to the burial chamber beneath the tumulus at Gavrinis is lined with intricately decorated stone slabs.

One of the alignments of menhirs (standing stones) at the Neolithic site of Carnac in Brittany.

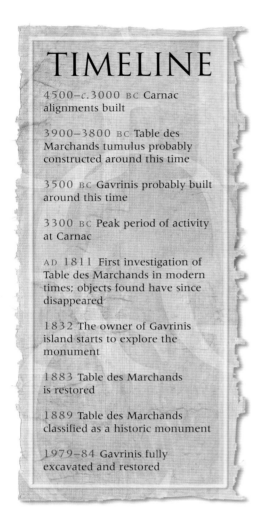

THE SECRETS OF THE CAPSTONE

In 1984 archaeologists examined the upper, hidden side of the capstone of the cairn of Gavrinis and found carvings on it that exactly matched those on two other great lengths of stone situated 2.5 miles (4 m) away in Locmariaquer.

Research determined that these three lengths of stone had originally formed one great standing stone, known as a menhir in France, that was 14 metres (46 ft) high. At some time in prehistory it fractured, or was deliberately broken, into three sections, which were then used to cover three different tombs. Near to this soaring menhir was another even taller, Le Grand Menhir Brisé ('the Great Broken Menhir'), which weighs 355 tons and now lies in four pieces. It was originally the highest of an alignment of 19 menhirs, and stood over 20 metres (66 ft) tall, making it one of Europe's greatest megaliths.

While one section of its smaller twin came to form the roof of Gavrinis, another capped the roof of a tumulus built beside the Great Broken Menhir. The entrance to this tomb is oriented to the summer solstice sunrise, and is known as the Table des Marchands, after the extraordinary stone of the same name that faces you once you enter its inner sanctum.

Originally this stone may well have been displayed in the open air, since both sides are carved. Hidden from view today is a central image of a square with a crescent-moon shape beneath and two semi-circles above. At its base, now buried in the earth, are the familiar symbols found in many examples of rock art: squiggly lines with 'heads' resembling sperm, and circles like ova. Although invisible to the human eye, it is tempting to believe that Stone Age people somehow intuited the presence of these primal forms.

The side of the stone that faces you is vibrant and emanates a sense of fertility, as if drawing upon the primal images concealed in the earth. No-one knows what, if anything, the rows of lines represent: they may be shepherds' crooks (like those that have been identified on other stones as far away as Portugal), plants or trees, or possibly even a depiction of the avenues of stones at Carnac.

THE GREAT AVENUES OF STONE

Carnac lies near the Atlantic coast, 8 miles (13 km) from the Table des Marchands. Here, more than 3000 standing stones are laid out in long lines, prompting the local legend that they are a Roman legion turned to stone by Merlin. Certainly they are reminiscent of the great terracotta army of China – 6000 pottery men and horses protecting the tomb of the emperor in Xi'an city.

These great rows of stones were erected in the Neolithic period, with the greatest period of activity probably being around 3300 BC. Today the existence of roads, fences around certain sections of the site and a village diminish the experience of being among the stones, but a day spent exploring the alignments is still highly rewarding.

As with so many features of the megalithic culture, we can only guess at the motivation and technology of the builders. Mysteriously, no trace of Neolithic dwellings remains in the area; there was also an abrupt cessation of activity in around 3000 BC, which may have occurred as the result of warfare or climate change. Some scholars have suggested that successive generations might have erected stones in honour of their ancestors, so that the site represents a vast tribute to the dead. Sacred sites researcher Paul Devereux speculates that the lines of stones, like their smaller cousins in England on Dartmoor, are 'spirit paths' or roads for the dead, built to help guide souls out of this world, or to assist the soul-flight of shamans during their trances. Quite why so many lines would be needed remains unclear, but what is certain is that this whole area around Morbihan was one vast sacred site for over a thousand years, Indeed, it still exerts a powerful influence on pilgrims today who visit these sites with an attitude of reverence and awe.

" You may forget but let me tell you this: someone in some future time will think of us. "

GREEK POET SAPPHO, 6TH CENTURY BC

Standing stones in the Kermario (or House of the Dead) alignment at Carnac, a fan-shaped arrangement of over 1000 stones.

CHARTRES CATHEDRAL

The magnificent cathedral of Notre-Dame de Chartres near Paris in France is considered one of the finest examples of Gothic architecture in the world, and has inspired artists as diverse as the French painter Camille Corot, the German poet Rainer Maria Rilke, and the American film director Orson Welles. The cathedral was built on the site of a pre-Christian shrine – a holy well and grotto that may also have been the site of Druid gatherings.

NOTRE-DAME DE CHARTRES, MORE COMMONLY KNOWN AS CHARTRES CATHEDRAL, is situated 56 miles (90 km) southwest of the centre of Paris, in relatively flat countryside. For miles around its great spires announce the presence of one of the finest cathedrals in the world – perhaps the finest. Twice as high as any cathedral built before it, the church boasts the most exquisite stained glass ever produced, and offers the visitor one of the best-preserved examples of a kind of medieval architecture which was termed 'Gothic' as an insult by critics in the 16th century, who found the style barbaric – as if produced by Goths or Vandals.

PAGAN ORIGINS

The cathedral, a quintessential symbol of mediaeval Christianity, is actually built over an ancient pagan shrine – a holy well in a grotto that tradition claims was a sacred site of the Druids. The ancient Celts worshipped water as a source of life and in particular revered wells and springs that bubbled out of the ground. Like milk flowing from the breast, they saw life-giving water flowing from the body of Mother Earth. Shrines grew up around such springs, which were also seen as mysterious portals to the Underworld – the realm of the gods and the ancestors.

Here at Chartres, in the grotto beside the well, they reputedly erected a statue of mother and child which some scholars believe provided the model for the Black Madonna, which stands in the crypt of the church.

The area around the well may have been the location referred to by Julius Caesar (100–44 BC) when he wrote, in his account of the Gallic War: 'At a certain time of the

CHARTRES CATHEDRAL

Chartres, France

The cathedral at Chartres soars above the surrounding city. The tower in the foreground dates from c.1150, while the other is a later addition in the 'Flamboyant' style.

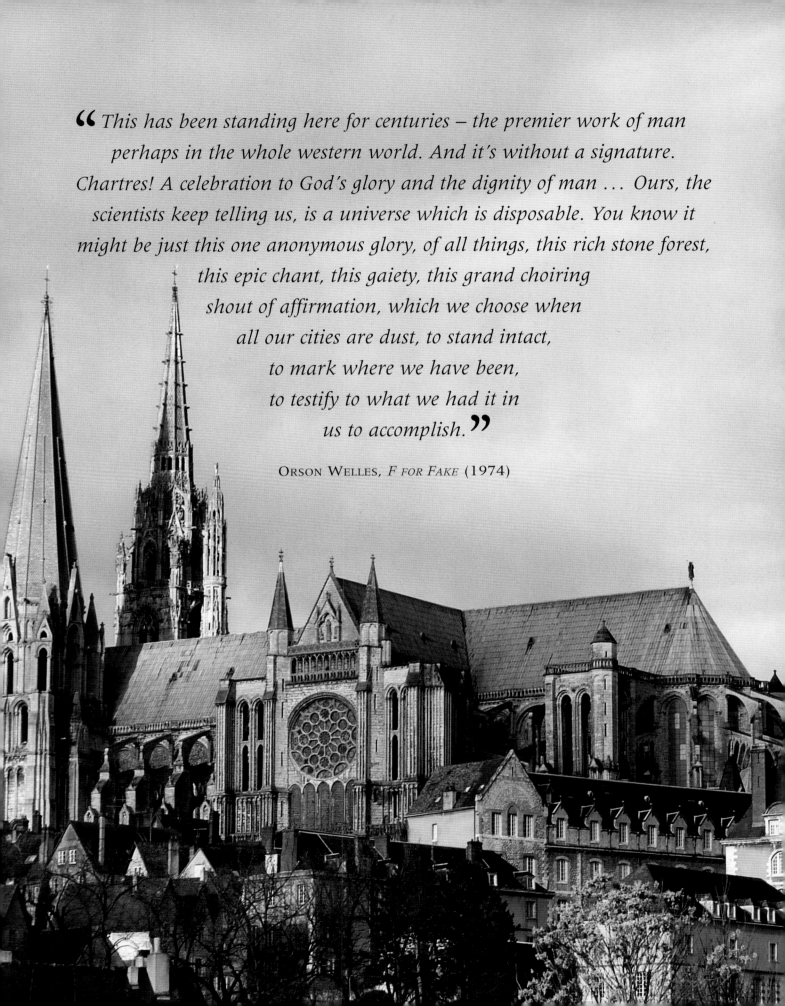

" *This has been standing here for centuries – the premier work of man*
perhaps in the whole western world. And it's without a signature.
Chartres! A celebration to God's glory and the dignity of man … Ours, the
scientists keep telling us, is a universe which is disposable. You know it
might be just this one anonymous glory, of all things, this rich stone forest,
this epic chant, this gaiety, this grand choiring
shout of affirmation, which we choose when
all our cities are dust, to stand intact,
to mark where we have been,
to testify to what we had it in
us to accomplish. "

ORSON WELLES, *F FOR FAKE* (1974)

year, they [the Druids] assemble in session on a consecrated spot in the confines of the Carnutes, which is considered the central region of the whole of Gaul'. Chartres was an important fortified town of the Gallic tribe of the Carnutes, and its sacred well atop a broad sloped mound would have been an ideal setting for a great convocation of sages.

A SYMPHONY IN STONE

The site's Christian heritage begins with the legend that, as early as AD 67, Saints Altinus and Eodaldus built a church over the Druid shrine in which Modesta, the virgin daughter of the governor, Quirinus, was martyred as a Christian when Gallo-Roman soldiers killed her and threw her body into the well. Emerging from the uncertainty of legend into the light of historical evidence, the first church on the site seems to have been built in the 4th century, and then to have begun a pattern of successive rebirths after being destroyed by fire: first in 743 by the duke of Aquitaine, then in 858 by Danish Vikings, who are also said to have thrown the bodies of their victims down the well. Over the next 300 or so years the church suffered fires another four times before it was rebuilt in its present form in the 12th century.

In 1145 work was begun on a new cathedral, fuelled by a wave of religious fervour. In what has become known as the 'Cult of the Carts', over one thousand people engaged in a mass act of penitence, dragging carts of stones and wood to help rebuild the church. In 1194 another fire destroyed all but the west front, and yet another rebuilding was carried out.

The construction of the present cathedral in the 13th century was informed by sacred geometry – a discipline based on a belief that a profound knowledge of numbers and proportion would reveal the structure of Creation. This knowledge manifests itself in the design of the stained-glass windows, particularly the Rose Window, whose dimensions are echoed in a tiled labyrinth on the floor of the nave. The rhythmic aspect that sacred geometry lent to Chartres cathedral's architecture has led several commentators to liken it to the most glorious music frozen in stone.

Beneath the nave the visitor can journey back in time by entering the vast 9th-century crypt of St Lupin, the largest in France and one of the few remaining parts of the original building.

THE LABYRINTH AND THE GODDESS

By 1220 the new cathedral was complete – and it included in the west end of the nave a labyrinth 13 metres (42 ft) in diameter. Here a pilgrim could undertake a symbolic journey to the Holy Land, covering the distance of a third of a mile in a contemplative journey designed to lead the soul closer to God.

Just as the holy well and the figure of the Madonna in the crypt bind Pagan and Christian practice together, so the use of the labyrinth bridges these two

TIMELINE

pre-Christian site of holy well and grotto

early 4th century AD the foundation of the primitive church of Chartres

743 Church destroyed by the Duke of Aquitaine

858 Church destroyed by Vikings

876 The cathedral begins to house the relic of the cloak of the Virgin Mary

1020, 1030, 1134, 1194 Fires destroy all or parts of the church

1194–1220 The final building is completed

1260 Cathedral is consecrated to the Virgin Mary

1979 Chartres cathedral is made a UNESCO World Heritage Site

The Rose Window in the north transept of Chartres cathedral was designed in accordance with what mythographer Joseph Campbell called 'a Platonic-Pythagorean concept of the laws of numbers governing the universe'.

great eras of the collective European experience. Like every religion, however much it may be based upon 'new revelation', the past provides a fertile matrix for its development. The pattern used for the labyrinth is known as 'Cretan' – after the Greek story of Theseus who arrived in Crete to slay the half-man, half-beast Minotaur who lived in the centre of a labyrinth built to contain him. The story travelled far – and coins from Crete dated between 430 and 67 BC show the design. This same pattern, though, has also been found on rock carvings in Sardinia that date back 4000 years and in India 3000 years. Meanwhile, in Italy the same design has been found dated to *c.*750–550 BC and in Egypt to 30 BC.

As a contemplative device for pilgrims, the resonances of the labyrinth run deep. As you walk the path that leads inexorably to the centre, you get tantalizingly close to your goal, only to be drawn back out to the periphery, until perhaps when you least expect it, suddenly there you are at the heart of the labyrinth facing the mystery of the Divine, and of your own Self too. Significantly, the Latin for 'to meditate' is *meditere*, which literally means 'to find the centre'.

In recent years there has been a renaissance of the use of the labyrinth as a device for spiritual and psychological development. In reaction to the pain and suffering in our life we are often tempted to turn outwards, but the labyrinth urges us to move inwards to explore the depths rather than the heights. And here lies a key to understanding the power of Chartres to stir the soul. Not only are Pagan and pre-Christian elements united in the building, but so too are the qualities of light, height and extension traditionally ascribed to the Masculine, or God, balanced and harmonized with the qualities of darkness, depth and inwardness traditionally ascribed to the Feminine, or Goddess. The labyrinth draws us to the centre as a place of the marriage of these two principles.

Layout of the floor labyrinth, or 'pavement', at Chartres. Anyone walking the labyrinth completes 11 full circuits and covers one-third of a mile. Unlike mazes, labyrinths have no false paths or dead-ends, but one clear route to the centre.

A PLACE OF PILGRIMAGE

Today Chartres has become a site of pilgrimage for Goddess worshippers in addition to the devout Christians who have been making pilgrimages here for centuries – either on their way to Santiago de Compostela in Spain or specifically to see the church's most precious relic – the Sancta Camisia. This is the Holy Cloak, said to have been worn by the Virgin Mary either at the Annunciation, when the Angel Gabriel foretold the coming birth of Christ, or at the time when she actually gave birth. It was given to the church in the 9th century by the French king and Holy Roman Emperor Charles the Bald (823–77). This donation began Chartres' association with the feminine aspect of divinity, and made it one of the first cathedrals to be dedicated to the Blessed Virgin Mary. The Holy Cloak survived the many fires and drew many pilgrims to Chartres throughout the medieval period and beyond – including King Henry V of England (r. 1413–22).

Pilgrims also came, and continue to come, to see the two Black Madonnas of Chartres. The 'Notre-Dame-sous-Terre', located in the crypt since earliest times, was joined in the 13th century by the statue of a second black virgin, which was installed in the main body of the church. There are over 180 of these black virgins in France, and some scholars believe they are evidence of pre-Christian goddess worship. Others claim that the images are black for more prosaic reasons, such as the type of wood used or as a result of the accumulation of candle-soot. Whatever their genesis, the fact remains that many of these images were associated with miracles and became important objects of devotion.

In addition to the many thousands who make their pilgrimages here each year to pray by the Madonnas, since 1982 15,000 or more supporters of a return to the traditional Latin Mass have undertaken a three-day-long walk from Paris to the cathedral every Pentecost (the fiftieth day after Easter Sunday). For a decade the cathedral was locked barring them entry, until the church finally allowed them access in 1992. Many thousands more are drawn to this site each year to marvel at the architecture and its intricate carvings, and to gaze up at the mandala of the great Rose Window, as if sensing that within this great building is encoded information that can lead to a spiritual renewal.

The 'rich stone forest' of Chartres is powerful because it seems to combine in one majestic structure elements that nourish and inspire mind, body, heart and spirit. The heart is opened in walking the labyrinth – taking the long journey closer and closer to the centre of being. The power of the abstract mind to expand and soar is stimulated by the architecture of the building itself – based as it is on the harmony generated by the use of sacred geometry. Our spirits are filled with awe as we gaze up at the radiance of the stained-glass windows, and our bodies are affirmed, blessed, and offered healing in the dark womb of the crypt, where the First Mother and the Druid well feed us with their primal energy.

At the heart of this Christian symbol of the power of the church, of patriarchy, of the fervour of medieval penitence and of florid Gothic architecture, there is the heartbeat of the Mother. No wonder the great mythographer Joseph Campbell (1904–87) called this sacred place 'the womb of the world'.

Black Madonnas are found not only in Chartres but at many other sites throughout France (such as here at Le Puy cathedral in the Auvergne) and worldwide. Some commentators have speculated that their origins lie in Earth-goddess figures or even the Egyptian deity Isis.

" Honey to all the Gods, but the most honey to the Mistress of the Labyrinth. "

13TH-CENTURY BC PRAYER TO THE GODDESS ARIADNE, FROM THE MINOAN SITE OF KNOSSSOS, CRETE

RENNES-LE-CHÂTEAU

Rennes-le-Château is a small, unassuming hamlet of 100 or so inhabitants in the southwest of France. But in recent decades, it has become a site of pilgrimage for thousands of people thanks to popular religious 'thrillers' such as The Holy Blood and The Holy Grail *and* The Da Vinci Code.

F UELLED BY ELABORATE HOAXES involving fraud and forgery over the last 50 years, writers have speculated that fabulous treasure may be buried in or near the village. Treasure hunters and mystery-seekers have come to Rennes-le-Château looking for the lost treasure of Solomon, the Romans and Visigoths, even the Ark of the Covenant. Some believe that Rennes-le-Château hides the last resting place of the family of Jesus, who, it is claimed, survived the crucifixion, married Mary Magdalene and had children.

Yet despite the increasing number of visitors who are drawn to the site each year (100,000 in 2007) and despite the tangled web of theories that surround the place, an extraordinary peace pervades the old church and garden, and the Magdala Tower, raised promenade and Orangery that were built in the opening years of the 20th century. There is gold here – but like the alchemists who discovered that true gold is spiritual rather than material, the pilgrim to Rennes needs to dig beneath the black hole of conspiracy theories and frauds to discover the real gift that Rennes-le-Château has to give to the world.

Rennes-le-Château is a small village perched on the top of a hill in the Languedoc region of the southwest of France. To the south lie the mountain ranges of the Pyrenees, which straddle the border with Spain, while to the east lies the 'Gulf of the Lion' – a section of the Mediterranean coast that stretches from Perpignan to the port of Marseille.

For centuries the village was all but forgotten. Even today many tourists who come to visit the region's Cathar castles and magnificent fortified towns leave this hamlet off their itinerary, since it seems to offer nothing of interest apart from a small church and museum, a café and a restaurant.

But ever since the 1950s this apparently insignificant village has seen a remarkable influx of visitors, who feel themselves impelled to make the pilgrimage to a site that has become synonymous with the word 'mystery'.

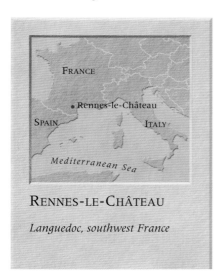

RENNES-LE-CHÂTEAU

Languedoc, southwest France

Rennes-le-Château began life as a prehistoric settlement – a Neolithic grave has been found in the village. Enjoying commanding views of the surrounding countryside, and blessed with its own spring water, it was ideally located for human habitation. There are records of its existence during the Roman occupation of Gaul, and it fell under Visigoth rule during the 6th and 7th centuries. The Visigoths were a Germanic people who sacked Rome in AD 410 and took control of much of the western territory of the Roman empire as it collapsed – including large parts of Spain and southwestern France.

During the following centuries a turbulent history unfolded in the region: as the Visigoth kingdom collapsed, this was followed by Muslim control under the Saracens, and invasion by the Franks in the 11th century. During the 12th century the Cathars (Albigensians) were a popular schismatic Christian sect that threatened the authority of the church to such an extent that an Inquisition and Crusade was waged against them for 20 years, between 1209 and 1229, ending in mass killings, with the last Cathar being burnt in 1321.

The village of Rennes-le-Château survived all these vicissitudes before succumbing to the plague in 1361. Little is then known of its history until a new priest was installed in 1885 to minister to its 298 inhabitants.

The neo-Gothic Magdala Tower at Rennes-le-Château, built by Bérenger Saunière to house his extensive library. Such major construction work fuelled speculation that Saunière had found hidden treasure.

THE MYSTERIOUS PRIEST

Father Bérenger Saunière (1852–1917) was a dynamic character. With one glass eye and engaged in a questionable relationship with his 18-year-old housekeeper, he was apparently fond of both alcohol and the lottery. Saunière inherited a church that was in a state of neglect. Consecrated to St Mary Magdalene in 1059, it may originally have been the chapel of the nearby medieval château. There is also evidence of another church in the village – dedicated to St Peter. Either one of them may already have been in existence in the 8th century. Saunière set to work renovating his church; in 1891 his diary mysteriously records that he explored a grave and uncovered a tomb. Ten years later, he embarked on a series of extensive building works: creating a raised walkway connecting a glass conservatory or orangery at one end with a tower that housed his library at the other. He also built and furnished a comfortable villa next to the church and a tower on a nearby hill.

There are two schools of thought on how Saunière found the money for these projects: he was either a fraudster, or he had stumbled upon hidden treasure and a secret that could rock the foundations of the established church.

> **"** *Most English-speaking people come to the mystery [of Rennes-le-Château] through reading* The Holy Blood And The Holy Grail … *They put the book down, wondering if there is any truth in it. Many of them go further and start to investigate for themselves.* **"**
>
> R. F. DIETRICH, *THE RENNES-LE-CHÂTEAU THEME PARK*

Saunière was an eccentric and charismatic figure who managed to attract donations from wealthy female admirers, and these donations, combined with the money he earned from a mail-order scam, probably generated the funds he needed for his building works. On realizing that he was allowed to accept payment for saying masses for the dead or for those in need of healing, Saunière started to advertise in Catholic newspapers around the world and soon money was pouring in for thousands of masses – far more than the three per day that he was permitted to perform. Once the bishop learned about this, he ordered him to stop and to transfer to another parish. Saunière refused to go, and the Bishop's Court in Carcassonne began an investigation into his trafficking in masses. In the ensuing ecclesiastical trial, Saunière was ordered to spend ten days in a monastery in penance.

In 1911 Saunière was stripped of his priesthood, and four years later was so desperate to pay off his debts that he started up his mail-order business again, despite the fact that he was no longer a priest. He did this for two years before taking a pilgrimage to Lourdes and dying in penury in 1917.

RUMOURS OF HIDDEN TREASURE

By the 1950s the story of a petty scandal in a French village was alchemically transformed through the inspiration of a local hotelier, Noël Corbu, keen to attract customers. He began spreading the rumour that Saunière had discovered hidden treasure and had become fabulously wealthy. Once the national press had picked up the story, the village's future was secured, as it became a magnet for conspiracy theorists, who began to link the 'unexplained wealth' of the priest with suggestions that the Visigoths had hidden treasure there that they had acquired from the sack of Rome. Since the Romans had

One of the decorations that the colourful Bérenger Saunière designed for the Church of St Mary Magdalene in Rennes-le-Château, showing a demon.

destroyed the second temple of Solomon, perhaps treasure from the temple – including the Ark of the Covenant – was also concealed in one of the limestone caverns beneath Rennes? Perhaps the buried treasure came from the Knights Templar whose headquarters had been on Temple Mount in Jerusalem?

An old maxim is that 'like attracts like' – and Saunière's dishonesty acted as the catalyst for a series of initiatives that ranged from the utter deceit of planting forged documents in the Bibliothèque Nationale in Paris by a group calling itself the 'Priory of Sion', which was formed as an elaborate hoax in 1956, to the disingenuousness displayed by many of the authors of the hundreds of books about the 'mysteries' of Rennes-le-Château that have since appeared.

Gérard de Sède (1921–2004) initiated this avalanche of books with *The Gold of Rennes, or The Strange Life of Bérenger Saunière, Priest of Rennes-le-Château* in 1967. The central thesis of the book was suggested by his friend Pierre Plantard (1920–2000) – an anti-semite and instigator of the Priory of Sion hoax, who believed he was the true heir to the throne of France and a descendant of Jesus

> *Believe that there is a secret and you will feel an initiate. It doesn't cost a thing. Create an enormous hope that can never be eradicated because there is no root. Ancestors that never were will never tell you that you betrayed them. Create a truth with fuzzy edges: when someone tries to define it, you repudiate him. Why go on writing novels? Rewrite history.*

UMBERTO ECO, *FOUCAULT'S PENDULUM* (1988)

Christ, who had avoided death on the cross, married Mary Magdalene and sired one or more children who had then married into the French royal bloodline.

These ideas were picked up and developed by the British authors of *The Holy Blood and The Holy Grail* – Michael Baigent, Richard Leigh and Henry Lincoln – which became an instant bestseller on its publication in 1982. They elaborated on the daring idea that the Holy Blood of Christ was a living bloodline, rather than the blood shed by a dying man, and that the Holy Grail could be understood not as a simple object but as the womb of Mary. After endless books had worked over the same ground, developing alternative theories or rehashing the same arguments, it was the success of Dan Brown's *The Da Vinci Code*, published just over 20 years later, that gave a further boost to the village's reputation as a place of mystery. Even though Brown does not mention Rennes-le-Château by name, he uses the name

The medieval fortified city of Carcassonne was a stronghold of the Cathars, who were forced to surrender to Simon de Montfort in 1209.

Saunière for one of the main characters in the book, cites the same bloodline argument and claims in a non-fiction preface to the novel that the Priory of Sion – inextricably linked to the village – was a genuine organization with an ancient lineage.

THE CATHARS' REVENGE

The central idea behind all these books is one that clearly holds immense appeal for many people: the idea that Jesus did not die on the cross, that he married and was a sexual being who fathered children. This is, after all, a central tenet of one of the world's fastest-growing Christian movements: the Mormon Church of Latter-Day Saints. Instead of Jesus being born of a virgin and dying a virgin himself in an agonizing death, he is seen as a partner to a holy woman. The universal archetype of a god and goddess who together are fertile, like Isis and Osiris, seems more satisfying to many people than the sterile figure of a lone god who fails to pass on his seed.

While it is sad that this idea needed the strange combination of a mail-order scam, a fraudulent claim to the French throne, and the lure of hidden treasure to gain currency, it is clearly an idea that inspires many people to revere the feminine principle of Deity and to question the authority of conventional Christian doctrine.

In the 13th century the Albigensian Crusade in southwest France resulted in the mass slaughter of the Cathars – heretics who dared to question Catholic doctrine. Perhaps it is poetic justice that such an idea has come to prominence in a region that suffered so much at the hands of the church.

TIMELINE

1059 The church at Rennes-le-Château is dedicated to Mary Magdalene possibly as the chapel of the nearby Château Hautpoul

1062 The region is invaded by the Franks

1130 Village falls under control of the count of Carcassonne

1361 The village is struck by plague

1885 Fr Bérenger Saunière arrives in Rennes-le-Château

1891 Saunière writes in his diary that he 'excavated a grave and discovered a tomb'

1901–05 Saunière builds his 'estate'

1910 An ecclesiastical trial orders Saunière to spend ten days in a monastery in penance

1911 Saunière defrocked

1917 Death of Saunière

1956 Newspapers print local hotelier Noël Corbu's tale of hidden treasure. Pierre Plantard and others found the Priory of Sion

1967 The story becomes famous in France with Plantard's friend Gérard de Sède's book *The Gold of Rennes*

1969 A British actor, Henry Lincoln, writes a book based on De Sède's work

1970s Lincoln presents two BBC documentaries on the 'mystery'

1982 Lincoln, Michael Baigent and Richard Leigh publish the bestselling *The Holy Blood and the Holy Grail*

2003 Dan Brown's *The Da Vinci Code* popularizes the story without mentioning the village

THE EXTERNSTEINE

The Externsteine, a group of extraordinary rocks in the heart of northern Germany peppered with caves, stairways and carvings, are redolent of mystery and legend. Some people believe the site was a Neolithic astronomical observatory and a site of Pagan worship long before it was used as a Christian hermitage.

SITUATED 73 MILES (117 KM) SOUTHWEST OF HANOVER in the northern region of Lower Saxony, the Externsteine are one of the most visited sacred sites in Germany. These strange rock formations act as a magnet for spiritual seekers, who are attracted both by their beauty, and by the healing power that is reputed to emanate from them. Some people claim to have been cured by rubbing the hard sandstone, while others come here to celebrate the old Pagan festivals of the solstices and Walpurgis night (a pagan spring festival, held on the night of 30 April and traditionally associated with witches). The Externsteine have also become a magnet for New Agers and, notoriously, neo-Nazis.

Geologically, the 13 rocks of the Externsteine are remnants of a hard sandstone plug that was forced vertically upward by a volcanic eruption some 70 million years ago, from a stratum that had been laid down about 50 million years earlier. The rocks are surrounded by a nature reserve, including meadows and woodland, which covers 57 hectares (142 acres). The lake that is now situated below the rocks is of relatively recent origin, created when the small Wiembecke river was dammed after the Second World War.

IRMINSUL, THE SAXON WORLD PILLAR

Many believe that this unusual geographical feature became a sacred site in prehistoric times and that pagan rites were practised there until the 8th century AD. In particular, the writings of the Lutheran theologian Hermann Hammelmann (1526–95) popularized the idea that the Externsteine were a centre of early pre-Christian religious activity among the Saxons who inhabited this region. However, no archaeological evidence supports this theory; the only artefacts uncovered at the site have been some stone tools from around 12,000 years ago, along with some pottery and other small finds, dated from the 10th to the 19th century.

Nevertheless, in the 1920s the German amateur archaeologist Wilhelm Teudt (1860–1942) suggested that the Saxon World Pillar or Irminsul – which the Saxons revered as the *axis mundi*, the centre of the Earth – was located at the Externsteine

The 'Teutonic' aura of the Externsteine has been lent extra weight by their proximity to the Battle of Teutoburg Forest, a crushing German victory over a Roman legion in AD 9.

until it was destroyed by Charlemagne (r. 768–814) in 772. The Irminsul was said to connect Heaven and Earth and was represented by a great trunk of oak, like a totem pole or maypole, which acted as an object of veneration.

HISTORY OF THE SITE

The known history of the site begins in 1093, when the land around the stones was bought by the Benedictine monastery of Abdinghof in Paderborn. The curious complex of niches and stairways cut into the rocks, some of which lead nowhere, was probably created either by the monks or by previous inhabitants. Teudt, and many since him, claimed that the area known as the 'roofless chapel', which is reached by a precarious bridge, was once a pagan shrine, since its circular opening points to the summer solstice sunrise and also to the most northerly rising point of the moon.

In addition to a series of caves used by the monks for contemplation – one of which carries an inscription stating that it was consecrated as a chapel in 1115 – a sarcophagus open to the elements was hewn out of the rock, along with several beautifully carved reliefs, including a famous one depicting Christ's descent from the cross (the Deposition). This Romanesque relief is heavily influenced by Byzantine art and is the only example of its kind in Germany. The sarcophagus may have been created as a shrine depicting Christ's tomb, although some authorities suggest that it could have been used for contemplation, or even for conducting initiation rites in pre-Christian times.

EXTERNSTEINE

Near Hanover, Lower Saxony, Germany

TIMELINE

THE *AHNENERBE* AND THE EXTERNSTEINE FOUNDATION

Wilhelm Teudt led excavations at the Externsteine until 1940, when responsibility for the site was transferred to the Nazi *Ahnenerbe Forschungs- und Lehrgemeinschaft* ('Ancestral Heritage Research and Teaching Society'). This institution was founded in 1935 by Heinrich Himmler, Hermann Wirth and Richard Darré. Wirth (1885–1981) was a Dutch historian obsessed with Atlantean mythology, while Darré (1895–1953) was a key architect of the Nazi 'blood and soil' (*Blut und Boden)* ideology. Himmler (1900–45) famously became second-in-command to Adolf Hitler and was in charge of the concentration camps, the SS and the Gestapo. He was fascinated with the occult and built a grail castle at nearby Wewelsburg for himself and fellow SS officers. Before founding the *Ahnenerbe*, Himmler had served on the board of the 'Externsteine Foundation', which sought to explore the site's significance and create a heritage park there.

The *Ahnenerbe* conducted anthropological and archaeological research that was designed to prove the supremacy of the so-called 'Aryan' race. Within a few years of its foundation, it became part of the SS and employed more than 130 historians, linguists, geographers, agronomists, folklorists and classicists. The *Ahnenerbe* undertook expeditions to try and trace the roots of the Aryan race, to places as diverse as Scandinavia, the Middle East and Tibet. These expeditions, often involving a motley crew of scientists and adventurers, inspired Steven Spielberg's 1981 film, *Raiders of The Lost Ark*.

Although the *Ahnenerbe* failed to find anything of significance at the Externsteine, the site still came to be regarded as a shrine of the Teutonic race; this status explains its continuing appeal to extreme nationalists and Nazi sympathizers. Fortunately, these 'pilgrims' are vastly outnumbered by the many tourists who visit the site, and the New Agers, Pagans and party-goers who camp in the meadow beside the stones to celebrate the traditional start of Spring on Walpurgis night – the eve of May Day, known as Beltane in other countries.

Gatherings also occur at both the winter and summer solstices. Sadly, though, the increasing popularity of pagan seasonal festivals has created its own problems, as this contributor to the website The Virtual Tourist reveals: 'Pros: Beautiful Landscape, Old Celtic Cult place, Freaky Crowd, Good Vibes, Very Mystic. Cons: On Walpurgis and Summer solstice there are too many people, polluting the place with electronic music and cans and bottles'.

LEY LINES AND STONEHENGE

The site also appears to fall on a number of ley lines or 'holy lines'. The theory of lines connecting ancient sites and landscape features was devised at around

" Stones of the Old Ones, let us be wise and listen to you,
Sharing the same heartbeat of the beautiful and beloved Mother Earth,
With the voices of trees whispering in our hearts. "

GERMAN DRUID VOLKERT VOLKMANN, *EXTERNSTEINE*

the same time by Teudt in Germany (who called them *heilige Linien*) and the British antiquarian Alfred Watkins (1855–1935), who coined the term 'ley lines'. Teudt was the first to suggest that the Externsteine stand at a junction of alignments, one of which extends as far as Stonehenge (which is located on virtually the same latitude). However, many scholars are deeply sceptical about the existence of such a phenomenon, pointing out how easy it is to plot lines that connect features in the landscape.

Whether or not the Externsteine were used as a sacred site prior to the arrival of the Benedictine monks, and whether or not they are connected to other sacred sites in a web of ley lines, their modern attraction as a place of pilgrimage is explained by their ineffable beauty and sense of mystery.

This medieval monastic relief on the sandstone face of one of the Externsteine shows the Deposition of Christ. It also includes a portrayal of Joseph of Arimathea and symbols of the sun and moon.

STONEHENGE

Stonehenge stands on Salisbury Plain, a grassy plateau covering 300 square miles (777 sq km) of the counties of Wiltshire and Berkshire in southern England. The plain has been declared an 'Area of Outstanding Natural Beauty' and much of it is in the care of three official bodies: English Heritage, the National Trust and the British Army.

FOLLOW THE OLD HIGHWAYS TO THE WEST COUNTRY OF ENGLAND, such as the Ridgeway along the Chiltern Hills just north of London, or the South Downs Way, which starts in Eastbourne in Sussex, and you come to a great chalk plateau about the size of the Isle of Wight known as Salisbury Plain.

The sparsely populated plain, which forms the largest remaining expanse of chalk grassland in northwest Europe, is home to over 450 monuments and the two great ritual landscapes of Avebury and Stonehenge, which have jointly been designated a World Heritage Site.

At its heart, though, Salisbury Plain is the most dangerous landscape in Britain. As one of the main training grounds for the British Army, and in particular its tank force, over the years the 'central impact area' on the plain has been hit by no fewer than eight million shells, 10,000 or so of which remain unexploded. One of the largest of 11 Romano-British villages found in this area by archaeologists lies in the zone of greatest danger. The village covers 26 hectares (64 acres) and explosions have thrown up the remains of houses, door latches, pottery and tiles. It is unlikely, however, that anyone will ever dare to undertake a proper study of the site.

Without a doubt, the most famous monument in this sacred landscape is the world-renowned megalithic site at Stonehenge, which attracts more visitors than any other place in Britain. But in addition to this, the plain is filled with many other places of historic and spiritual significance. Traces of 6000 years of history can be found here, and the ancient monuments reveal a past that continues to exert a peculiar fascination on tourist and spiritual seeker alike.

Mysteries abound on Salisbury Plain. Most crop circles in Britain occur within a triangle between Winchester, Warminster and Wantage. Circle-watchers are joined by leyline-hunters and UFOlogists, looking for ancient energy lines or extraterrestrial visitors, whom some people suggest are drawn to the area because of its unusual power.

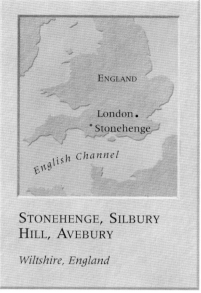

STONEHENGE, SILBURY HILL, AVEBURY

Wiltshire, England

SILBURY HILL

Walking along the Ridgeway towards Salisbury Plain from the northeast, you pass Dragon Hill, the carved chalk horse at Uffington and the massive longbarrow of Wayland's Smithy before entering a great rolling landscape that, in this northern part of the plain, appears to be one vast ritual site. Ruling over it all is the massive mound of Silbury Hill, the tallest Neolithic structure in Europe. This huge man-made construction of 340,000 cu metres (12 million cu ft) of chalk was built in c.2700 BC. It was long thought to be a burial mound, but archaeologists have tunnelled into it and found no remains. These investigations showed that the mound was made of chalk blocks arranged in a honeycomb lattice. Organic material such as the bodies of buried insects enabled the site to be dated and, amazingly, turf found within the hill still retained its greenish colour after 5000 years of burial.

Flat-topped artificial mounds such as that at Silbury can be found all over Britain and around the world. They may have been constructed as ritual sites where people could reach up to 'touch the heavens', intercede with the gods and make offerings to them and to survey the surrounding landscape.

Stonehenge at sunset. Many legends surround this famous site: the 12th-century Welsh chronicler Geoffrey of Monmouth claimed the stones were originally brought from Ireland by King Arthur's magician Merlin.

TIMELINE

*c.*8000 BC Date of four large Mesolithic postholes found under the car park at Stonehenge

*c.*4000 BC Round barrows appear and cursuses (ditched and banked enclosures whose purpose remains a mystery) are created in the area and the forest is cleared

3100 BC The first stage in the construction of Stonehenge. The ditch and bank and 56 post holes ('Aubrey holes') that held timber uprights date from this period

2500 BC Bluestones from the Prescelli Mountains in Pembroke, South Wales 245 miles (380 km) away are erected at Stonehenge

2300 BC The largest stones (sarsens) are dragged from the Marlborough Downs, 20 miles (32 km) away, and erected along with the bluestones with lintels to form 'trilithons'; Woodhenge is built around this time

1600 BC The last signs of construction at Stonehenge

AVEBURY AND PAGAN RITES

Below Silbury is the stone circle of Avebury. Remarkably, it is so large that an entire later village grew up within it. Any visitor to Avebury at one of the old pagan festival times will have a chance to experience the joyful, sometimes chaotic, sometimes moving, celebrations of Druids, Wiccans and other followers of ancient rites. These old ways in their new form are characterized by an open-minded spirituality and a rediscovered reverence for the planet.

While a summer solstice ceremony at Avebury will typically involve just a few hundred people, move south across the plain to that other ritual complex of Stonehenge and your experience will be very different. Walking there, along the great avenue of stones that snakes up from the ritual circle of Avebury towards the hilltop site known as 'The Sanctuary' you may first wish to visit West Kennet Long Barrow. Here, as at Wayland's Smithy, the ancestors feel very close. Although these barrows were used as repositories for earthly remains, archaeologists think that the sites did not remain sealed, but instead became places for ritual and communion with the dead. In addition to being tourist attractions, such sites have also become places of pilgrimage for contemporary Pagans.

WOODHENGE AND STONEHENGE

Arriving in the southern part of the plain you come first to Woodhenge. This was built around the same time as Stonehenge, which is just 1.2 miles (2 km) away. Today all you can see are stumps to mark where six concentric circles of wooden posts once created the supports for a building about the size of Stonehenge. Like its stone twin, it is surrounded by a bank and ditch, and its entrance points northeast to the place of the rising sun at midsummer.

Stonehenge itself may at first sight seem disappointing. It lies squeezed between two roads and looks surprisingly small from a distance. It is only when you get close to the stones that you appreciate their grandeur. To open to their spiritual power may need some effort of will or surrender. The constant drone of traffic, the scores of tourists buying snacks

The original purpose of the 40 m (130 ft) high artificial chalk mound near Avebury known as Silbury Hill is unknown.

and books and listening to guided tours in various languages on portable headsets, all seem determined to remind you that you are living in the industrial age. But at certain moments, if you are fortunate, you will gaze up at the great trilithons and your mind will cease to ask such pragmatic questions as: 'How on Earth did they build this?', and 'Who were these people who dragged huge stones from Wales to create this?' Instead you will find yourself basking in the atmosphere they generate, and their quiet, resolute power.

AN ALTERNATIVE BRITAIN: ALBION

Theories abound as to the purpose of this enigmatic circle. Writers such as the archaeologist Terence Meaden believe it was constructed as a sanctuary for the celebration of the sacred marriage between the Earth Goddess and the Sun. Legend tells us that the wizard Merlin transported and erected the stones here. Astroarchaeologists claim that the site is precisely aligned with movements in the heavens, while archaeologists inform us that the bank and ditch around the stones was created in about 3100 BC and that the stones were raised around 2200 BC, with the last construction work occurring at the site in c.1600 BC.

Over the last 50 or more years the site has become a quintessential symbol of alternative Britain, of a spiritual Albion that exists beneath the humdrum surface of an increasingly overpopulated and materialist society. Every summer solstice thousands flock to the stones to experience the solstice dawn.

Although they are often cheated of the visual magic of this moment by the fickle British weather, when the sun does stream across the landscape, the mystery of this time is revealed in all its simple, primal splendour here in Merlin's stones on Salisbury Plain. In Newgrange in Ireland, a shaft of sunlight penetrates the womb of the Goddess at the moment of the winter solstice dawn. Here, in complete reversal, at the summer solstice dawn the dark shadow of the Heel Stone cast by the rising sun penetrates the cauldron of stones, the inner circle. The sacred marriage is consummated. All will be well for another turning of the wheel of the year.

The sarsen-stone circles and earthworks at Avebury, which date to around 3000 BC. Many of the sarsens were destroyed from the 14th century onwards to provide building materials for houses in the village and to clear the ground for farming.

"The construction at Stonehenge is a working display and artistic statement of the life-generating union of sexual opposites which, by their conjunction, keeps the cosmic cycle in motion. Representing the whole Goddess in this drama, Stonehenge is an awe-inspiring tribute to Nature worship and love."

TERENCE MEADEN, *STONEHENGE: THE SECRET OF THE SOLSTICE* (1997)

115

THE CERNE ABBAS GIANT

Two chalk-carved giants grace the hillsides of southern England. In Sussex, the Long Man of Wilmington – an outline of a figure holding a staff in each hand – stands 70 m (227 ft) tall. Meanwhile, the Cerne Abbas Giant in Dorset has the following vital statistics: 55 m (180 ft) tall, with eyes 1 m (3.3 ft) in diameter and shoulders 14 m (45 ft) broad, he holds a fearsome club measuring 36 m (120 ft). But the most striking feature of the giant's anatomy is 7.2 m (30 ft) long, and has earned him the nickname 'The Rude Man'.

CHALK HILL FIGURES ARE A UNIQUE FEATURE OF THE HILLSIDES of southern Britain. The earliest known example, the White Horse at Uffington on the downland near Wantage in Oxfordshire, has been dated to the Early Iron Age or Late Bronze Age, between 1400 and 600 BC. Many of the 100 or more figures that we know about are of more recent origin. Some have been cut into the earth very recently, such as the giant caricature of British Prime Minister John Major (b.1943) wearing only underpants and a traffic cone on his head, cut into the turf outside Brighton by the cartoonist Steve Bell (b.1951) in 1994 in protest over the Conservative government's road-building programme. Others were created during the 18th and 19th centuries or earlier, but the recent scientific dating of the Uffington horse has now proved that the tradition of creating vast figures on hillsides is indeed ancient, and that for at least 3000 years the inhabitants of southern Britain have been engaged in a spectacular form of landscape art.

The Uffington horse forms part of a sacred landscape that includes the Neolithic long barrow of Wayland's Smithy, the flat-topped tump of Dragon Hill beneath the horse, and the Bronze and Iron Age hill fort known as Uffington Castle beside it. Likewise, the Long Man of Wilmington stands above its own small tump, and beneath tumuli that crown Windover Hill in Sussex.

But for centuries, the most famous and controversial chalk carving has been the giant priapic figure that stands on a hill overlooking the small Dorset town of Cerne Abbas. In its time, the Cerne Abbas Giant has excited a mixture of emotions – ranging from awe at this obvious symbol of fecundity to the prudishness of the Victorians, who saw the giant's member as an affront to public decency and allowed vegetation to obscure it.

The Cerne Abbas Giant continues to exercise a powerful hold on the public imagination. Recent archaeological research suggests that an animal skin may once have been shown hanging from the left arm, thus reinforcing the association with Hercules.

"The Giant survives as an image redolent with meaning concerning warrior-heroes, fertility, aggression, the tenacious adherence of rural communities to a totem, a Father-Protector. He has handed us back a portion of the past that would otherwise have been grassed over and been lost forever."

PAUL NEWMAN, *THE LOST GODS OF ALBION* (2000)

CELEBRATING FERTILITY

The stylized figure on the slopes of the Iron Age hill fort at Uffington in Oxfordshire has been identified as a horse since the 11th century. It is thought to be a tribal symbol of the former occupants of the fort.

The erect phallus is still considered so provocative an image that photographs or artworks depicting it are considered obscene by many and can stir up great controversy – witness the furore that arose even in the late 1990s over male nude studies by the American photographer Robert Mapplethorpe (1946–89). However, Victorian sensibilities aside, the Cerne Abbas Giant has long since become embedded in folk consciousness and greeted with tolerance, even reverence: in an old custom, childless women would spend a night asleep on the giant's member, while couples supposedly made love on it to increase their chances of conceiving.

In more recent times, the giant has become a focus of celebration by those who are inspired by natural spirituality – be they pagans, Wiccans, Druids or simply people who feel no affinity with conventional religions but find spiritual sustenance in an appreciation of nature. Those adopting such a worldview are happy to affirm the inherent sexuality of life rather than denying it, and thus the Cerne Abbas Giant has become a totemic image of fertility and sexuality.

We now know that the giant's penis has increased in length over time. Depictions from the 18th century, and postcards as late as 1901, show a navel with the tip of the penis just below it. But by 190. the image was so overgrown a subscription was raised in the neighbourhood and the giant was scoured and the trenches fill ith fresh chalk. By the time the archaeologist Flinders t (1853–1942) surveyed the site in 1926 the giant had surpas he ambition of most men – his organ had eclipsed his navel, ing grown by 1.83 metres (6 ft).

THE VISIT OF SAINT AUGUSTINE

Legend claims that, in 603, St Augustine of Canterbury (d. *c.*604) and fellow Benedictine monks visited the village of Cerne Abbas while on a mission to convert the Anglo-Saxon tribes of southern Britain to Christianity. They were given a hostile reception by the locals, who fastened cows' or fishes' tails to themselves as a mark of disrespect, jeered the missionaries and drove them out of the village. But, so the story goes, the villagers finally relented and destroyed the idol of their pagan deity Heil (or Hegle). At the place where they smashed the idol, a spring miraculously rose from the ground, so permitting their baptism.

The spring at Cerne Abbas can still be found in a corner of the cemetery that was once the abbey churchyard. Shaded by lime trees, it is protected by a wishing stone on which i carved an eight-petalled flower or wheel. Some see in it a Catherine wheel commemorating the martyrdom of St Catherine of Alexandria, who was tied to a spiked wheel before being beheaded. Others prefer to see it as a symbol of the pagan wheel of the year, marking the eight annual festival days of seasonal celebration. Traditionally the well was known as Silver Well, perhaps after Sylvanus the Roman god of forests, groves and fertility. Its waters were believed to have healing properties and were said to aid fertility and well-being – particularly in women.

MAY DAY AND MORRIS MEN

One of the eight feast days of pre-Christian (and now contemporary pagan) practice is Beltane on 1 May. This is an occasion for celebrating the burgeoning fertility of the land, and Cerne Abbas provides an ideal setting for festivities. Even the village's name is appropriate, since it is thought to derive from the Celtic fertility god Cernunnos, who was traditionally associated with horned male animals such as the stag. For the last 30 years or more the Wessex Morris Men have climbed Giant Hill to dance with a strange horned creature called the Ooser – half man, half bull, and made of painted wood with a horsehair beard – which is lent to them by the Dorset County Museum.

The Morris Men dance in the so-called 'Frying Pan' or 'Trendle', an earthwork above the giant's head. This tradition derives from a report in 1901 by the former sexton of Cerne that villagers were in the habit of dancing around a maypole erected there in

TIMELINE

603 St Augustine's mission destroys the 'idol of Heil or Hegle' at Cerne

987 Cerne Abbas Abbey founded

1654–62 The land is owned by Denzil Holles (1st Baron Holles)

1694 First record of the giant – the church warden pays 3 shillings 'for repareing ye Giant'

1754 Dr Richard Pococke states that the lord of the manor pays for the lines to be scoured (cleared) every 7 or 8 years

1764 The earliest published account of the giant in *The Gentleman's Magazine*. William Stukeley puts forward the idea that he represents Hercules

1774 The historian John Hutchins reports the story that the Parliamentarian Denzil Holles' servants cut the giant in mockery of Oliver Cromwell

1868 First recorded scouring opposed by the local vicar

1880 General Pitt-Rivers inherits the land, scours the giant and encloses him in a six-sided pen to protect him from revellers at the Jubilee bonfire of 1887

1908 Another scouring undertaken, probably increasing the size of the giant's penis

1926 Sir Flinders Petrie conducts a survey of the site

1939–45 The figure is hidden under brushwood to stop German planes from navigating by it

1979 Five contractors take 11 weeks to scour the figure

1996 Bournemouth University holds a Commission of Enquiry at Cerne Abbas into the age of the giant

former times. Later, other villagers disputed this, saying that the maypole was erected beside the pond in the middle of the village. This difference of opinion brings to light a strong dichotomy within the spiritual landscape of Cerne: the powerful masculine presence of the giant on the slope is balanced by an abundance of the feminine element of water at the foot of the hill – not only in the form of the town pond, but also in the watercress beds of the River Cerne and, of course, in Silver Well. Intriguingly, the remains of a possible sanctuary or reception area for pilgrims beside the spring can be discerned in a number of earthworks that show up on satellite images of the abbey field.

Some people believe that the Dorset Ooser represents the Devil, though this fearsome apparition may also derive from the Celtic deity Cernunnos.

A PLETHORA OF THEORIES

The historian Rodney Castleden believes the whole area was a sacred site of the Durotriges tribe who cut the giant figure during the Iron Age as a symbol of ferocity, fertility and healing. According to Castleden, the Frying Pan was a temple or shrine to the god Helis, or perhaps to the Celtic god Nodens, who was worshipped by the Durotriges. A bronze handle ploughed up at nearby Blandford Forum, which depicts Nodens naked with a club in his left hand and the fertility symbol of a hare in his right, suggests a connection with the Cerne giant. This link has been reinforced by archaeological surveys suggesting that the giant originally held something in his free hand – though frustratingly only a few lines, and no clear image, are discernible.

Aside from the Cerne Abbas Giant, the Long Man of Wilmington in East Sussex is the only other ancient human chalk figure in England.

Many other theories have been advanced to explain the giant's origin. At a meeting of the Society of Antiquaries in 1764, William Stukeley (1687–1765), the founding father of archaeology, was the first to suggest that it might be the Graeco-Roman hero Heracles/Hercules. Worship of Hercules arrived in Britain with the Roman invasion of AD 43, and he is thought to have become amalgamated with Cernunnos over time. An elaboration of Stukeley's theory was offered by archaeologist Stuart Piggott (1910–96), who helped restore the giant after it was covered up during the Second World War to prevent German bombers from using it as a navigation point. Piggott traced the origins of the giant to the reign of the emperor Commodus (r. AD 180–192). The Hercules cult experienced a strong revival once Commodus, after having beaten the Scots in 184, began to style himself 'Hercules Romanus', even dressing accordingly (in a lion skin, and wielding a club) to engage in gladiatorial contests.

The archaeologist Paul Newman is unconvinced, noting not only that Commodus' reign was brief and unpopular, but also that it is highly unlikely he would have been portrayed with an erection. Newman thinks the giant may well be older, and cites in evidence the fact that a proud physique and huge club would have been wholly out of keeping with the later eras suggested by some scholars.

Others take the figure as a sort of Chaucerian jest – cut into the turf in 1539, during Henry VIII's dissolution of the monasteries, when the church's power began to wane. Four years prior to this the abbot at Cerne was accused of keeping concubines in the abbey's cellar, entertaining them at table, and allowing the monks to play cards all night. Perhaps, then, the figure was carved either by the monks or by critics deriding the lewd abbot.

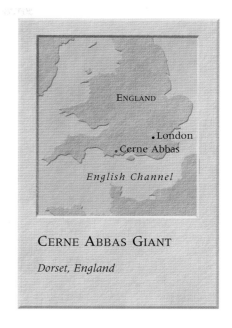

CERNE ABBAS GIANT

Dorset, England

Finally, the historian Ronald Hutton (b.1954) advanced the theory that the figure was cut in the 17th century by local landowner Baron Denzil Holles (1599–1680) as a lampoon against Oliver Cromwell (1599–1658); Cromwell's detractors took to mocking him as 'the English Hercules' for his increasingly autocratic behaviour.

Until the figure can be dated precisely, we are free to speculate that the historians may all be wrong and that local folklore is correct – namely, that what we see is the outline of a real giant who was captured and pinned down by villagers as he lay sleeping after a meal of many sheep.

Yet whatever we choose to believe about its past, the Cerne Abbas Giant still undoubtedly conveys a complex and powerful message. With his club raised in defiance, he symbolizes the paradoxical nature of human sexuality – that it can be both an animal and a spiritual experience, and that it can be both

creative and destructive. The erect penis can be a vehicle for love, pleasure and procreation, but it can also be used to violate and abuse. As long as something remains hidden it can never be fully understood, and men have for centuries surrounded the image of the erect penis with taboos and legal restraints. It epitomizes male power – and yet authoritarian patriarchy also demands that it remain hidden. As we move into a more egalitarian age, we can start to look at this image and all that it represents with a greater degree of detachment – to demystify it, to free ourselves, perhaps, from our fear or envy of it, and to celebrate it too, as a source of pleasure.

GLASTONBURY

Glastonbury, in southwest England's cider-making region of Somerset, is known to spiritual seekers as Avalon, the 'isle of apples'. Standing on Glastonbury Tor when the mists have rolled in and only hilltops are visible, it is easy to imagine the area as it once was – islands and lake villages on stilts surrounded by water. In medieval times the town and its abbey rivalled Canterbury as a destination for pilgrims.

CHRISTIAN PILGRIMS STILL COME TO THE TOWN but they are now greatly outnumbered by Pagan and New Age pilgrims and other spiritual seekers drawn here by the numerous legends that have grown up around key features of the town and surrounding countryside, concerning the Druids, Joseph of Arimathea and Jesus and King Arthur and his queen, Guinevere.

Avalon is a gathering place – every year the Glastonbury festival attracts thousands of music lovers, and hundreds are drawn to the Goddess Conference and gatherings of the Order of Bards Ovates and Druids. It is a place of meeting of the inner and outer worlds too, of the essence of Paganism and Christianity, which merge in the story of the grail, and of the God and the Goddess embodied in Glastonbury Tor and Chalice Hill.

Glastonbury is considered by many to be one of the most sacred spots on Earth. To the west of the town lie Exmoor, Dartmoor and Bodmin Moor. To the south stand the hills of Dorset and the rampant figure of the Cerne Abbas Giant (see pages 116–121). To the east lies the great sweep of Salisbury Plain in Wiltshire with its barrows and circles of stone – Avebury and Stonehenge (see pages 112–115). To the north is the mouth of the river Severn and beyond it, the southern coast of Wales.

Visiting the town today you could be forgiven for finding it unremarkable at first glance. But spend a little while here, explore the old churches and the countryside around the town, and read about its history and the legends associated with it, and the façade of an English provincial town starts to fall away. In its place somewhere quite different – and profoundly sacred – emerges.

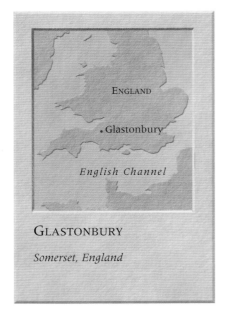

GLASTONBURY

Somerset, England

View towards Glastonbury Tor in Somerset. Some people believe that the regular terracing on its slopes are the remains of a Neolithic initiatory labyrinth.

"*There is on the confines of western Britain a certain royal island, called in the ancient speech Glastonia, marked out by broad boundaries, girt round with waters rich in fish and with still-flowing rivers, fitted for many uses of human indigence, and dedicated to the most sacred of deities.*"

ST AUGUSTINE OF CANTERBURY, 6TH CENTURY AD

TIMELINE

c. 3rd century BC The lake villages of Glastonbury and Meare created

AD 37 According to legend, Joseph of Arimathea brings the Holy Grail to Glastonbury

63 Joseph of Arimathea and 11 companions supposedly build the first church in Britain on the site of Glastonbury Abbey

1135 Geoffrey of Monmouth writes 'Arthur's last earthly destination was Avalon'

1184 Fire destroys much of the Abbey; it takes 120 years to rebuild

1190 Two oak coffins found under a slab and lead cross whose inscription reads: 'Here lies buried the renowned King Arthur with Guinevere in the Isle of Avalon'

1275 Earthquake destroys church of St Michael on Glastonbury Tor

1582 Dr John Dee, Queen Elizabeth I's astrologer, announces he has found the Elixir of Life at Chalice Well

1750 Chalice Well becomes popular as a healing spa

1892 Glastonbury Lake Village is discovered by Arthur Bulleid

1912 Celtic revivalist Alice Buckton buys Chalice Well

1914 Composer Rutland Boughton initiates the first Glastonbury Festival

1935 Katherine Maltwood discovers the 'Glastonbury Zodiac'

1958 Chalice Well Trust founded

1971 The first modern Glastonbury Festival is held at nearby Pilton; it is now the biggest rock festival in Europe

One such sacred site is the Holy Thorn tree on Wearyall Hill. It was here that legends say Jesus was brought to Glastonbury as a boy by his uncle Joseph of Arimathea during the 'silent years' – the time between the ages of 12 and 33 when the Bible says nothing of his life. Some believe he spent these years studying in the desert with the ascetic Essenes. Others suggest he may have been in training here with the Druids in Britain. His uncle brought him, so the legend runs, on his travels as a tin trader, when he sailed across the Mediterranean, around Cornwall, and over the sea that swept in across the Somerset Levels.

Joseph stuck his staff into the ground at Wearyall Hill, where it miraculously sprouted into a living tree once more. It was felled by Reformation zealots wanting to rid the town of 'superstitions', but monks had carefully preserved cuttings of the original, and the Holy Thorn tree you see today is said to be a direct descendant of that first tree. Once more it has become a place of devotion. Clooties (prayer-ties) hang from its branches, while messages and offerings are tucked into its bark or left by its roots.

A LANDSCAPE OF ISLANDS

Until the Levels were drained for farming from the late 19th century onwards, this was a landscape of islands, teeming with fish and game. It was dotted with villages supported on wooden platforms over the shallow waters, while wooden trackways allowed villagers to walk across the flooded land.

John Michell (b.1933), author of the 1960s cult classic *A New View Over Atlantis,* which introduced a generation to the idea of Britain's sacred landscape and reawakened their interest in its pre-Christian heritage, claims that seven islands in particular were held in great reverence. In ancient times they would have been sacred to the Druids and inhabited by hermit sages. By the medieval era, the great abbey of Glastonbury stood on the Isle of Avalon, while the other six islands – God's Island, Beckery, Martinsea, Meare, Panborough and Nyland – each housed a small chapel.

GLASTONBURY AND KING ARTHUR

Michell has noticed that these seven islands form a pattern that mirrors the positions of seven stars in the constellation of the Great Bear. This he believes points to one of Glastonbury's great secrets – its relationship with that spiritual hero of Albion, King Arthur (whose name means 'bear-like').

The town's fame as a major site of Christian pilgrimage in medieval times derived from this association with the semi-legendary king, which began when two bodies were discovered in the abbey grounds, supposedly of King Arthur and Queen Guinevere. The Arthurian romances had already fused with the grail legend and the story was told that Joseph of Arimathea, accompanied by 11 missionaries, had returned to Glastonbury after the crucifixion, bearing the Holy Grail. Some believe the grail lies buried to this day beneath Chalice Hill, whose gentle rounded form provides a perfect image of femininity in contrast with the rugged hill surmounted by a tower that is Glastonbury Tor.

AVALON AND THE TOR

We may imagine the Tor as a god, and Chalice Hill as a goddess. And the wooded region where they meet – the 'centre of their ecstasies', as the German poet Rilke would put it – is the place of their marriage, and perhaps the most sacred spot of all in Glastonbury.

Arriving there, as if at a sacred grove, you will find yews and oaks, and other trees and plants in profusion, guarding a sanctuary of two springs – the White Spring that gushes perpetually from the side of the Tor, and the Chalice Well with its red, iron-rich water. Today a lane separates the two, but their waters eventually flow together. The White Spring cascades through a series of channels and pools to an old water authority building that has become a shrine filled with images of the Goddess. Nearby a footpath leads to the Tor, past the former house of one of Britain's greatest magicians, Dion Fortune (1890–1946).

At the summit of the Tor stands a tower – all that remains of the 14th-century church of St Michael, built to replace its predecessor destroyed by an earthquake in 1275. In the countryside you might make out the signs of the zodiac that the artist and sculptor Katherine Maltwood (1878–1961) discovered in the 1930s, etched in the landscape – the boundaries of fields, rivers and ancient lanes marking out the figures and making Avalon a sacred land that mirrored the perfection of the heavens and united the land and sky in a mystical union.

But this marriage of Heaven and Earth can best be experienced back in the Chalice Well Gardens. Flowers and shrubs chosen for their colour associations to the *chakras* – spiritual energy centres of the body – lead you past pools, a waterfall and channels to the wellhead. Its cover stands open and proclaims that this is the place of Mystical Marriage, where paradise on Earth is found. Its design of two circles merging provides the clue: a 'Vesica Piscis' is formed where they meet – this fish-shaped form variously symbolizes the Philosopher's Stone, Christ, or the vulva of the Goddess.

The wellhead at Chalice Well Gardens in Glastonbury, showing the 'Vesica Piscis' or mandorla design from medieval sacred geometry.

The ruins of the abbey at Glastonbury. When the institution was dissolved in 1539, the abbot, Richard Whyting, was hanged, drawn and quartered on the Tor.

NEWGRANGE

Newgrange is the largest and most impressive of several dozen prehistoric monuments found in the Boyne Valley 20 miles (32 km) northwest of Dublin in Ireland. Famous for being oriented to the winter solstice sunrise, Newgrange was constructed 5000 years ago, and forms part of a sacred landscape that includes the nearby site of Tara, seat of the ancient kings of Ireland.

TWELVE MILES (19 KM) SOUTHWEST OF TARA, the River Boyne snakes across the land to form a bowl about 3 miles (5 km) wide and 1 mile (1.61 km) deep. This area, known as the Brugh na Bóinne, 'The Palace of the Boyne', is one of the most impressive sacred landscapes and archaeological sites in all of Europe. Twenty-six passage tombs dated to the Bronze Age are sited in this part of the valley, leading some scholars to call it Ireland's own 'Valley of the Kings', in allusion to the royal cemetery in Upper Egypt. But many now believe that it is more than just the resting-place for the bones of an ancient people who lived in this fertile region.

The most striking of all the monuments in the Boyne Valley is Newgrange – an enormous artificial mound built in around 3250 BC and covering an acre of land. It has now been dramatically renovated with blocks of white quartz, which gleam brightly in the sun. Its entrance reveals at once the mystery that many people feel inhabits the heart of this sacred landscape.

Newgrange and the surrounding countryside are steeped in myth. The River Boyne is named after the goddess Boann, and its source is the magical Well of Segais. Nine hazel trees grow around this well, dropping their ripe nuts into the waters below to feed the 'salmon of knowledge' that swim in its depths. And just as salmon are plentiful in this stretch of the river, so stories of otherworldly figures and the accounts of their loves and lives have grown up around it. One such legend tells how the river goddess Boann mated with the father-god Dagda to give birth to Aenghus Og, the god of love, who then tricked his father out of possession of the house he had built. Gazing at it now, we can sense Aenghus Og's presence even today.

A PLACE OF MYSTERY

As you walk towards the monument on the hill you notice at once how around the base of the mound many of its 97 large granite kerbstones are carved with geometric designs of spirals, lozenges, zigzags and other symbols, reminiscent of the patterns found on the stones at the mound of Gavrinis in Brittany (see pages 92–95). Facing the white wall of stone as you walk towards the entrance you come to the most magnificent kerbstone of all, with its swirling carvings of a triple spiral, double spirals, concentric semi-circles and lozenges.

This is the first clue, perhaps, that this is a place of mystery – a place of return to the centre, of spiralling in to the heart of life. But then look up to the entrance itself and notice the peculiar opening above it. This feature, known as the 'roofbox', is a chamber that runs above the entrance passageway and brings light to the innermost sanctuary of the mound. Here is the second clue: this chamber is oriented to the winter solstice sunrise – the time of the longest night in December, when the sun is reborn from its winter sleep and the days start growing longer again.

When Newgrange was rediscovered in the modern era, by local landowner Charles Campbell in 1699, the roofbox remained hidden. However, later archaeological restoration started to reveal the grandeur of this monument. It is now estimated that 200,000 tons of granite from Dundalk Bay, 75 miles

NEWGRANGE

County Meath, near Dublin, Ireland

The prehistoric mound at Newgrange, with its controversial modern facing stones of white quartzite.

TIMELINE

*c.*3250 BC Newgrange is constructed

AD 1699 Entrance to Newgrange discovered accidentally when Charles Campbell digs material from hillside for road-building

1725 Thomas Molyneux writes that Newgrange was built by the Danes between the 8th and 9th centuries

1890 Irish archaeologist George Coffey begins work on the site

1962–75 Michael O'Kelly of University College, Cork, leads major excavation and rebuilding works, including restoring the quartzite facing stones – a controversial move that has upset some scholars

1967 O'Kelly experiences the sun's penetration of the inner chamber on the winter solstice

1983 Martin Brennan's book *The Star and the Stones* suggests Newgrange is a solar temple rather than a burial mound

(120 km) away, together with white quartz brought from the Wicklow Mountains, 50 miles (80 km) distant, were used to create the great cairn, which was surrounded by a circle of standing stones. Originally this circle probably comprised 38 stones. Today only 12 remain.

THE SUNRISE INITIATION

The roofbox was discovered by Professor Michael O'Kelly and his team during major restoration works carried out in the 1960s. They unearthed the opening to the shaft to find that it was half-obscured by a square block of quartz. There were scratches on this stone as if it had worked as a shutter that had often been slid to and fro. Kelly recalled a local tradition that the sun always shone into the tomb at midsummer, but checking the orientation of the shaft showed that it faced not the midsummer, but the midwinter sun.

On the winter solstice of 1967 O'Kelly crawled along the 19-metre (60-ft) passageway into the main chamber of Newgrange and waited in the dark until sunrise. He was rewarded with an experience which has led him to return to the mound every winter solstice since then:

'I was literally astounded ... the [sun]light began as a thin pencil and widened to a band of about 6 inches. There was so much light reflected from the floor that I could walk around inside without a lamp and avoid bumping off the stones. It was so bright I could see the roof 20 feet above me. I expected to hear a voice, or perhaps feel a cold hand resting on my shoulder, but there was silence. And then, after a few minutes, the shaft of light narrowed as the sun appeared to pass westward across the slit, and total darkness came once more.'

Soon scholars began to speculate that O'Kelly had experienced one of the main purposes of the temple, as a place of initiation into the mysteries of rebirth during the time of greatest darkness. The entry of the midwinter sun occurs for five days, from 19 to 23 December, and it is now possible to enter your name in a draw to be among the ten people who are allowed to sit in the chamber on one of these five nights, awaiting the arrival of the sun. So popular is this experience that in 2006 no fewer than 27,485 names were entered in the lottery, which is drawn by local schoolchildren.

Swirling spiral and lozenge motifs adorn the threshold stone at Newgrange. Such patterns reappear at megalithic sites elsewhere.

The Fairy Mound of Darkness

As if to capture the magical, fertilizing power of the midwinter sun, the entrances to a number of sites around Newgrange are also oriented in its direction. Once the rising solstice sun has left Newgrange, it finds its way into a number of satellite cairns during the day until at sunset it enters the large cairn of Dowth, known locally as the Fairy Mound of Darkness.

Deliberately or not, the Ancients succeeded in recreating the drama of the creation of life in stone and in light. With tons of material hauled and erected with great effort they built a cave, a womb, of the Mother Goddess that would receive the seed of the Sun God. It is as if they believed that the answer to one of life's greatest mysteries – the mystery of death – could be found by re-enacting the process of conception on the grandest of scales. Perhaps safe within the dark womb of the Earth Mother, fertilized by the bright ray of the Sun Father, both the dead and the living could be recreated, reborn. Newgrange's symbolic encapsulation of the magical power of the sexual act is further heightened by the aforementioned myth identifying it as the dwelling of the god of love Aenghus Og.

The solstice phenomenon may have been created exclusively for the dead in the hope of their rebirth in this or another world, but it may also have been used to provide living members of the tribe with an experience of initiation. Such an experience could have been enhanced by the unusual acoustic effects that occur within the monument. In addition, some writers have speculated on the ability of the geometric carvings on the stones to bring about changes in consciousness. Others have wondered about the ritual use of the mysterious stone basins that were found in the side alcoves.

View of the corbelled roof over the chamber inside Newgrange, lit by candlelight.

IONA

The tiny island of Iona in the Scottish Hebrides is believed by many to be one of the most sacred places on Earth. It may have been a holy site of the Druids before becoming the centre from which St Columba converted most of Scotland and northern England to Christianity. Monks from Iona created the Book of Kells *and founded Lindisfarne monastery in Northumbria. As its fame as a centre of learning spread, Iona became a place of pilgrimage and royal burial. A Benedictine monastery and nunnery later replaced Columba's settlement, which was destroyed by the Vikings.*

TRAVELLING TO THE WESTERN ISLES OF SCOTLAND is like a journey out of darkness, for, as you head west towards the Atlantic Ocean, the quality of light changes fundamentally – becoming translucent, more heavenly and less earthly. At the same time the sea mists produce rainbows of every kind – either short and transient, or vast and arcing across the sea. Iona, which is only 1 mile (1.6 km) wide and 3.5 miles (5.6 km) long, is reached by two sea crossings – first from the Scottish mainland at Oban to the island of Mull, and then across the Sound of Iona on a ferry that is often filled with the pilgrims and tourists who come in their thousands every year to this wild and, at first sight, unremarkable spot.

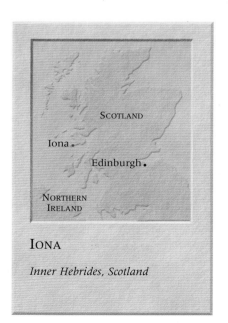

IONA

Inner Hebrides, Scotland

IONA'S EARLY HISTORY

The reason why so many are drawn to Iona becomes apparent when you investigate its history. Formed from some of the oldest rocks in the world – Lewisian gneiss from the Neoarchean eon some 2700 m.y.a., the island looks for all the world as if it has been birthed from nearby Fingal's cave on Staffa. The island was reputed to have once been filled with stone circles, and to have

A coloured engraving (c.1820) of the ruined Benedictine abbey on the Inner Hebridean island of Iona by William Daniell.

been a Pagan religious centre long before Christianity reached its shores. One of its old names was Isla na Druidhneach – Isle of the Druids. Although there are now no traces of Megalithic structures, this name alone appears to indicate that the island was once deemed sacred.

In AD 83, the Roman emperor Nerva (r. 79–98) commissioned the grammarian Demetrius of Tarsus to draw a map of the north of Scotland. Returning from his mapmaking voyage, Demetrius told the historian Plutarch (c.46–120) – who had also mapped this area – that on sailing around the north coast of Scotland he had discovered an island that was a retreat for holy men who were considered inviolate by the local people. Some scholars believe this island was Iona.

THE ARRIVAL OF COLUMBA

By the sixth century any reputation the island may have had for fostering pagan sages was eclipsed when the Christian missionary Columba (521–597) arrived from Ireland with 12 companions. He had taken the name Columba, Latin for 'dove', as a religious name, preferring it to the one he had been given at birth – Crimthann, Gaelic for 'fox'. After studying in monastic schools, Columba founded the monastery of Derry in Ulster at the age of 25. He then travelled the length and breadth of Ireland for 15 years preaching and founding hundreds of churches and monasteries.

One version of St Columba's life claims that his insistence on keeping a copy he had made of a psalter belonging to the scriptorium of St Finnian provoked a bloody battle in 561, in which many men were killed. According to this account, as a penance, Columba exiled himself from his homeland in order to work as a missionary in Scotland. Another version simply states that Columba and 12 companions sailed in search of unbelievers to convert.

The 13 Christians arrived in a coracle at the southern tip of the island in 563, and set about creating a church and monastery complete with kitchen, kiln, stables, mill and guesthouse – all surrounded by a defensive bank and ditch that excluded both women and cattle, since Columba believed 'where there is a cow there is a woman, and where there is a woman there is mischief'. Despite these restrictions, the community prospered, new followers joined, and two years later Columba travelled to the mainland to successfully convert the king of the Picts, having first engaged in a magical battle with the king's druid.

Soon monks from Iona were travelling all over Scotland, building churches and preaching the gospel. Three prelates from Iona founded the monastery of Lindisfarne in Northumberland, which became the most important Christian centre in northern Britain. Columba gained a reputation for both saintliness and strong leadership, and clan chiefs and kings eagerly sought his advice. On one occasion, in the earliest recorded mention of the Loch Ness monster, Columba was said to have saved a man's life by ordering the creature to depart.

THE BOOK OF KELLS AND THE STONE OF DESTINY

Today Iona seems remote from civilization, but in Columba's time the Hebridean islands were hives of activity, being far easier to defend than mainland strongholds. The island became a powerhouse in the spread of the new religion. Ionian monks produced the famous illuminated manuscript known as the

Book of Kells. In addition, a tradition of royal burials developed on the island, with a total of four Irish, eight Norwegian and 48 Scottish kings laid to rest there, including Macbeth (d.1057) – made famous by William Shakespeare.

A legend reinforces the connection between royalty and the island by stating that a standing stone called the Lia Fáil, which had once been used as a

Illumination showing St Matthew, from the Book of Kells. *The manuscript was taken from Iona to Kells, County Meath, for safekeeping in 807.*

133

coronation stone for inaugurating the High Kings of Ireland – also known as the 'Stone of Scone', 'Stone of Destiny' or 'Coronation Stone' – was brought to Iona by Columba, who then used it as a travelling altar on his missionary activities to the Scottish mainland.

By the eighth century the island was being raided by the Vikings, and Kenneth MacAlpin (d.858), the first king of the Scots, may have taken the stone for safe-keeping to Scone, near Perth, where it was used for coronations. Columba himself had died in 597 having prophesied, according to tradition: 'In Iona of my heart, Iona of my love, instead of the chanting of monks shall be the lowing of cattle. But before the world comes to an end, Iona shall be as it was.'

Viking raiders began a long series of attacks on the west coast of Scotland, including Iona, in the early 790s. In 806 they slaughtered 68 monks on the island, and within 20 years the community there had disbanded. In 1098 Iona fell for a time under Norwegian rule until 1156, before St Ronan established a Benedictine abbey and monastery on the site of Columba's church in 1204, while his sister Beathag established a nunnery nearby. Columba had apparently banished all women to the small island in the sound known to this day as the Isle of Women. The mounds of pebbles still found on the island are said to have been created in penance by those monks who had succumbed to their temptations, but by the time of Beathag women were able to worship on Iona itself. On one wall of the nunnery ruins you can see the worn image of what was probably a Sheela-na-Gig – a squatting female figure displaying her genitals that is either a pagan fertility symbol or a medieval morality icon warning against the dangers of lust.

THE SECOND COMING OF CHRIST ON IONA

The spiritual associations between women and Iona are reinforced by the legend that Mary, the mother of Jesus, visited the island, and by a prophecy mentioned by the author William Sharp (1855–1905), writing as Fiona Macleod in 1910:

'When I think of Iona I think often, too, of a prophecy once connected with Iona … the old prophecy that Christ shall come again upon Iona, and of that later and obscure prophecy which foretells, now as the Bride of Christ, now as the Daughter of God, now as the Divine Spirit embodied through mortal birth in a Woman, as once through mortal birth in a man, the coming of a new Presence and Power: and dream that this may be upon Iona, so that the little Gaelic island may become as the little Syrian Bethlehem'.

Statue of St Aidan (d.651) on the Northumbrian island of Lindisfarne (Holy Island). Aidan was an Irish monk who studied under Columba on Iona before founding the Lindisfarne monastery.

Iona was admired by Samuel Johnson (1709–84) when he spent a night on there in 1773 and by Felix Mendelssohn (1809–47), who captured the atmosphere of the region in his *Hebrides Overture*, composed between 1830 and 1832.

THE ISLAND TODAY

In the modern period the island has taken on a new lease of life, having become a place of pilgrimage not only for Christians, but also for Pagans, Druids and followers of New Age beliefs.

" *This island set apart, this motherland of many dreams, still yields its secret, but it is only as men seek that they truly find. To reach the heart of Iona is to find something eternal.* "

G.E. TROUP, *SAINT COLUMBA*

It has also once again become a vibrant centre of the Christian faith. At the start of the 20th century, work began on restoring the abbey ruins, and in 1938 the Rev. George MacLeod (1895–1991) founded the Iona Community, which continued the work of restoration. The Community has since developed into an ecumenical group committed to seeking new ways of Christian expression. It is politically active, promoting the ideals of economic and ecological justice; it opposes nuclear weapons and campaigns against racism and the arms trade. It is also active in inter-faith dialogue and in work with young people.

Today, most visitors come to the island just for a few hours, touring the ruins of the nunnery and visiting the rebuilt abbey and the local shops before leaving. But to truly appreciate its unique atmosphere you need to spend time in its wilder places. Then, perhaps, you will find yourself agreeing with Fiona Macleod:

'None can understand it who does not see it through its pagan light, its Christian light, its singular blending of paganism and romance and spiritual beauty. There is, too, an Iona that is more than Gaelic, that is more than a place rainbow-lit with the seven desires of the world, the Iona that, if we will it so, is a mirror of your heart and of mine'.

Iona Abbey as it appears today, having been restored by the Iona Community in the mid-20th century.

WALDEN POND

Walden Pond is situated just outside the small town of Concord, Massachusetts in the northeastern United States. It was here that Henry David Thoreau wrote his seminal work Walden *– an account of his sojourn beside the lake. This book continues to inspire readers, thanks to the constant topicality of its message about the human race's need to respect the natural world and resist the pressures of consumerism.*

IN THE HEART OF THE NEW ENGLAND COUNTRYSIDE, 20 miles (32 km) northwest of Boston and 15 miles (24 km) east of Harvard, lies a place that has played a key role in the political, cultural and spiritual history of the United States. Today Concord in Massachusetts is a small town of 17,000 inhabitants, but every year it attracts over a million visitors. Many of them are making a pilgrimage to a spot they consider the birthplace of the nation, since it was here – in 1775 – that the first major set-piece battle took place in the American War of Independence against the British.

Other visitors to Concord come on a literary pilgrimage. The town acted as a magnet for a number of important American

writers in the 19th century, including the philosopher Ralph Waldo Emerson (1803–82), the novelist Nathaniel Hawthorne (1804–64) and Louisa May Alcott (1832–88), author of *Little Women*.

A third group of visitors are on a spiritual quest; a 40-minute walk, or a 5-minute drive down Walden Street, brings you to their particular place of homage – Walden Pond, where the author and naturalist Henry David Thoreau (1817–62) famously set up home. The literary fruit of his residence there has inspired many generations of spiritual seekers and lovers of the natural world.

Thoreau has been called America's first environmentalist, but he was much more than that: his support of the anti-slavery movement, and his philosophy – and practice – of civil disobedience profoundly influenced such diverse figures as Leo Tolstoy (1828–1910), Mohandas Gandhi (1869–1948) and Martin Luther King (1929–68). Thoreau's genius lay in his ability to combine his interests in living with integrity according to moral principles with a study of the world around him and an appreciation of life's inherent spirituality.

WALDEN POND

Near Concord, Massachusetts, USA

A LIFE OF SIMPLICITY

'Pond' is something of a modest description of what is really a substantial body of water – Walden Pond is a lake covering 25 hectares (61 acres) and up to 31 metres (102 ft) in depth. Beside it, Thoreau built a log cabin and lived there for two years and two months, from July 1845 to September 1847. Every day the water inspired him, and he wrote eloquently of its beauty: 'A lake is the landscape's most beautiful and expressive feature. It is Earth's eye; looking into which the beholder measures the depths of his own nature.'

On the shores of the tranquil Walden Pond in Massachusetts, Henry David Thoreau tried to escape the dehumanizing effects of the Industrial Revolution.

TIMELINE

1803 Ralph Waldo Emerson born in Boston

1817 Henry David Thoreau born in Concord

1836 Transcendental Club formed

1836 Emerson's *Nature* published

1840–4 Publication of the Transcendentalist magazine *Dial*

1841 Transcendentalist community Brook Farm founded at West Roxbury, Massachusetts

1841 First series of Emerson's Essays published

1843 Transcendentalist community of Fruitlands established at Harvard, Massachusetts

1845 Thoreau begins his stay at Walden Pond

1846 Thoreau jailed for refusal to pay poll tax

1847 Thoreau returns from Walden Pond to stay with Emerson's wife and children, while Emerson travels to Europe

1849 Thoreau publishes 'Resistance to Civil Government'

1854 Publication of Thoreau's *Walden: or, Life in the Woods*

1854 Emerson meets the poet Walt Whitman, who espouses many of his ideas on nature

1862 Thoreau dies in Concord

Thoreau's sojourn beside Walden Pond was a deliberate attempt to put into practice his philosophy of living a simple life close to nature. His friend and mentor Emerson let him build on land he owned beside the pond. Thoreau's account of his experiment in natural living – *Walden* – opens with a detailed description of how he constructed his cabin and how much it cost – US$28 and 12 cents. The hut measured 4.5 m (15 ft) by 3 m (10 ft) with a storage cellar 2.1 m (7 ft) high beneath it. He felled pine trees to erect the frame and bought floorboards and secondhand bricks for the chimney at local stores. He furnished his cabin with a bed, two chairs, a table and a copy of the *Bhagavadgita*, the Hindu epic on the life of Lord Krishna.

Although Thoreau was living beside a lake in second-growth forest he wasn't out in the wilderness – his nearest neighbour was only a mile (1.6 km) away. During his stay at the cabin, he was in the habit of walking into Concord every two days or so. Also, the track of the Fitchburg Railroad, laid only the year before Thoreau took up residence here, passed close to his cabin, providing a constant reminder of the increasing human exploitation of the land. Thoreau found himself profoundly out of sympathy with the *laissez-faire* capitalism that characterized his age. His refusal to pay poll tax in protests against slavery and the Mexican–American War led to a very brief spell in gaol. This experience prompted him to write the essay 'Resistance to Civil Government' (later known as 'Civil Disobedience') in 1849. In it, he argued that the dictates of an individual's conscience should never be overruled by the demands of the state. The essay contains the famous statement: 'That government is best which governs least.'

Reading partly like a journal, and collapsed into the span of a year to follow the seasons, some have called *Walden* an early example of a 'blog', both in its directness and in the intensely personal nature of its musings. Lyrical, naturalistic observation and practical information about building and farming are combined with philosophical and psychological reflections – prompting Thoreau expert Thomas Blanding to recommend that we read the book as poetry or scripture. Even though *Walden* was written more than 150 years ago, its message about our relationship with the Earth is more relevant today than ever before.

CONCORD TRANSCENDENTALISM

If a spirituality based on a reverence for the natural world required a Bible, then *Walden* would furnish us with all we need. By combining the everyday with the philosophical, earthiness and practicality with aesthetics and spirituality, Thoreau succeeded in bringing to life the ideas expressed by Emerson in his essay *Nature*, published nine years before

Thoreau came to Walden Pond. Emerson's text articulated for the first time the tenets of a spiritual philosophy that came to be variously known as American Transcendentalism, New England Transcendentalism, or Concord Transcendentalism. This movement encouraged people to take individual intuition as their spiritual and moral compass rather than the doctrines of established religion.

After leaving the pond, it took nine years and seven edits by Thoreau before *Walden* was finally published. In the meantime, the cabin was sold and disassembled to patch a barn and roof a pig sty. Thoreau went to live with his parents in a third-floor attic room and devoted the remaining years of his life to an intense study of the natural world, dying of tuberculosis in 1862, aged just 44.

At the site of the cabin Thoreau's friend and fellow Transcendentalist Bronson Alcott (1799–1888), father of writer Louisa May, built a cairn of stones, which has since been added to by pilgrims who come to walk in the woods, to gaze at the pond, and to stand at a place that proved such a powerful inspiration. Nearby stands a replica of the cabin, with a statue of the author beside it.

One of Thoreau's most famous sayings was that 'the mass of men lead lives of quiet desperation and go to the grave with the song still in them'. Thoreau may have gone to the grave too early, but part of his appeal today resides in the fact that he refused to compromise his ideals. He was a man whose song emerged so powerfully and clearly that we can still hear it and be inspired by it today.

Title page from the first edition of Walden, *published in 1854.*

> 66 *I went to the woods because I wished to live deliberately, to front only the essential facts of life, and see if I could not learn what it had to teach, and not, when I came to die, discover that I had not lived. I did not wish to live what was not life, living is so dear; nor did I wish to practise resignation, unless it was quite necessary. I wanted to live deep and suck out all the marrow of life …* 99

HENRY DAVID THOREAU, *WALDEN* (1854)

DENALI

North of Anchorage in Alaska an extensive National Park surrounds and protects North America's highest mountain – Denali, or Mount McKinley. A single road winds through part of this huge reserve, but even this is closed to private cars for most of the year as a way of preventing tourism from blighting this magnificent wilderness.

MANY MOUNTAINS IN NORTH AMERICA ARE CONSIDERED SACRED and places of special power, including Mount Shasta in California, Mount Rainier in Washington State, Pilot Mountain in North Carolina and Tso'dzil (Mount Taylor) in New Mexico. However Denali stands as the most spectacular sacred peak of them all.

If you believe those mystics who maintain that a country's spiritual centre is found on its highest peak, then to find the spiritual centre of North America you must first travel four hours north of Anchorage, Alaska's largest city, before entering the Denali National Park, a wilderness of 24.3 million hectares (60 million acres). Venturing deep into this vast land you finally arrive at the peak itself. Rising to 6194 metres (20,320 ft), this is one of the world's 'Seven Summits' – that is, the tallest mountains on each continent, which include Everest in Nepal at 8850 metres (29,035 ft), and Aconcagua in Argentina at 6962 metres (22,841 ft).

Denali soars straight up from the surrounding tundra, making it a breathtaking site every bit as impressive as the Grand Canyon in Colorado. The mountain appears even taller than Everest, since its vertical relief is higher: whereas Everest rises 3658 metres (12,000 ft) from the Tibetan plateau, Denali's steep southern face rises uninterrupted for fully 5500 metres (18,000 ft). Five glaciers flow down the mountain, while permanent snowfields cover more than half its slopes. The ice is hundreds of feet thick in many places, and so fierce is its weather, with winter temperatures dropping to –75°F (–50°C), that it is arguably the coldest mountain in the world.

Despite its remoteness and relative inaccessibilty, Denali National Park still attracts thousands of visitors each year, who come to catch glimpses of grizzly bears, caribou and wolves and to gaze in awe at the mountains and glaciers.

DENALI

North of Anchorage, Alaska, USA

The forbidding south face of Denali. Its position just below the Arctic Circle and the severe wind-chill factor make Denali one of the most hostile environments on Earth.

" *The crest of Denali is considered to be the throne of Sa, the solar shaman and Master of Life. Annually he conquers Dzadu of the north, the demon of snow, and renews life with warming rains, green growth, spawning fish, migrating waterfowl, roaming caribou, sheep, moose and animals awakened from their winter's sleep.* "

LaVedi R. Lafferty

TIMELINE

1867 The land that became Alaska is purchased by the US from the Russian empire for $7,200,000

1903 First attempt on Denali's summit by Judge James Wickersham

1906 Frederick Cook falsely claims the first ascent of McKinley

1912 Alaska becomes an 'organized territory' of the US; the Parker-Browne expedition almost reaches the South Summit

1913 First successful ascent by Hudson Stuck, Walter Harper, Harry Karstens and Robert Tatum

1932 Second ascent, by Alfred Linley, Harry Liek, Grant Pearson and Erling Strom

1947 Barbara Washburn becomes the first woman to reach the summit

1959 Alaska becomes the 49th state of the United States

Every year, more than one thousand climbers attempt to reach the summit of Denali. Just over half of them are successful, but it is an unforgiving mountain that has claimed the lives of more than 100 people since detailed records began in 1932.

THE GREAT ONE

The mountain has been given a variety of names in the past. Today it is most commonly called Denali, which in the local Athabascan language means 'The High One' or 'The Great One': the Athabascans believe that the mountain is home to Sa, the solar shaman and Master of Life.

Early Russian explorers named it Bolshaya Gora ('Great Mountain'). Tsarist Russia sold the territory of Alaska to the United States in 1867, and in 1889 a party of American gold prospectors christened the peak Densmore's Mountain after one of their group. Eight years later the mountain was officially renamed Mount McKinley, in honour of the Republican president-elect William McKinley (1843–1901).

Later, though, a number of critics began to voice their opposition to this name, as an example of colonialist appropriation. The eminent American naturalist Olaus Murie (1889–1963) claimed that naming natural features after human beings was an example of human arrogance. Murie was one of the great heroes of wilderness preservation. Like many others, he felt that his experience of the natural world was essentially a spiritual one. In 1920, while camping in the Denali region during his landmark study of the Alaskan caribou, he wrote:

> *'I guess I am still enrolled in the Lutheran Church at home, but there is no one church or creed with which I fully agree. For one thing, I am crazy about Nature, and almost worship it, but isn't Nature the direct work of God?'*

Here it is hard not to feel the presence of God or the Goddess, or powerful spirits of nature. The wilderness around the mountain is rich in wildlife: grizzly bears, caribou, wolves, moose and Dall sheep roam the tundra. There are foxes, pine martens, lynx and wolverines in abundance too, as well as smaller creatures, such as snowshoe hares, hoary marmots, arctic ground squirrels and beavers. Sadly, as a result of climate change, over the course of the 21st century it is possible that the tundra will largely disappear from the Alaskan landscape, along with many of the animal and plant ecosystems that rely upon it.

ATTEMPTS ON THE SUMMIT

In 1903 Judge James Wickersham (1857–1939) made the first recorded attempt to climb the peak via its treacherous North Face. He never reached the summit, and the route was not successfully climbed until 1963. Yet Wickersham gave to posterity something far more valuable than a personal achievement. In a story entitled 'The Sage of Kantishna – Legends of Denali', in his book *Old Yukon – Tales, Trails and Trials,* he recounts how a local blind

> **" *Keep close to Nature's heart … and break clear away, once in awhile, and climb a mountain or spend a week in the woods. Wash your spirit clean. None of Nature's landscapes are ugly so long as they are wild.* "**
>
> JOHN MUIR, *OUR NATIONAL PARKS* (1901)

medicine man called 'old Koonah' told him the myth of Denali's creation: Yako, the ancient founder-hero of the Tena (an Athabascan tribe) magically created the Denali massif from giant sea waves sent to destroy him by Totson the Raven Chief.

The summit of Denali was first reached by an expedition organized by an Episcopalian archdeacon, Hudson Stuck (1865–1920). Born in London, Stuck fell in love with Alaska on a visit in 1904 and hardly ever left the territory thereafter. In 1913 he and three others embarked on a three-month ascent of the peak. In his moving account *The Ascent of Denali*, Stuck describes how Walter Harper, a member of the indigenous Athabascan peoples, was the first man to reach the summit on 7 June:

A bull caribou grazing on the tundra in Denali National Park in Alaska. This wilderness is home to a wide variety of animals annd plants but is under threat from global warming.

> *'With keen excitement, we pushed on. Walter, who had been in the lead all day, was the first to scramble up. A Native Alaskan, he is the first human being to set foot upon the top of Alaska's great mountain.'*

Astonishingly, Walter Harper had never climbed a mountain in his life before, and five years later he died in a shipwreck. But for that one moment in his life he had reached the throne of Sa.

Mato Paha
(Bear Butte)

In South Dakota, Mato Paha – most commonly known as Bear Butte – rises out of the Great Plains as part of the isolated mountain range of the Black Hills. The mountain has long been regarded as sacred by many Native American peoples of the region, including the Lakota, Cheyenne, Arapaho, Kiowa, Kiowa-Apache, Mandan and Arikara.

D RIVING NORTH FOR TEN MINUTES OUT OF THE SMALL TOWN OF STURGIS, you come to the wildlife refuge of Bear Butte Lake on your left, before you suddenly notice, to the right, Bear Butte rising out of the surrounding plain to a height of 382 metres (1253 ft).

A butte is a small hill with steep sides and a flat top, and the Lakota or Sioux call this place Mato Paha – Bear Mountain. The Cheyenne name for it is Noahvose – the good or beneficent mountain. They believe it was here that Maheo (God) gave the mythical hero Sweet Medicine the knowledge that forms the basis of their religious, political, social and economic customs.

Today Bear Butte is a site of pilgrimage for ceremony, prayer and meditation. Offerings are often left at the top of the mountain, and prayer cloths and bundles are tied to the branches of trees on its slopes. The tranquillity and atmosphere of the site are at risk from commercial developments that seek to exploit the land around the mountain, but there is a vigorous campaign in place to restore the land to Native ownership and to protect Bear Butte from desecration.

Some 50 miles (80 km) to the south of Bear Butte lies the Mount Rushmore national monument, famous around the world for its giant sculptures of the faces of four US presidents, and visited by three million sightseers every year.

An 1888 photograph of the settlement at Fort Meade, with Bear Butte looming in the distance, shows the extent of White incursion onto Indian lands by the late 19th century.

Nearby stands the Crazy Horse memorial, in honour of the Lakota warrior (1842–77) who fought to preserve the Native American way of life from White encroachment. The life's work of Korczak Ziolkowski (1908–82) a sculptor who worked on the Mount Rushmore project, it was begun in 1948 and is still unfinished. Once complete, it will be the largest mountain sculpture in the world.

BEAR BUTTE

South Dakota, USA

A PLACE OF VISION AND PRAYER

For the Lakota and Cheyenne, and other Plains Indian tribes, the mountain has always been seen as sacred, and as a place of vision and prayer. There is evidence of human occupation here dating back 10,000 years, and over the centuries the tribes living in the area have changed. By the 15th century the Arikara inhabited the region, and were followed by the Cheyenne, Crow, Kiowa and Pawnee. In 1765, a Lakota exploring and raiding party led by Chief Standing Bear discovered the Black Hills, and by 1776 the Lakota Sioux had taken control of the region.

In 1857 tribal rivalries were set aside by the common threat of the growing incursion of white settlers in the Black Hills, and a council of many Indian nations met at Bear Butte to discuss the problem. Within a decade, the Fort Laramie Treaty was agreed between the US government and the Oglala and Lakota tribes, with Chief Sitting Bull (c.1831–90) signing this treaty on their behalf. Land in South Dakota, west of the Missouri River, was given to the

TIMELINE

8000 BC Earliest date of human artifacts found on or near Bear Butte

AD 1500 The Arikara arrived in the Black Hills by this time, followed by the Cheyenne, Crow, Kiowa and Pawnee

1776 The Sioux take the region from the Cheyenne

18th century The Lakota arrive from Minnesota driving out other tribes

1857 A council of many Indian nations meet at Bear Butte to discuss the growing presence of White settlers in the Black Hills

1868 Treaty of Fort Laramie confirms the Lakota (Teton Sioux) ownership of the mountain range

1874 General Custer leads an expedition to the Black Hills, and confirms rumours of gold in the Black Hills, sparking a gold rush

1876 Lakota Sioux and Cheyenne wipe out General Custer's force at the Battle of Little Bighorn

1948 Sculptor Korczak Ziolkowski and Lakota Chief Henry Standing Bear inaugurate the Crazy Horse Memorial project in the Black Hills to honour North American Indian culture, tradition and living heritage

1961 Bear Butte becomes a State Park

1965 Bear Butte registered as a National Historic Landmark

1980 The US Supreme Court rules that the Black Hills were illegally taken

2005 The Intertribal Coalition to Defend Bear Butte is formed to develop and engage in action to protect the sacred site

surviving Indians in the area, but within a few years the cavalry commander General George Custer (1839–76) entered the territory, apparently camping on the slopes of Bear Butte. Custer confirmed that there was gold to be found in the Black Hills and soon the area was overrun with prospectors. The government reneged on its treaty obligations and drove the Indians on to reservations, such as Pine Ridge.

THE VISION OF CRAZY HORSE

Such an outcome had already been seen in vision three years before Custer's exploratory mission of 1874. Crazy Horse, the Oglala Lakota war leader, famous for his statement 'We do not inherit Mother Earth from our ancestors, we borrow Her from our children', went up to Bear Butte, and after much praying and fasting he was given a vision of the future. As a great thunderstorm accompanied by hailstones and lightning crashed around him, he was shown how Native American tribes would be marginalized, how poverty and alcohol would affect them, and how war would be followed by a time of 'crazy water'. But he was reassured by a voice saying that the dark times had to be, but will pass away, 'for all the people of Earth must gather together like the geese that fly together in the springtime'.

And it was Crazy Horse who would play a key role in the death of Custer, at the Battle of the Little Bighorn, in 1876 – just two years after his mission to the Black Hills. Of this famous battle, commonly known as 'Custer's Last Stand', Crazy Horse said:

> 'A very great vision is needed and the man who has it must follow it as the eagle seeks the deepest blue of the sky. I was hostile to the white man … we preferred hunting to a life of idleness on our reservations. At times we did not get enough to eat and we were not allowed to hunt. All we wanted was peace and to be left alone. Soldiers came and destroyed our villages. Then Long Hair (Custer) came … They say we massacred him, but he would have done the same to us. Our first impulse was to escape but we were so hemmed in we had to fight'.

THE FIGHT FOR JUSTICE

In 1980 the federal courts ruled that the seizure of the Black Hills was illegal, and monetary compensation of over US$100 million was offered to the Lakota, which they turned down. Rick Two-Dogs, Oglala Lakota medicine man, expressed the feelings of many of his people when he said: 'All of our origin stories go back to this place. We have a spiritual connection to the Black Hills that can't be sold. I don't think I could face the Creator with an open heart if I ever took money for it'. Nearly 30 years later the Lakota are still demanding the return of their land, and refusing the compensation award, which has now grown to US$600 million.

Today the fight by the Indians, who want to be left in peace to follow their own way of life, continues; in particular Bear Butte has become a focal point for many tribes in their united opposition to an annual bikers' rally held at nearby Sturgis, which has taken place for two weeks in August for over 60 years. Native Americans feel that the rally desecrates the peaceful atmosphere of the mountain. Huge campsites accommodate the visitors and commercial interests are constantly seeking to encroach upon land near the site. Those who revere Bear Butte as a sacred place long for the time when once again the mountain and the land around it is treated with reverence and restored to its spiritual guardians.

The Crazy Horse Memorial in the Black Hills of South Dakota. Although it was inaugurated by a Sioux chief, some Native American activists believe that this monument violates the sanctity of the land.

"*Miracles and prophecies have revealed themselves; the White Animals are showing their Sacred Color to give us the message of change and sacrifice. Throughout the world, people have made spiritual commitment to bring peace, harmony and restoration back to our lives. Faith must continue to live in the hearts of the People – to gather at our Sacred Sites and heal our Grandmother Earth.***"**

CHIEF ARVOL LOOKING HORSE, *LETTERS TO THE PEOPLE*

YOSEMITE

Yosemite National Park in the High Sierras of northern California is the epitome of the American wilderness. Ever since its natural beauties began to be described in the mid-19th century, visitors have flocked to experience the rugged grandeur of its scenery. Enthralled by its towering granite peaks with their sweeping panoramas, its alpine meadows, rushing waterfalls, crystal-clear lakes and giant redwood trees, many people have experienced Yosemite as one of the most sacred places on Earth.

W E ARE ALL WEARY OF TRAVEL BROCHURES CONSTANTLY WAXING LYRICAL about places that are supposedly 'breathtaking' and 'out of this world', but Yosemite truly is one place where only superlatives will suffice. One of its earliest and greatest champions, the preservationist John Muir (1838–1914), called it 'the grandest of all special temples of Nature', and such is its beauty that it is tempting to see the whole of Yosemite as one vast natural sacred site.

AN ALL-TOO POPULAR DESTINATION

Designated a UNESCO World Heritage Site in 1984, Yosemite National Park covers an area of over 1000 square miles (2600 sq km) in the Sierra Nevada Mountain range, just four hours' drive east of San Francisco. Ninety-five percent of the area is categorized as wilderness, but although there are over 800 miles (1287 km) of hiking trails through the park, most visitors confine their explorations to the 7 square miles (18 sq km) of Yosemite Valley that are easily accessible. And yet the sheer magnificence of the natural spectacle at Yosemite is so seductive that it has created a major problem of its own; the annual influx of over three million tourists prompted the environmentalist David Brower (1912–2000) to say, 'My complaint is that it is too damn beautiful'.

Most visitors enter by following the course of the Merced River into the broad, steep-sided Yosemite Valley. This was formed about 1 million years ago when, with ice sheets up to 1200 metres (4000 ft) thick, great glaciers carved their way into the rock to sculpt the landscape of the High Sierras.

On the flat valley floor the Merced River meanders through woods and meadows, creating an ideal

YOSEMITE NATIONAL PARK

California, USA

The 3000-ft (910-m) sheer southwest face of El Capitan in Yosemite National Park. First scaled in 1958, this peak is now a favourite venue for rock climbing.

"*Yosemite Valley, to me, is always a sunrise, a glitter of green and golden wonder in a vast edifice of stone and space.*"

ANSEL ADAMS

A giant sequoia tree in Mariposa Grove. One Native American term for this species of redwood is Wawona, the name of the valley where the grove is situated.

environment for the day visitor, who can walk and picnic amidst magnificent scenery, which includes some of the highest waterfalls in the world tumbling from great granite cliffs. Tour buses provide transport around the valley and to lookout points above. Although there are camping facilities, most visitors come only for the day, leaving the incomparable experience of Yosemite by moon and starlight to those who choose to camp or stay at one of the lodges or motels, or at the Victorian Wawona Hotel, built in 1878.

THE SEQUOIA GROVE

Near this hotel are the soaring sequoias of Mariposa Grove, including the 'Grizzly Giant', which stands 63 metres (207 ft) tall. This, the oldest tree in the grove, is between 1600 and 2000 years old.

Spring is a favourite time to visit Yosemite because the valley meadows are filled with wild flowers, the dogwood is in bloom and the waterfalls are in full flood. Yosemite Falls plunges over 740 metres (2425 ft) and is the third largest waterfall in the world, while Sentinel Falls cascades over 610 m (2000 ft). Towering over the landscape are the great summits of Half Dome and El Capitan, about which an early writer on the park, Herbert Earl Wilson, wrote in his 1922 book *The Lore and Lure of the Yosemite*:

> *'To apply human standards of measurements to this monarch of mountains is sacrilege. To attempt by mere words and figures to convey some idea of its stupendous massiveness, its nobly-defiant impressive individuality, is rankest folly.'*

Once you leave the valley and hike or go on horseback up into the High Country, the trappings of mass tourism fall away and the numerous natural sanctuaries of Yosemite start to reveal themselves more easily in the solitude found here. Hikers will often avoid the valley altogether and drive instead straight into the High Country to the Tuolumne Meadows area at elevations of 2560 metres (8500 ft) to 3048 metres (10,000 ft). Here, in one of the largest sub-alpine meadows in the Sierra Nevada, a campsite acts as a base for hikers on the John Muir or Pacific Crest Trails.

A LAND OF BEARS

The name Yosemite means 'they are killers', and derives from *yosse'meti*, a term used by the Southern Sierra Miwok people to describe the warlike Ahwahneechee tribe that once inhabited

the Yosemite Valley. Some writers have incorrectly stated that the name comes from the Miwok word *išïïmati*, meaning 'grizzly bear', since grizzlies used to roam the valleys of this region until the last one was shot in 1895.

Although the California grizzly is now extinct, bears are still very much a presence in the National Park. The 300–500 American black bears that live in Yosemite sometimes break into tourists' cars or roam the campsites in search of food, but mostly live peacefully in the wilderness. According to native legend, bears have been here since the beginning of time, and the great cliff face of El Capitan was supposedly created when a grizzly and her two cubs fell asleep upon a large, flat rock. It was the grizzly bear that taught the indigenous people of the region that acorns were a source of food.

The Ahwahneechee harvested the acorns, hunted and fished, and traded with the Mono Lake Paiute people for obsidian, rabbit skins and pine nuts. Sickness reduced their numbers in the 19th century, and they left the valley to join with the Paiutes. Later around 200 of them returned to the valley; however, after they attacked gold prospectors, they were hunted down in 1851 by a detachment of soldiers, who entered the valley on their trail with the aim of forcing them onto a reservation.

Yosemite Falls in autumn. This waterfall, which cascades in two stages, is the highest in North America.

THREE CONSERVATION PIONEERS

The conservation of Yosemite – and indeed of great wildernesses throughout the American West – was championed by three pioneers of the American conservation movement: John Muir, Galen Clark (1814–1910) and Ansel Adams (1902–84). These men were dynamic heirs to one of the United States' greatest gifts to the world – the nature-loving spiritual tradition of American Transcendentalism (see pages 136–139).

In 1853, the homesteader Galen Clark came to live in the clear mountain air of the Wawona Valley in an attempt to cure his terminal tuberculosis. He can fairly lay claim to being the founding father of Yosemite National Park; Clark spent his time exploring and climbing in the area, and proselytizing about its beauty. He discovered the Mariposa Grove and was influential in persuading President Abraham Lincoln (1809–65) to protect the land by granting it to the State of California for public use and recreation. Once Clark was made the first 'guardian of the grant', he opened a hotel and wrote about the sequoias, the local indigenous peoples and the valley itself.

John Muir wrote that Clark was 'one of the most sincere treelovers I ever knew'. Muir, a Scotsman, came to the USA when he was just 11 years old. At the age of 30 he visited Yosemite, and instantly fell under its spell, writing: 'No temple made with hands can compare with Yosemite'. One of Muir's heroes, the Transcendentalist writer Ralph Waldo Emerson (1803–82) came to the park in 1871 and visited Muir. Muir became one of the first modern preservationists and a passionate defender of wilderness, being instrumental in helping the area become a National Park in 1890. Two years later, he founded the American environmental organization, the Sierra Club, and famously took President Theodore Roosevelt (1858–1919) camping with him in the back country of the park in 1903. Muir's great gift for articulating his love of nature and his awareness of the intrinsically spiritual power of the wild, as well as his environmental activism, was so influential that hiking trails, a park, a college, a school and an asteroid have all been named after him.

In 1919, after visiting Yosemite, a 17-year-old joined Muir's Sierra Club to become the third of the park's most famous champions. Ansel Adams was to become America's greatest landscape photographer and a fierce advocate for the preservation of wild places. Every year for the rest of his life, he returned to the park to photograph its vistas and changing moods, trying to capture what he termed the 'spiritual-emotional aspects' of the landscape. He once described how, when photographing in the park, he 'dreamed that for a moment, time stood quietly and the vision became but the shadow of an infinitely greater world, and I had within the grasp of consciousness a transcendental experience.'

In the tradition of the New England Transcendentalists who combined nature mysticism with social activism, Adams, along with Clark and Muir, was not only spiritually nourished by his contact with the beauty and power of Nature, but actively campaigned to preserve the wilderness he loved, and fought tirelessly against over-development of the park.

Thanks to these men and many other activists, it is still possible to find solitude and tranquillity in Yosemite. If you are able to strike away from the crowd and take 'the path less travelled', Yosemite offers a powerful experience of the inherent sanctity of nature, of place and of the world.

John Muir (left) and the American naturalist John Burroughs (1837–1921) pause to take in the beauty of the scenery at Yosemite in 1909.

"It's so good and wonderful and so other-earth-other-sky transcendentally different in Yosemite that I could spend a dozen karmic cycles there and not exhaust the place."

MOUNTAINEER MIKE BORGHOFF

CHACO CANYON

The stark desert landscape of the Four Corners area of the American southwest, where the borders of Utah, Arizona, Colorado and New Mexico converge, was once home to the Ancestral Puebloan peoples, also known as the Anasazi. Pueblo Bonito and other buildings in Chaco Canyon, New Mexico, form part of a vast ceremonial complex built by these ancient peoples and oriented to the sun and moon.

THE NAVAJO NATION, WHO TRACE THEIR ANCESTRY BACK TO THE PUEBLOANS, now occupies 27,000 square miles (70,000 sq km) of the Four Corners – an area larger than many US states – and it is here that the most remarkable and well-known examples of these peoples' ancient culture can be found: Mesa Verde in Colorado and Canyon de Chelly in Arizona, with Chaco Canyon a little to the east of Navajoland in New Mexico.

Mesa Verde and Canyon de Chelly are famous for their spectacular cliff dwellings, built within caves and under cliff outcrops. Chaco Canyon at first sight seems less spectacular and is less visited, but research over the last 30 years suggests that the

canyon was the centre of a fascinating and complex civilization that flourished for about 250 years before vanishing in the 12th century.

Here, in the desert steppe of the Chaco Culture National Historical Park, 4000 archaeological sites have been recorded, mostly dating to between AD 900 and 1130.

THE GREAT HOUSES AND THE SOLAR DAGGER

The most striking of these sites are large D-shaped buildings known as 'Great Houses', 150 of which have been identified. At the heart of the Chaco Canyon area lies the largest and most impressive of them – Pueblo Bonito. Sited in front of the north wall of the canyon, much of this huge complex was originally five storeys high, and contained as many as 800 rooms. Two great *Kivas* (vast ceremonial rooms) and 37 smaller ones suggest this was a site of much ritual activity.

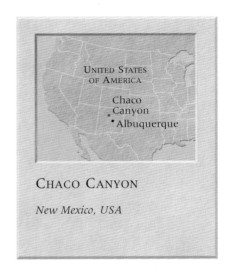

CHACO CANYON

New Mexico, USA

Today only a rough dirt track leads to Pueblo Bonito – deterring all but the keenest visitors. There are controversial plans afoot to resurface the road, inevitably bringing more tourists to the site, but this move is being vigorously opposed by Pueblo Bonito's guardians. For now only the intrepid can enjoy campfire talks by the enthusiastic astronomer and park guide G.B. Cornucopia, who for nearly 20 years has regaled visitors with insights into the extraordinary history of this place and provided telescopes for them to view the night sky.

Sunrise and sunset and the cold desert night bring relief from the sometimes searing heat of the place, affording the visitor to Pueblo Bonito an opportunity to appreciate the way in which the Anasazi built their structures to be in harmony with the rising and setting of the sun and the movements of the moon.

In 1977 an archaeoastronomer, Anna Sofaer, climbed Fajada Butte opposite 'Downtown Chaco' – Pueblo Bonito – and discovered a spiral carving which, either by chance or synchronicity, was being illuminated by a dagger-like sliver of sunlight at the very moment she arrived. Careful study revealed that the carving was a complex device that used slits in the rock above it to mark the solstices and equinoxes.

The Chacoan 'Great House' at Pueblo Bonito. It is believed to have been built in stages beginning around AD 919.

Over the years it has emerged that the whole site was laid out according to astronomical principles. In 1978 Sofaer launched the Solstice Project, a group dedicated to studying, documenting and preserving the Solar Dagger. The project

TIMELINE

*c.*10,000 BC Nomadic Clovis hunters arrive in the southwest

900 BC Cave-dwelling hunter-gatherers inhabit the area

AD 800 'Basketmaker' farming peoples begin building crescent-shaped structures in Chaco Canyon

900–1130 Major period of construction as the site develops as a hub of ceremony, trade and administration in the Four Corners

10th century Evidence of turquoise-processing industry here

1130 Worst drought in 2000 years hits the region

1140 Chacoan society begins to disintegrate, and migrations begin

1849 Site rediscovered by US soldiers, but vandalized over the next 70 years

1907 Established as a National Monument

1920 Excavation and reconstruction of the site begins

1937 Civilian Conservation Corps plants 100,000 cottonwood, tamarisk, plum and willow trees throughout the canyon, and improves roads and trails

1947 Tomasito, the last Navajo in Chaco Canyon, moves away

1971 National Parks Service and University of New Mexico survey Chacoan 'roads'

1978 The Solstice Project formed by Anna Sofaer

1987 Designated a UNESCO World Heritage Site

2005 A study projects that visitor numbers will soar fivefold if road is paved; many groups, including the Sierra Club, oppose paving

produced a film, *The Mystery of Chaco Canyon*, narrated by the actor Robert Redford (b.1936) and now available online, which explains the astronomical background to Pueblo Bonito.

A number of rock paintings have also been found in the canyon. One, known as the Supernova Petroglyph, may depict the stellar explosion that was seen on Earth on 4 July, 1054 and which was responsible for creating the Crab Nebula.

SPIRIT PATHS

Radiating from the Chaco complex is a mysterious network of straight lines that extend from 10 to 20 miles (16–32 km) into the desert. Reminiscent of the Nazca lines in Peru, hundreds of miles of these tracks have now been identified from aerial photographs.

Although some of these tracks may have served a utilitarian function, it seems more likely that they were used ceremonially. A tradition of the Hopi of northeastern Arizona (another people descended from the Anasazi) requires that initiates run in straight lines to shrines to plant prayer sticks. Moreover, a Navajo legend tells of the lines being 'tunnels' that the Ancient Ones used to travel in safety. The fact that the tracks are often bordered with stones and broken pottery suggests a connection with the ancestors, since smashed pottery was customarily placed as grave goods in burials as an offering to the ancestral spirits. The British Earth Mysteries expert Paul Devereux (b.1945) suggests that they may have developed as a result of shamanic trances, in which initiates undertook 'spirit flights' – out-of-body experiences of flying in straight lines over the landscape.

THE PLACE BEYOND THE HORIZON

Many Navajo and Hopi clans feel a strong spiritual connection to Chaco Canyon, and pay homage to the site in their prayers and songs and by making pilgrimages here. The Hopi call Chaco Canyon *Yupkoyvi*, 'the Place beyond the Horizon', and still perform their ceremonial dances at the site.

Although now deserted, Chaco Canyon is filled with a sense of life and of the presence of the spirit world. As the Hopi say,

A petroglyph at Chaco Canyon. Such images are thought to have been important forms of visual communication. Some represent clan symbols, while others record events during migrations or recall folk myths.

'the people never left'. Of course, at a mundane level they did indeed leave the site. Having spent several hundred years hauling vast quantities of wood and stone for miles through the desert to create this city, in the 12th century the population migrated, carefully sealing their buildings before abandoning them. Although there is some evidence that massacres involving cannibalism occurred in the area, these happened later and the most likely explanation for their departure comes from evidence of a severe drought that began in 1130 and lasted for at least half a century.

Chaco Canyon holds a fascination for many people. At the New Age spiritual event known as the Harmonic Convergence, which took place on 16 and 17 August, 1987, thousands of people were drawn to meditate and pray for a new era of peace and harmony here. To preserve the site, fewer visitors rather than more are needed, but by learning about Chaco Canyon – through reading, or watching *The Mystery of Chaco Canyon* – we can come to a deeper appreciation of our place in the world.

Civilizations rise and fall like the passing of the seasons and though we might be tempted to mourn this, on a deeper level this knowledge can become a source of strength, since it reminds us that the true wellspring of the human spirit lies beyond its outer forms, however magnificent. The ceremonial city in the canyon may lie in ruins, but its spirit remains. The people never left.

Just southeast of Pueblo Bonito, Chetro Ketl is one of the largest pueblos in Chaco Canyon. This is one of 12 kivas there.

“*The cardinal directions connect people, the seasons, the Sun and Moon's patterns, time, nature, the environment, the cosmos, and ceremonial systems. Observance of the cardinal directions and the Sun essentially ensured life by knowing when it was time to plant, harvest, and hunt for example. Pueblo Bonito is a physical manifestation of these ideas.*”

DR SHELLEY VALDEZ, A MEMBER OF THE PUEBLO LAGUNA TRIBE

PALENQUE

In the dense, humid rainforest of southern Mexico, the ancient 'lost city' of Palenque represents one of the finest examples of Mayan art and architecture. Palenque flourished for about 400 years, from the fourth to the eighth century. Over a dozen temples in this sacred city have been discovered, but much still remains buried in the surrounding jungle.

THE CHIAPAS REGION OF MEXICO LIES AT THE COUNTRY'S SOUTHERN TIP, south of the Yucatán Peninsula and just before the border with Guatemala. To the north the sparkling waters of the Gulf of Campeche might tempt you to the coast, but 80 miles (130 km) inland, 2743 metres (9000 ft) above sea level, a thick forest of mahogany, cedar and sapodilla surrounds a place that offers the traveller a far deeper and more memorable experience.

There, the Mayan sacred city of Palenque nestles in the foothills of the Sierra Madre mountains. The Yucatán Peninsula to the north is home to many Mayan sites, including the Temple of the Magician, dedicated to a legendary dwarf king, and Tulum, the 'Place of the Dawn'. There are still more in Guatemala. But of all the Mayan ruins it is Palenque that has stirred people's imaginations. This is undoubtedly due in part to the city's extraordinary setting and the atmosphere it exudes. But mostly it is attributable to the aura of mystery surrounding one of its rulers – Pacal II ('the Great'; r. 615–683) – who was entombed there 1300 years ago.

A RIP IN THE FABRIC OF TIME

To reach the ruined city you walk uphill through rainforest, following a footpath alongside a stream and past giant fig trees. Every so often you notice small ruins covered with lichen; to date, only about 10 percent of the city has been cleared and studied. As you reach a plateau, you enter a glade hacked out of the jungle. You might feel, as one recent traveller reports, that you are 'peering through a rip in the fabric of time'.

This clearing is the site of a white ziggurat, popularly known as El Templo de Comte (the Temple of the Count), after a self-styled French nobleman who stayed here in the early 19th century – just one of the many dreamers and adventurers who have been drawn to Palenque over the centuries.

THE TEMPLE OF THE INSCRIPTIONS

From the top of El Templo de Comte you can make out two huge temples in an adjacent clearing. One, the royal palace, has a four-storey tower and is carved with

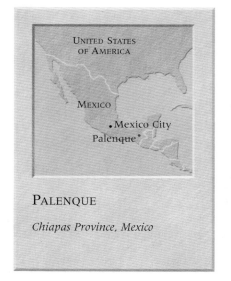

PALENQUE

Chiapas Province, Mexico

symbols of Venus. A labyrinth of decorated passages leads to living rooms and steam baths, which were used for ritual purification. But it is the other building that is the source of most of the modern speculation about Palenque – The Temple of the Inscriptions.

Here, after you have climbed 220 steep stairs to the top of the pyramid, the whole ceremonial complex unfolds before you. Beyond it lies the ocean. In 1952, the Mexican archaeologist Alberto Ruz Lhuillier (1906–79) discovered a hidden chamber within the ziggurat. After four seasons of digging in the floor of the temple he finally broke through into a burial chamber. His astonishment rivalled that of Howard Carter on opening the tomb of Tutankhamun:

> 'Out of the dim shadows emerged a vision from a fairy tale, a fantastic, ethereal sight from another world. It seemed a huge magic grotto carved out of ice, the walls

View of the Mayan site of Palenque in Chiapas province. On the left is the Temple of the Inscriptions, while to the right is the royal palace.

Far right: the burial chamber and sarcophagus of Pacal the Great in the Temple of the Inscriptions in Palenque. Erich von Däniken claimed that the engraving of Pacal on the lid resembled an astronaut in a 1960s Mercury space capsule.

sparkling and glistening like snow crystals. Delicate festoons of stalactites hung like tassels of a curtain, and the stalagmites on the floor looked like drippings from a great candle. The impression, in fact, was that of an abandoned chapel. Across the walls marched stucco figures in low relief. Then my eyes sought the floor. This was almost entirely filled with a great carved stone slab, in perfect condition.'

This turned out to be the lid of the sarcophagus of Pacal the Great, who ruled Palenque for almost 70 years in the seventh century AD. Today the chamber is sealed, but a replica of the lid can be seen in the National Museum of Anthropology and History in Mexico City.

Experts on Mayan art explain that the image on the lid is a representation of Pacal entering the Maya underworld. Beneath it was found the body of Pacal, wearing a jade mask and bead necklaces, surrounded by sculptures and stucco reliefs depicting figures from Mayan mythology, and Pacal's transition to divinity. Ascending the throne at the age of 12 and dying at the age of 80, Pacal and his two sons who ruled after him ensured that the city experienced a century of flowering before it was sacked in 711. By the ninth century it was abandoned and left to the forest. The Mayan account of creation and history, the *Popol Vuh*, records a legend that their cities were abandoned because the divine cycle had been completed and the moment of dispersion had arrived. According to this interpretation, then, Pacal the Great had already become a god who could speak to his descendants.

An exterior view of the Temple of the Inscriptions. Construction of this building began in c.675.

FROM ATLANTIS TO THE APOCALYPSE

First visited by a European in 1567, Palenque became the subject of several outlandish theories from the 18th century onwards. The first of these was expounded by the traveller Ordoñez y Aguilar, who was taken to the site by local hunters in 1773, and who wrote that he had discovered a lost city of Atlantis. From 1831 to 1833, a French antiquarian and *soi-disant* aristocrat, Jean-Frédéric Maximilien de Waldeck (1766–1875), lived on top of El Templo de Comte. On his return to Europe, Waldeck produced a lavish tome, illustrated with his own lithographs, which was a heady

TIMELINE

AD 431 The first recorded king of Palenque ascends the throne

599 Palenque is attacked by the city of Calakmul and its client states

611 Calakmul and its client states attack the city again

615 Pacal the Great ascends the throne and presides over nearly 70 years of rebuilding

799 The last recorded king ascends the throne

800–900 The city is abandoned

1567 Father Pedro Lorenzo de la Nada becomes the first European to visit the ruins and publish an account

1773 Father Ordoñez y Aguilar rediscovers the site

1831–33 The 'Baron' de Waldeck lives on a ziggurat at Palenque for two years, while compiling a fanciful book about the city

1948 Alberto Ruz Lhuillier begins excavating the floor of the Temple of the Inscriptions

1952 Alberto Ruz Lhuillier finds the tomb of Pacal the Great

1968 Erich von Däniken popularizes the tomb by suggesting its lid depicts an ancient astronaut

1973 The first Mesa Redonda conference brings together a diverse group of archaeologists, linguists, artists and enthusiasts to study the site

1979 Alberto Ruz Lhuillier dies and is buried facing the temple

1980s The ruins are partially cleared for tourists

mix of fact and speculation and sold extremely well. Waldeck's principal claim was that Palenque had been built by one of the lost tribes of Israel.

In 1968 the book *Chariots of the Gods?* by the Swiss author Erich von Däniken (b.1935) became an instant bestseller. Von Däniken's sensational claims that Palenque was partly built by extra-terrestrials and that Pacal's sarcophagus lid might well depict an ancient astronaut were timed to perfection – images of spaceflight filled the world's television screens in the 1960s. The first space walk had been accomplished in 1965, while in 1967 both the USA and Russia suffered the first human fatalities in their space programmes.

Forty years on, von Däniken's theories still attract a loyal, if dwindling, band of devotees. 'Mystery Park', an ambitious theme park in Switzerland, complete with displays on Palenque, was built to promote his ideas. The attraction opened in 2003, but closed after only three years because of a lack of visitors. A leading member of the Swiss Academy of Sciences memorably called it a 'Cultural Chernobyl'.

In the late 1980s the American art historian José Argüelles (b.1939), who claims to be a direct spiritual descendant of Pacal, developed theories about the Mayan Calendar that predict major changes for civilization in 2012.

> *"What impresses you when you enter the tomb of mighty Pacal? The silence. The void that comes with time, too dies. For 1300 years Pacal had reposed here in absolute silence, in total darkness."*
>
> HOWARD LAFAY, *THE MAYA, CHILDREN OF TIME* (1975)

WIRIKUTA, THE FIELD OF FLOWERS

The Huichol people, living mostly in the Western Sierra Madre of Mexico, have managed to preserve much of their religious and cultural heritage from pre-Columbian days, and central to their traditions is a pilgrimage of over 250 miles (400 km) to a desert region east of the Sierra Madre, known as Wirikuta, the 'Field of Flowers'.

EVERY YEAR, IN AUGUST, MILLIONS OF BRIGHT ORANGE AND BLACK MONARCH butterflies begin their long migration south from the Rocky Mountains as far north as Canada to their winter home in the Oyamel fir and pine forests just south of the Sierra Madre mountains in Mexico.

Every year, a group of indigenous Huichol people make an equally colourful pilgrimage for 250 miles (400 km), from the Western Sierra Madre, on the border of Jalisco and Nayarit states, and across the Chihuahuan Desert to the sacred area of Wirikuta, the 'Field of Flowers'. Surrounding the former silver-mining town of Real de Catorce in the state of San Luis Potosí, the 140,000 hectare (345,800 acre) site of Wirikuta is one of the most biologically rich and diverse tracts of desert in the world, teeming with plant, bird and animal life.

A RICH CEREMONIAL LIFE

The Huichol – or Wixarrica, as they call themselves – are a community of around 20,000 people who have retained much of their original pre-Columbian culture and spiritual beliefs, thanks both to their geographical isolation and to their resistance to conversion. Around half the population still live in the traditional way – in extended families inhabiting 'rancho' settlements. There, nuclear families live in individual stone or adobe houses while sharing a communal kitchen and family

The sacred site of Wirikuta in the Chihuahuan Desert. This area of rich biodiversity contains almost one-quarter of all the world's cactus species.

shrine. With an extensive mythology and full annual cycle of religious festivals, which feature dance, music, and all-night chanting, the Huichol represent one of the richest examples of indigenous ceremonial life in the Americas.

Pilgrimages are central to this life, and their landscape is filled with numerous sacred places. These are used by the Huichol to commune with their deities – whom they feed with offerings, such as chocolate, and entertain with song and dance.

At the centre of their world is Teekata, where a sacred fire is kept burning. Four other sites stand at the cardinal directions. To the west: Haramara, Isla del Rey, the dwelling-place of the sea goddess and queen of the five-coloured corn. To the north: Hauxa Manaka, Fat Hill, where the canoe of the goddess Nakawé, mother of all gods, finally rested and where the wind and the royal eagles, her messengers, were born. To the south: Xapawiyeme, Scorpion Island in Lake

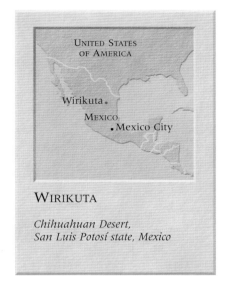

WIRIKUTA

*Chihuahuan Desert,
San Luis Potosí state, Mexico*

❝ *For the Huichol, art is prayer and direct communication with and participation in the sacred realm. It is meant to assure the good and beautiful life; health and fertility of crops, animals, and people; prosperity of the individual, the kin group, and the larger society.* ❞

ANTHROPOLOGIST PETER FURST, *VISIONS OF A HUICHOL SHAMAN* (2007)

TIMELINE

Chapala, where the farmer Watákame touched first ground after the universal flood. And to the east: Wirikuta, the final destination of the ancestors and deities in the Huichols' first pilgrimage, which was made to witness the birth of the sun. And it was at Wirikuta that the first deer hunt took place, and from the deer's footprints peyote, the sacred cactus, was born. The Huichol say that both the sun and their people were born here; this is their land of origin.

SHAMANISM AND CONSERVATION

The Huichol believe that the pilgrimage route to Wirikuta follows the path of the legendary *kawi* – a caterpillar that crawled out of the ocean in the west and was transformed on arrival at Wirikuta into a butterfly as the sun rose. Those who wish to undertake the journey to the Field of Flowers must prepare offerings, and abstain from both sex and salt. In former times pilgrims would walk to Wirikuta, but today the journey is made with the help of transport. Along the way, sacred sites are visited and ceremonies are performed, in which the elder shamans (*marakames*) transmit the tribe's legacy to the young initiates (*jicareros*) through chanting, story-telling and ritual. For this reason, the pilgrimage has been described as an 'itinerant Mesoamerican university'. The pilgrimage culminates in the picking of the hallucinogenic peyote, which is revered for its curative and enlightening properties. Some of the pilgrims, who have undergone rigorous preparation, then ingest the peyote to commune with the ancestors and deities, and the visions they receive inspire brightly coloured pictures made with dyed yarn.

The psychedelic revolution of the 1960s, and the popularity of books by the South American anthropologist and author Carlos Castaneda (d.1998), which glamourized Mexican shamanism while presenting fiction as fact, fuelled an interest in the Huichol that has proved a mixed blessing. Visitors in search of psychedelic experiences have often failed to respect the Huichols' traditional culture, and unrestrained picking of cacti is disturbing the distribution of the plant. However genuine appreciation of the Huichol culture has also been stimulated, bringing economic benefit to them through the sale of their visionary yarn paintings and handicrafts.

Sadly the Wirikuta region is threatened by over-grazing, over-exploitation of underground aquifers, and illegal trafficking in wildlife. However, the World Wide Fund for Nature (WWF) has identified the region as one of the 'most biologically diverse and important natural sites in the world' and the UN-backed Project for the Conservation of Biodiversity-Rich Sacred Natural Sites has chosen to assist the region. The Alliance of Religions and Conservation has been instrumental in producing

a full geographical survey of the entire pilgrimage route, and the Landmarks Foundation is assisting in both the purchase of land and the installation of gates in cattle fences to permit the free passage of pilgrims.

Today the culture of the Huichol who follow the path of the caterpillar and butterfly is under threat – as is the Mexican forest habitat of the Monarch butterfly. And yet, with sufficient care and well-targeted direct action, both may still be saved.

An embroidery panel produced by the Huichol people of central Mexico. The colourful scenes such craftworks depict come from the heightened state of awareness induced by consuming peyote.

❝*Deer-Person, the supreme teacher of the Huichol, teaches songs, reveals himself to shamanic healers through his Peyote spirit, and punishes those who violate his moral precepts. 'It is because of the wisdom of Deer-Person,' we are told, 'that shamans exist. That is how we Huichols are able to diagnose diseases with our visionary ability and soul, which are the eyes of Deer-Person. That is our method of curing'.***❞**

J.C. FIKES, *CARLOS CASTANEDA – ACADEMIC OPPORTUNISM AND THE PSYCHEDELIC SIXTIES* (1993)

SIERRA NEVADA
DE SANTA MARTA

*The indigenous inhabitants of the Sierra Nevada on the Caribbean coast
of Colombia escaped the domination of the Spanish in the 16th century,
and thanks to their extreme secrecy and isolation have managed to retain
their ancient traditions, which include making offerings at the many
sacred sites that exist in the region.*

IN NORTHERN COLOMBIA, JUST WEST OF THE BORDER WITH VENEZUELA, the world's
highest coastal mountain range of the Sierra Nevada de Santa Marta is held in
great reverence by certain of its inhabitants, and increasingly by many people
around the world. To the north its tropical jungle meets the turquoise waters of the
Caribbean along a shoreline of white beaches. Four indigenous peoples who share
the same cultural and spiritual traditions live in this remote and beautiful region:
the Kogi, the Wiwa, the Arhuaco and the Kaukaumu. Until recently, little was
known about these people, who were determined to safeguard their way of life by
keeping their contact with the rest of the world to an absolute minimum.

In the late 16th century, as descendants of the ancient Tairona (or Tayrona)
civilization, these peoples abandoned their cities, now mostly reclaimed by the
jungle, to escape the Spanish Conquistadors, and migrated to the higher reaches
of the Sierra, taking with them a sophisticated cosmology
and set of spiritual practices.

Their elders or priests, known as Mamas, undergo a long
process of initiation from childhood, often carried out in
the dark, during which they are taught how to work in
Aluna, the inner world of soul and thought that unites
all Nature. They learn about the ninefold structure of the
Universe and its primordial creator, whom they call 'The
Mother', and are instructed in how to bless the harvest,
all human endeavour and the natural world.

The Tairona developed a network of sacred sites in the
Sierra. At these sites, gold statuettes were placed in pots,
which were buried but visited frequently thereafter with
votive offerings. The Mamas believe that these sites
exude a special essence that maintains the equilibrium
of the world, but ever since the Spanish – and later
archaeologists and thieves – began digging up these

SIERRA NEVADA DE SANTA MARTA

Colombia, South America

figures, the world has been out of balance. Even so, they continue to make offerings at the sites and practise a form of divination to guide the life of their communities by observing the bubbles that rise from beads dropped into bowls of water.

A MICROCOSM OF THE WORLD

The 8,000 square miles (20,000 sq km) of the Sierra Nevada de Santa Marta are home to a phenomenally rich variety of wildlife, with much of its plant and animal species unique to the region. Its profusion of ecosystems makes it virtually a miniature version of the planet. Here you can find mangrove swamps and coral reefs, deserts and woods, rainforests and plains, glaciers and snowfields. The snow-capped peaks of the mountain range rise up to 5750 metres (17,000 feet) and lie only 30 miles (48 km) from the coast.

A deceptive idyll – Taganga Bay near Santa Marta may look inviting, but exploitation of this region has seen its indigenous peoples' way of life threatened and left its landscape polluted.

167

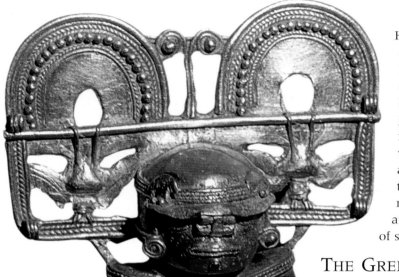

Human life in the region, while equally diverse, is also the source of its problems. Here there are not only indigenous communities, but also incoming farmers known as *colonos*, who clear the land of trees, guerrillas and government soldiers endlessly in conflict, drug barons who farm coca and who grew marijuana in the 1960s and 1970s, and tomb-robbers who shamelessly plunder the old sacred sites. The Sierra is indeed a microcosm of our world both in its beauty and variety, and in the ignorance and greed of some of its inhabitants.

THE GREEDY YOUNGER BROTHER

By the end of the 1980s, the Mamas had grown increasingly alarmed at the despoliation of the Sierra. Up on the heights they noticed that the glaciers were retreating. With every passing year less snow remained on the peaks, while throughout the Sierra more and more commercial logging and farming were taking place. The Mamas see their people as the 'Elder Brothers', who are charged with caring for the well-being of the heart of the world, and they regard the rest of humanity as the 'Younger Brother'. They were convinced that if the Younger Brother continued to act so rapaciously the Earth would suffer and die. And so they resolved to break with their tradition of secrecy to communicate their concerns to the outside world.

This Tairona metal statuette depicting a high priest was created sometime between AD 900 and the beginning of Spanish encroachment in the Santa Marta region in the 1520s.

Since the 1940s, the 'father of Colombian archaeology' Gerardo Reichel-Dolmatoff (1912–94) and his wife had been studying Kogi culture and were deeply impressed by their understanding of ecological principles and great reverence for the Earth. In 1986, another admirer of Kogi culture, the photographer Juan Mayr (b.1952), who was later to become Colombia's Minister for the Environment, helped to form the Fundacion Pro-Sierra Nevada de Santa Marta to tackle the environmental and social problems on the mountain. The following year, a group of Mamas founded an organization called the Gonawindúa Tayrona to communicate their message to the Younger Brother, and to start the long process of trying to reverse the degradation of their environment.

In 1988 the Kogi gave access to a film crew from the BBC. This visit resulted in director Alan Ereira's powerful and moving 1990 documentary 'From the Heart of the World – The Elder Brothers' Warning'. This and the accompanying book presented the Kogi's plight and their message to the western world, which was just waking up to the severity of the global environmental crisis. Ereira subsequently founded the Tairona Heritage Trust, and more publicity and charitable work followed – the French writer Eric Julien, who stayed with the Kogis in 1985, produced a documentary and book and formed an association to help purchase land. In 2004, *National Geographic* featured the Sierra and its people, posting an informative video and audio material on its website.

THE KOGI'S URGENT MESSAGE

Since the Mamas first decided to communicate their concerns, the increasing pace of global warming and species extinction has shown that their message cannot simply be dismissed as scaremongering, and over the last 20 years the story of the Sierra Nevada has unfolded in ways that are both tragic and hopeful.

The discovery that so-called 'primitive peoples' were in possession of an ancient and profound understanding of the workings of Nature has inspired greater respect for indigenous cultures worldwide, and as a result of the publicity given to the Elder Brothers' warning, substantial amounts of land have been purchased for them: 27,000 hectares (67,000 acres) are now in collective ownership, permitting reforestation and the elimination of illicit coca plantations without the use of herbicides. Now some of the rivers are cleaner as drug factories cease their pollution, while some of the old sacred sites are back under the control of the Mamas.

Despite this encouraging news, in 2005 Ereira went back to Colombia to find that 'the situation in the Sierra has changed fundamentally: Military bases have been established in indigenous territory ... There is no hidden world any more.' Two years later, he reported that the invasion of the Sierra was continuing unabated, that the glaciers had almost disappeared and that within a few years no snow would remain on the Sierra's peaks.

When faced with a situation that is tragic we have two stark choices – to despair or to seek out the rays of hope that exist and focus on them, without, however, denying the gravity of the situation. Despite all the clear indications of the effects of global warming and the growth of armed activity in the region, thousands of acres of land are being brought back to life. The Kogi, Arhuaco, Kaukaumu and Wiwa do not need or want us to visit them, but if we can help them restore the Heart of the World, we should.

> " *The Kogi make no predictions. They say only that if we do not change, they truly believe that the world will die. It will cease to be fertile.* "

ALAN EREIRA, *THE HEART OF THE WORLD*

TIMELINE

900 A hierarchical network of villages whose culture has come to be known as Tairona emerges in the Sierra

1498 Alonso de Ojeda is probably the first Spaniard to discover the area

1525 The Spanish town of Santa Marta is founded; some trading, and fighting, occurs between the Tairona and the Spanish

1600 At around this time the Tairona flee the Spanish and retreat to the Higher Sierra

1940s–1970s Gerardo Reichel-Dolmatoff and his wife Alicia conduct anthropological and archaeological fieldwork in the region and produce the definitive ethnographic work on the Kogi

1986 The region is classified a Human and Biosphere Reserve by UNESCO. Juan Mayr starts the Fundacion Pro-Sierra Nevada de Santa Marta

1988 Alan Ereira visits the area for his documentary 'From the Heart of the World: the Elder Brothers Warning'

1999 The Biopolitics International Organisation award the Bios Prize to the Kogi community

2000 French NGO 'Tchendukua' buys land by the sea for the Kogi and names it La Luna

2004 Dyncorp, a private military contractor of the US government, sprays the land in the 'War on Drugs', contaminating the soil and water for years to come; children are born deformed or develop cancers

2007 UNHCR reports that armed conflict in Colombia has resulted in 2 million displaced indigenous people

MACHU PICCHU

Over 2000 feet (600 metres) above the swirling Urubamba River that flows through the Peruvian Andes of South America lies one of the most famous sacred sites in the world – Machu Picchu, which means 'Old Peak'. Only rediscovered in 1911, it had been preserved from the ravages of the Spanish Conquest by its remote mountain-top location.

MACHU PICCHU WAS BUILT AROUND THE MID-15TH CENTURY, probably both as a royal estate for the Inca emperor and as a site of ritual significance. However, it flourished for only 80 years before the Inca empire collapsed under the onslaught of Spanish conquistadors commanded by Francisco Pizarro (c.1475–1541).

From the deep valleys below, the city remains completely hidden from view. This explains why the Spanish never found it, despite the fact that they easily overran the nearby Inca capital of Cuzco and the Sacred Valley in 1533.

THE ORIGINAL INDIANA JONES?

When the American academic and explorer Hiram Bingham (1875–1956) stumbled upon the site of Machu Picchu in 1911, he only spent a few hours there before pressing on in search of the supposedly 'lost' Inca cities of Vitcos and Vilcabamba. The true impact of what he had seen at the vertiginous site above the Urubamba gorge took some time to dawn on Bingham, and it was only later he realized that Machu Picchu might actually be the very place he was searching for. He returned one year later with a grant from the National Geographic Society and Yale University, investigated the site, and later wrote a bestseller about his discoveries.

In his book, *Lost City of the Incas* (1948), Hiram Bingham explained just what captivated him about Machu Picchu:
'In the variety of its charms, the power of its spell, I know of no place in the world which can compare with it. Not only has it great snow peaks looming above the clouds more than two miles overhead; gigantic precipices of many-coloured granite rising sheer for thousands of feet above the foaming, glistening, roaring rapids, it has also, in striking contrast, orchids and tree ferns, the delectable beauty of luxurious vegetation and the mysterious witchery of the jungle.'

MACHU PICCHU

Near Cuzco, Peru, South America

The imposing site of Machu Picchu. All buildings there were built with mortarless dry-stone masonry, so exactly cut that a knife cannot even be inserted into the joins.

“*Come up with me, American love.*
Kiss these secret stones with me.
The torrential silver of the Urubamba
makes the pollen fly to its golden cup.
The hollow of the bindweed's maze, the petrified
plant, the inflexible garland, soar above the silence
of these mountain coffers.”

PABLO NERUDA, 'THE HEIGHTS
OF MACHU PICCHU' (1943)

Today over half a million visitors a year follow in his footsteps. Up to 500 people a day make the arduous hike along the Inca Trail to arrive at the Gate of the Sun, ideally at dawn, before entering the city. The rest take a train from Cuzco that carries them ever higher up the Sacred Valley of the Incas until it reaches Aguas Calientes. From here they take a bus that zig-zags its way up the mountainside before arriving outside the city, 2430 metres (7970 ft) above sea level.

WHY WAS MACHU PICCHU BUILT?

Archaeologists have discerned three distinct zones within the 5 square miles (13 sq km) covered by Machu Picchu: the Popular District, which housed the general populace; the District of the Priests and the Nobility; and the Sacred District.

The Intihuatana stone at Machu Picchu. At the equinoxes, the Incas held ceremonies here in which they 'tied' the sun to the stone to arrest its northward motion across the sky.

Overlooking the site is 'Young Peak' – Huayna Picchu – with its Temple of the Moon and dazzling views of the city and the mountains beyond. The temple is in the form of a cave, with a mysterious seat carved out of rock.

The majority of bodies unearthed at the site were originally identified as female by Bingham's team, leading them to speculate that the site may have been a sacred city inhabited by priestesses or 'Virgins of the Sun'.

Later research has shown that there is in fact no gender imbalance in the remains found at the site, and recently two Yale scholars, Richard Burger and Lucy Salazar, have suggested that the city was not in fact a religious centre but a retreat for the emperor Pachacuti (1438–71) and the Inca aristocracy – a retreat in the highlands, away from the hustle and bustle of Cuzco, 44 miles (70 km) away to the south. But for the Incas there was no rigid separation between secular and spiritual, and the city was probably both a highland estate for the ruling class and a sacred centre at the same time.

Within Machu Picchu's Sacred District there are several notable ritual sites, all of which were probably dedicated to the Inca sun god Inti. In addition to the

" Since ancient times, this land has been preserved as sacred. The guardian spirits do not want roadways or industry, or people who pollute the land. These are sacred areas. It was there the deities built the ancient city of Machu Picchu. "

INDIGENOUS INHABITANT OF THE VALLEY BELOW MACHU PICCHU

Temple of the Sun, these include the Temple of the Three Windows – which Bingham linked to an Inca legend telling how their ancestors emerged from a cave with three windows – and the Intihuatana stone, popularly known as the 'Hitching Post of the Sun'. Likewise, the House of the Chosen Women here recalls similar structures found elsewhere in the Inca empire, built as sanctuaries for women who had dedicated their lives to the service of the Sun.

In common with many sacred sites around the world, it seems that the layout of Machu Picchu may well have been influenced by astronomy; for example, the Intihuatana stone is positioned to mark the equinoxes, while one window in the semicircular Temple of the Sun (or Torreón), which is thought to have functioned as a solar observatory, is placed so as to mark the winter solstice on an altar stone. Another of its windows points directly towards the summer solstice sunrise and at night frames the constellation of the Pleiades. Right up to modern times in the Andes, the Pleiades are an important astronomical symbol, used to calculate the onset of rains and the optimum time to plant crops.

Researchers of sacred sites believe that even the geology and topography of Machu Picchu may be spiritually charged. The city is built on, and of, granite and positioned above a fault line in the Earth's crust; such features are thought to engender a sense of well-being, high energy and what psychologists call 'peak experiences'.

Moreover, Machu Picchu forms just part of an entire sacred landscape in the High Andes, which takes in the idyllic Sacred Valley and the monumental fortress-temples of Ollantaytambo, Saqsayhuaman and Pisac, as well as the city of Cuzco. Cuzco means 'navel of the Earth' in the Quechua language of the Incas, and they conceived of their thriving capital city as an umbilical life-giver to the rest of the empire. In the dense jungle beyond Machu Picchu, explorers have found other sites and it is likely that there are still more ancient cities waiting to be discovered.

A SOURCE OF INSPIRATION

In 1943 the renowned Chilean poet Pablo Neruda (1904–73) visited Machu Picchu on horseback. While he was there he could feel the suffering of the labourers and craftspeople who had built this city for their masters, but he also sensed its numinous power. Neruda experienced the site as a royal palace and as spiritual sanctuary, and the poem that he wrote about it, 'The Heights of Machu Picchu', has been compared in its impact on South American culture to the influence that T. S. Eliot's 'The Waste Land' of 1921 had on English literature.

The lost city of the Incas may only have been inhabited for a relatively short time, but it will continue to inspire poets and spiritual seekers for as long as its great walls stand.

TIMELINE

early 13th century The Inca empire develops in the highlands of Peru

1438 The Inca empire expands to include a large portion of western South America

c.1450 Machu Picchu built

1526 First incursion of Spanish conquistadors into Inca territory

1532 The Spanish return and begin conquest with just 180 men, 27 horses and 1 cannon

1533 The Spanish take the Inca capital Cuzco. Machu Picchu is abandoned around the same time

1572 The last Inca stronghold is taken, and the last ruler executed

1904 An engineer, Franklin, spots the ruined city from afar and tells a missionary, Thomas Paine

1906 Paine and Stuart McNairn, another missionary, climb up to the ruins

1911 Explorer Hiram Bingham is shown the site by locals

1912 The National Geographic Society and Yale University give US$10,000 each for Bingham to return to Machu Picchu

1948 Hiram Bingham's *Lost City of the Incas* becomes a bestseller

1983 Machu Picchu designated a UNESCO World Heritage Site

2006 Limitations imposed on visits to Huayna Picchu; only 400 visitors are allowed each day and must begin hiking by 1 p.m.

2006–7 Yale returns 300 antiquities removed from the site by Bingham after pressure from Peru

SILLUSTANI

On a plateau 4000 m (13,500 ft) above sea level near Lake Titicaca in the Peruvian Andes, there is an ancient burial site called Sillustani. Overlooking the tranquil Laguna Umayo, lonely funeral towers that once housed the mummified families of nobility stand empty and half-destroyed by tomb-robbers. A rare example of a binary stone circle – two adjacent rings of stone similar to the Megalithic circles of Europe – bears witness to ceremonies once held here.

HIGH IN THE SOUTH AMERICAN ANDES stands Lake Titicaca, its western waters belonging to Peru, its eastern to Bolivia. Here there are islands sacred to the sun and the moon, and floating villages of reeds inhabited by families who fish the waters of one of the highest lakes in the world.

The Incas, who ruled the High Andes from AD 1438 to the Spanish Conquest, believed that their ancestors emerged from Lake Titicaca as 'Children of the Sun'. In 2000, during a series of 200 dives into the lake's icy depths, a team of archaeologists uncovered a submerged temple.

Yet some 20 miles (32 km) inland from Titicaca, not far from Puno, is a much smaller and far less well-known lake – Umayo. According to a legend of the Pukara, a pre-Incan civilization that began settling the Andes from around 1000 BC onwards, this body of water came into existence when a princess named Ururi cried so much after losing her

SILLUSTANI

Near Lake Titicaca, Peru

One of the destroyed chullpa funerary towers at Sillustani in the Peruvian Andes.

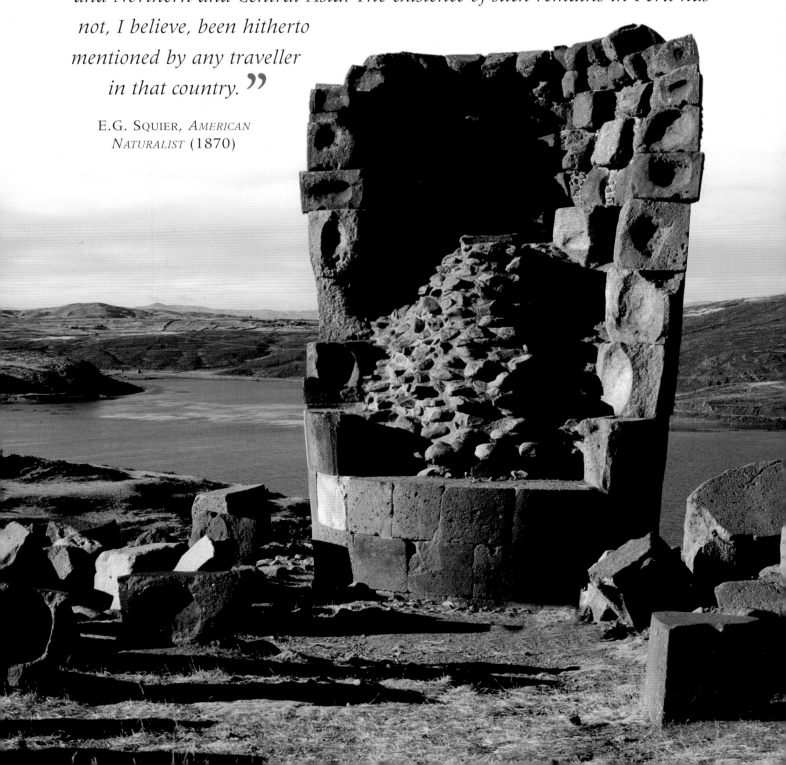

> *There is a class of stone structures in Peru belonging to what is regarded through the world as the earliest monumental period, coincident in style and character with the cromlechs, dolmens, and 'Sun' or 'Druidical' circles, so called, of Scandinavia, the British Islands, France, and Northern and Central Asia. The existence of such remains in Peru has not, I believe, been hitherto mentioned by any traveller in that country.*

E.G. SQUIER, *AMERICAN NATURALIST* (1870)

TIMELINE

1500 BC The Pukara culture establishes itself in the region

AD 1200 The Colla and Lupaca cultures establish themselves here

1445 The Incas conquer the area

1533 Spanish conquistadors, led by Francisco Pizarro, overrun the Inca Empire

1870 E.G. Squier visits the site and reveals it to the world in the *American Naturalist*

2000 Ancient temple found submerged in Lake Titicaca

love that her tears formed a salty lake. Rising from Umayo a solitary island, bare and uninhabited, stands as a silent guardian of the lake's tranquillity.

On a windswept red sandstone plateau overlooking the water is the ancient sanctuary of Sillustani—a necropolis and ritual site dating back thousands of years. Sillustani has been spared an excessive number of visitors by its isolated location, well off the beaten tourist track. Who would want to wander in a vast cemetery in a barren landscape, when a trip to a floating island or a day spent in the colourful market at Puno is on offer instead? Recently another site has also lured tourists away – the 'Temple of Fertility' at Chucuito – whose 24 giant stone phalli are the subject of controversy.

A PLACE OF DEATH AND REBIRTH

The Pukara civilization was supplanted by cultures such as the Tiwanaku (*c.*200 BC–AD 800), which honeycombed the plateau with tunnels and subterranean tombs. But it was the later Aymara kingdom of Collas that was responsible for building the plateau's most striking features – the funerary towers known as *chullpas*. Each tower probably acted as a family tomb for members of the nobility. Their mummified corpses were placed in the foetal position within

Faking the past – the 'Inca' Temple of Fertility at Chucuito was almost certainly built around 1993, by local people wanting to cash in on the burgeoning tourist trade in the High Andes.

> " *Having made pilgrimages to the sacred places of the Earth Mother, one begins to notice a lingering enchantment, as if a music heard before arises of itself in the silence of the mind, and paints the common scene with a richness of meaning hitherto unperceived.* "
>
> FREDERIC LEHRMAN, *THE SACRED LANDSCAPE* (1988)

interiors designed to represent the uterus. Some commentators have suggested that the towers themselves represent the phallus. Clothing and everyday items were also included as grave-goods.

Reaching a height of up to 12 metres (40 ft), each *chullpa* has a small doorway, facing east and just large enough to crawl through. Often the carving of a lizard can be found on one of the outer stones. Since some lizards can regenerate their tails (a capacity known as autotomy), it is thought that they were carved as a symbol of rebirth. Most *chullpas* are round, but some are square. On one, two pumas – one male, one female – have been carved on either side of the doorway. Sadly, all of the *chullpas* have been desecrated, with grave-robbers sometimes using dynamite in their attempts to uncover any treasures concealed with the bodies or within the walls of the towers.

This stone with a spiral carving at the entrance to the necropolis at Sillustani deflects compass needles, probably as a result of the high iron content of the rock.

Two great stone circles, yet to be dated, stand in this magnificent setting. The 19th-century American archaeologist E.G. Squier (1821–88) – renowned for investigating sites of the ancient 'Moundbuilder' cultures in the Mississippi Valley – was the first to note their startling similarity to European megalithic circles. The two circles standing side by side are reminiscent of the circles of the sun and moon at Avebury in Wiltshire, England (see pages 112–115).

THE POWER OF THE LIZARD

Standing on the plateau of Sillustani, we are evidently at a place of mystery. A lone rock stands carved with a spiral and is said to exhibit a magnetic anomaly that can be detected with a compass. Once a year, a local shaman apparently sacrifices a pregnant llama, removing its foetus to present it as an offering for the fertility of the land. Here the controversial British writer David Icke (b.1952) claimed to have experienced a powerful awakening that resulted in his promotion of one of the most bizarre conspiracy theories of all time: that the world is run by a powerful élite of reptilians disguised as humans.

As New Age visitors meditate amongst the ruins, and tourists listen to commentaries on the archaeology of the site, the spirit of the Collas' lizard is alive and well here, inspiring or deluding whoever is brave or foolish enough to wander in a sacred burial ground of an ancient people.

Rapa Nui

Isolated in the vast expanses of the Pacific Ocean, the small island of Rapa Nui (Easter Island) is now a World Heritage Site. Its mysterious moai *statues, Birdman carvings, caves and stone buildings stand as monuments to a civilization that at its height, in the 14th century, may have numbered as many as 20,000 people.*

T HE WORLD'S MOST ISOLATED INHABITED ISLAND, RAPA NUI, lies roughly midway between Chile and Tahiti in the South Pacific Ocean. Its nearest neighbour is Pitcairn Island, some 1290 miles (2075 km) to the west, most of whose 48 inhabitants are descended from the mutineers who seized HMS *Bounty* in 1789.

To its original inhabitants, the island was known as Te pito o te henua ('The Navel of The World') or Te pito o te kainga a Hau Maka ('The Little piece of land of Hau Maka'). It was named Easter Island in 1722 by the Dutch explorer Jacob Roggeveen (1659–1729) because he found it on Easter Sunday, but it is now increasingly referred to by the Polynesian name the islanders prefer – Rapa Nui.

BASALT, OBSIDIAN AND VOLCANIC TUFF

The story of Rapa Nui is one of great tragedy shot through with mystery. The 64 square mile (165 sq km) island was probably first discovered by Polynesians arriving by canoe sometime between the fourth and tenth century AD. Here they found an island lush in vegetation and covered in subtropical forest that included palms, ferns, shrubs and herbs, and set about growing sweet potatoes, harpooning dolphins and raising poultry.

The basalt, obsidian and softer volcanic tuff that made up the island's geology proved excellent materials for building and carving. Over the next 500 years a phenomenal amount of stonework was carried out – 1000 ritual sites were carved with over 4000 petroglyphs, 1233 stone chicken houses were built, 313 temple platforms (*ahus*) were created and – most famously of all – 887 giant figures were carved out of the tuff.

Ever since its discovery, Rapa Nui has become synonymous with these mysterious figures, which are known as *moai*. The largest is 20 metres (65 ft) high, though most average 4 metres (13 ft). Their

A moai *on Rapa Nui. The volcanic crater at Rano Raraku, where these huge figures were quarried and carved, is one of the most sacred sites for the island's current inhabitants.*

eye sockets were originally filled with white coral or red scoria rock, and they had topknots of red scoria. At the time the statues were created, in the volcanic crater of Rano Raraku, some trees were still standing on the island, and logs with ropes fashioned from *hau hau* bark or tree daisies were probably used to move and erect them.

ECOLOGICAL AND SOCIAL DISASTER

The civilization on Rapa Nui was at its height during the 14th century, when the island is thought to have supported a population of between 7000 and 20,000. But presently all the forest was exhausted and ecological disaster struck – the springs dried up, the topsoil eroded and, with no wood to build boats, fishing gradually became impossible.

Almost overnight the creation of the *moai* ceased, and the process of hauling them abruptly halted. Many of the figures visible today on Rapa Nui – especially the 394 in the quarry at Rano Raraku – are

EASTER ISLAND

Off Chile, South Pacific Ocean

TIMELINE

400–900 Disputed dates for first Polynesian migrants reaching Rapa Nui

800 Pollen records show the destruction of the forests is well underway

1000–1500 The *ahu* and *moai* are created; deforestation is complete by the end of this phase

1300 The Birdman cult probably begins at this time

1722 Dutch explorer Jacob Roggeveen lands on the island on Easter Sunday

1770 Rival clans start to topple each other's statues

1862 Slave raiders abduct or kill half the island's population

1864 By now the last statue is toppled and desecrated

1868 The British get 200 men to haul two *moai* on to HMS *Topaz* for transport to Britain

1870–77 Island controlled by French despot Dutrou-Bornier

1888 Chile annexes the island

1893 The last king is poisoned and most of the island is used as a sheep ranch

1914 Katherine and William Routledge spend over a year on the island recording, surveying and excavating

1950 Thor Heyerdahl's best-selling *Kon-Tiki* is published

1953 Chilean navy takes over the administration of the island

1966 Chilean troops withdraw

1980s Sheep removed to conserve archaeology

incomplete, while others lie abandoned. We may never know why this occurred, but the most likely explanation seems to be that fighting broke out between clans as competition grew for scarce resources. This feuding resulted in clans toppling each others' *moai* and engaging in slavery and cannibalism. As food sources dwindled, the population plummeted dramatically. Those who survived moved to fortified settlements and caves near the coast.

The Birdman cult, which may have begun as early as the 1300s and was practised until the 1860s, is thought to have assumed greater importance during this time of upheaval, as warlike skills became more greatly prized. This cult involved the worship of a fierce deity, half-man, half-bird, and each year rival warriors would swim to a nearby islet to find the first sooty tern egg of the season and claim the title of 'Birdman'.

FROM EUROPEAN 'DISCOVERY' TO THE PRESENT DAY

By the time the Europeans arrived Rapa Nui was in serious decline. The Dutch, the first to land here, in 1722, found that 'its wasted appearance could give no other impression than of a singular poverty and barrenness'. A French expedition of 1786 left goats, pigs and sheep to help the islanders, and in 1805 an American ship arrived and took 22 slaves. In 1862 Peruvian slavers abducted, captured or killed 1500 people – half the island's population – leaving tuberculosis to cut a swathe

through those remaining. Among the enslaved were the king and the priesthood, but after protests by the French and by ordinary Peruvians, the 100 slaves who had survived were sent home. On the voyage back to Rapa Nui, smallpox decimated this group, and the 15 who were spared duly infected many of the islanders who had not already succumbed to tuberculosis. Soon Rapa Nui's population stood at just 110.

Today the island is beginning to thrive once more, with a population of around 4000 and a burgeoning tourist industry.

A Birdman cult petroglyph. The winner of the annual 'Birdman' title (tangata-manu) gained his clan the sole right to collect eggs from the islet of Moto Nui.

Although Chile 'owns' Rapa Nui, the indigenous people are pressing for autonomy. They have rediscovered and embraced their spiritual and cultural heritage, gaining strength from the presence of their ancestors all around them, and from the power that radiates from the silent *moai* who stand guard on their island home. To date, 50 of the statues have been re-erected.

THOR HEYERDAHL'S KON-TIKI THEORY

The controversial Norwegian ethnographer Thor Heyerdahl (1914–2002) believed that the island's Birdman cult and the building style of some island walls supported his 'Kon-Tiki' theory, which proposed that a mysterious race of White people had lived in Peru during the Neolithic era. Kon-Tiki was their high priest and sun king. According to Heyerdahl, this race built massive stone monuments and taught the Incas, but was almost totally wiped out in a battle on an island on Lake Titicaca. Kon-Tiki and his close companions managed to escape and took to the sea, eventually colonizing much of Polynesia, including Rapa Nui.

Heyerdahl's theory is now dismissed by archaeologists and anthropologists, who point to the overwhelming evidence in support of the Southeast Asian origins of Polynesia's first populations.

This hand-coloured illustration, from Islanders and Monuments of Easter Island *(1788) by Gaspard Duche de Vancy shows islanders and French explorers examining* moai, *two of which have scoria topknots.*

“ *In this place I can sense the spirits of my ancestors and take strength from the ancient Moai statues.* **”**

CONTEMPORARY INHABITANT OF RAPA NUI

HALEAKALA AND KAHO'OLAWE

The remote archipelago of Hawaii in the North Pacific lies 2300 miles (3700 km) from the nearest landmass, North America. There are many sacred sites here, but two in particular have been much in the public eye in recent years: the volcanic peak of Haleakala on the island of Maui, and the island of Kaho'olawe, which lies just off Maui's southwestern shore.

MOST SCHOLARS NOW THINK THAT THE POLYNESIANS – those seafarers who became the first inhabitants of Hawaii – probably originated in Southeast Asia or Taiwan over 10,000 years ago. Merging with Austronesian tribes of Papua New Guinea to form a people we now term Polynesian, they colonized first the islands of Fiji, Samoa and Tonga before moving on to Hawaii in around AD 400 and finally New Zealand between AD 800 and 1300.

While the details vary from place to place, the main features of Polynesian culture and religion are constant across the vast distances that separate the islands of the region.

Almost three-quarters of the Hawaiian island of Maui is made up of the massive volcano called Haleakala. At the summit of this mountain is a huge crater, measuring 7 miles (11 km) long by 2 miles (3 km) wide and up to 800 metres (2600 ft) deep. In Polynesian mythology, Haleakala was once home to Pele the fire goddess and the demigod Maui, and the peak is one of the most sacred on the islands.

The crater on the summit of Haleakala. The peak offers wonderfully clear views of the night sky, though light pollution from the growing population of Maui is an increasing problem.

HALEAKALA AND
KAHO'OLAWE

Hawaiian Islands, Pacific Ocean

Only found on the slopes of the 'House of the Sun', the Haleakala silversword plant almost became extinct in the early 20th century as a result of overgrazing by cattle and goats. It is now a protected species.

To the southwest of Maui, the island of Kaho'olawe shares a dubious distinction with another sacred area on the other side of the world. In common with much of Salisbury Plain (near the mesolithic site of Stonehenge), the island has been used for decades as a weapons range. But unlike its English counterpart, Kaho'olawe is now in the process of being reclaimed for nature.

MAUI'S 'HOUSE OF THE SUN'

Haleakala rises to more than 3050 metres (10,000 ft) above sea level and covers an area larger than Manhattan Island in New York. It last erupted in around 1790, and has hurled its lava into the air at least ten times since AD 1000. Over a million visitors drive to the peak each year – many to catch the sunrise from the summit. Most come as tourists, but for many Hawaiians and spiritual seekers the journey is a pilgrimage to the 'House of the Sun'. The volcano's name derives from the fact that this was where the Polynesian trickster figure and demigod Maui ensnared the sun. According to one version of the myth, Maui's grandmother lived in the crater and baked bananas in an oven near a wiliwili tree where the sun was in the habit of stopping for a meal. One day, Maui lay in wait there before suddenly leaping out and lassoing the sun. His aim was to slow it down so that the days would become longer, allowing people more light to germinate their crops and dry their *kapa* – cloth made from the bark of the paper mulberry tree.

According to some, Maui's other volcano, to the west, is the 'House of the Moon', and is regarded as being a female presence and the navel of the Earth, as a counterpoint to the male presence of Haleakala. One of Haleakala's cliffs traditionally provided the best rock on the island from which to make adzes – tools used for smoothing rough-hewn wood. Legend relates that the cliff was created when Maui struck the mountainside with his penis. This location was also the site of secret graves of local chieftains.

The volcano of Haleakala was also home to the fire goddess Pele. Chased from her original volcanic home on Kauali, or the star-land of Kahiki, by her sister Namakaokaha'i, goddess of the sea, Pele went first to Oahu and then here to Haleakala where she lived for a time before moving to Kilauea Volcano on the Big Island. Intriguingly, the mythology mirrors geological fact: Pele journeys across the archipelago in the same sequence that the volcanoes were formed.

The upper reaches of Haleakala are traditionally considered the abode of spirits. Here, in the strange landscape of red volcanic rock with vegetation including silversword, lobelia and sandalwood, archaeologists have found numerous stone platforms, which are the remains of temples known as *heiau*. They have also uncovered the remains of cairns, markers, shrines and wind breaks for people travelling over the mountain. Several of the sites were clearly connected with the traditional practice of umbilical cord offerings, while others were ritual and family burial sites.

Haleakala is still used today by *Kahuna* (priests) for initiations, ceremonies and prayers. Some modern *Kahuna* maintain that the mountain's power derives not only from its mythological and religious significance, but also because its density and high iron content makes it 'a vortex of gravity and electromagnetism'.

In a strange twist of fate, the place where Maui once caught the sun has been chosen by astronomers as the best location for the world's most powerful solar observatory. The National Park, the authors of an environmental impact assessment and many islanders, including the *Kahuna*, are opposed to the project, which they feel will desecrate the site. Time will tell whether the House of the Sun will be preserved as it is, or whether it will have to play host to a new 'house' that gazes up at the sun to measure its flares and storms.

KAHO'OLAWE – THE ISLAND OF SAILORS

While Haleakala still faces an imminent threat to its hallowed ground, the situation regarding the island of Kaho'olawe is far more optimistic.

> **"** *Majestic Haleakala*
> *Beautiful mountain of Maui*
> *Prized by you, Hawai'i*
> *Glorious Maui, is the very best.* **"**
>
> JOHN KAPOHAKIMOHEWA

The remoteness and elevation of the islands that form the Hawaiian archipelago make them ideal observatory sites. This is the telescope on the dormant Mauna Kea volcano on Big Island.

TIMELINE

Covering an area of just 45 square miles (116 sq km), Kaho'olawe is considered sacred by many Hawaiians and contains no fewer than 544 archaeological and historical sites. In former times the island was dedicated to Kanaloa, the god of the ocean and navigation. The western tip of the island and the outlying channel was named Kealaikahiki, meaning 'Pathway to Foreign (or Mythical) Lands', and was used by early sailors as a training ground for learning navigation by the stars. In their pioneering voyages across the huge expanses of the Pacific Ocean, ancient Polynesian navigators relied upon a thorough understanding of the movement of the stars and sun and a detailed knowledge of sea conditions to reach their destination.

However, by the mid-20th century Kaho'olawe had become a very different kind of naval training ground. From December 1941 onwards, when the Japanese precipitated America's entry into the Second World War by launching a surprise attack on the US fleet at Pearl Harbor on nearby Oahu Island, Kaho'olawe was used for target practice by the US Navy, with countless bombs falling on it, while shells and torpedoes hammered its coastline. In 1976 members of the grassroots local group Protect Kaho'olawe 'Ohana filed a suit against the navy and gained a series of victories over the ensuing years, which finally resulted in all use of the island as a weapons range being stopped in 1990.

Even before the US Navy began pounding Kaho'olawe, the degradation of the island's ecology had begun in the early 19th century, when it was used as a penal colony. After this institution closed in 1853, cattle, sheep and goats were grazed on the island.

BACK TO NATURE

In 1993, the Hawaiian State Legislature designated Kaho'olawe a reserve for the 'preservation and practice of all rights customarily and traditionally exercised by the native Hawaiians for cultural, spiritual, and subsistence purposes'. Some US$400 million of public funds were set aside for the navy to clear the land; the contractor commissioned to carry out the work reported in 2001 that

> 'Over 1.5 million pounds of ordinance has been recovered, in what navy officals call the largest project of its kind undertaken by the US military. Over 4600 items … have been found thus far. They range in size from 40-mm grenades and small cluster-bomb submunitions to bombs as large as 2000 lbs.'

Reforestation projects are already well under way and Protect Kaho'olawe 'Ohana (two of whose leaders were once lost at sea while on their way to protest on the island), have built altars to the god Lono at certain points around the island

where they make offerings. Every November, a five-day ritual begins with a purification ceremony called *hiuwai*. Alone in the ocean at night, initiates are called out of the sea by the sound of a conch shell and a cry to Lono. Offerings are made and the ritual ends with the ascent of a sacred mountain. Visits to the island always begin with a traditional prayer-request followed by a welcome sung in return: 'You are almost here, almost here, you brave ones so buoyant on the sea of Kanaloa.'

The coast of Maui: legend tells how the demigod Maui raised the Hawaiian islands from the sea.

" *The land is not just full of sacred paths, where every rock and flower is significant, the land itself is sacred … Everything is sacred and so everything needs to be acknowledged. That is why every kind of wind, every group of rocks, every clump of trees has its name in Hawaii. Each place also has its own chant, and particular associations with myths and gods. Every time a place name is spoken, the meaning of that name is activated, revitalizing the connection between the speaker and the land.* "

RIMA MORRELL, *THE SACRED POWER OF HUNA: SPIRITUALITY AND SHAMANISM IN HAWAII* (2005)

TONGARIRO AND TAUPO

Lake Taupo lies in the centre of the North Island of New Zealand like a tranquil sea, while in the mountains nearby, fire and water combine to form a dramatic, primal landscape that is sacred to the Maori. Like slumbering dragons, Mount Tongariro and other active volcanoes exhale steam from their slopes, while lakes of emerald water are held up by the rocky plateau like chalices offered to the sun and moon.

THE MAORI NAME FOR NEW ZEALAND IS AOTEAROA – 'Land of the Long White Cloud'. The first humans who set foot here, between AD 800 and 1300, came from Eastern Polynesia, probably the Society Islands. Some scholars believe that the island of Rai'atea in this group might be the legendary Hawaiki, which many Polynesian cultures, including the Maori, regard as their land of origin.

While retaining many of the fundamental elements of Polynesian civilization, Maori society began to evolve its own unique expresssions in the new and different environment of Aotearoa. For the Maori, all of the land is sacred. Even so, particular regions and landscape features became the focus for legends and hence the development of sacred sites. So it was in the centre of North Island, where three volcanoes – Ruapehu, Ngauruhoe and Tongariro – and the great lake of Taupo became a sacred landscape for the Maori. In addition, two new sacred sites – the Tauhara Centre and Zuvuyaland – have recently grown up beside the lake.

'SEIZED BY THE SOUTH WIND' – TONGARIRO

One of the first canoes to arrive from Hawaiki was called Te Arawa, and the tribe descended from the pioneer settlers that it brought peopled the area around Tongariro. According to legend, when Ngatoroirangi, the high priest and navigator of that canoe, climbed to the mountain top, a strong south wind began to blow, nearly freezing him to death. Flinging his arms to the sky, he called out for help from his sisters in Hawaiki, far across the ocean. Heeding his call, they came in the form of fire within the Earth, from White Island and Rotorua out to the east, leaving a trail of geysers and volcanoes in their path.

TONGARIRO AND TAUPO

North Island, New Zealand

The peak of Mount Ngauruhoe, a secondary cone of Mount Tongariro on North Island. This volcano last erupted in 1975.

"kimihia te kahurangi;
ki te piko tou matenga,
ki te maunga teitei

If you bow your head
Let it be only to a
*great mountain.***"**

MAORI PROVERB

TIMELINE

*c.*2 m.y.a. Volcanic activity begins in the region

*c.*260,000 y.a. The first estimated eruption of Tongariro

c. AD 800–1300 The first settlers arrive in New Zealand from eastern Polynesia

1800s European settlers start to arrive

1887 Peaks are gifted to the crown by Maori Chief Te Heuheu Tukino IV

1894 The region becomes a national park

1922 The park is extended

1975 Last eruption of Tongariro; park boundaries extended again as more land is purchased

1978 Tauhara Centre founded at Lake Taupo

1990 UNESCO nominates the park as a World Heritage site

1991 Zuvayaland created at Lake Taupo

1993 UNESCO renominates the park for its value as an 'associative cultural landscape' – a category that recognizes sites that possess 'powerful religious, artistic or cultural associations of the natural element rather than material cultural evidence'

1995, 1996 Ruapehu erupts

2006 The great-great grandson of the chief who donated the land to the Crown asks for greater Maori control of how the park is managed

2007 Ruapehu erupts

To this day, the volcanoes of the region remain among the most active in the world – Ruapehu last erupted in 2007 – and although thousands of visitors make the Tongariro Alpine Crossing every year on one of the world's most spectacular day walks, there is always the danger that the gods will flex their muscles once again.

In 1887, the area around Tongariro was given to the British Crown (which had dominion over New Zealand at that time) by Chief Te Heuheu Tukino IV (1821–88), to protect the land from being carved up by European settlers. Although his descendants now question the terms of his gift, his gesture saw the creation of only the fourth national park in the world – and the first to be gifted by an indigenous community.

In a country where the ocean seems otherwise ever-present, Tongariro suddenly strikes the visitor as being surprisingly remote and landlocked. Driving between the two main cities on North Island, Wellington and Auckland, you begin to climb steadily until you find yourself in a mountainous wilderness of volcanic rock and snow-capped peaks. Most of the 1 million or so people who make the journey here annually come to ski or trek on the mountain slopes. However, for the Maori and all those who are alive to the area's deeper significance, Tongariro is first and foremost a place of spiritual pilgrimage.

Today, the Tongariro National Park is managed by the New Zealand Department of Conservation in consultation with local Maori tribes to ensure that leisure use does not

" *The name Tongariro formerly included in Maori usage all three peaks – Tongariro Range, Ngauruhoe and Ruapehu – all three were considered as one, the sacred* kopu, *the belly of this island-fish, the abode of the fire-gods, ever afterwards to be regarded as the holy of holies of the Arawa nation.* "

JAMES COWAN, *FAIRY FOLK TALES OF THE MAORI* (1925)

compromise this area of outstanding natural beauty or violate its status as a sacred site. The region was designated a UNESCO World Heritage Site in 1990.

TAUPO – LAKE OF FIRE AND WATER

About 16 miles (25 km) north of the park the crystal-clear water of Lake Taupo also attracts many visitors to its scenic beauty. Here – as at Tongariro – the calming presence of water is indissolubly linked with the volatile power of fire.

The lake was formed about 26,500 years ago when a massive volcanic eruption created a caldera (a huge depression in the land) that filled with water. Since then the volcano has erupted a further 27 times – most recently in AD 186, when a grade 7 explosion ejected 24 cubic miles (100 cu km) of material into the atmosphere. A grade 7 explosion is described by vulcanologists as 'super-colossal', to distinguish it from the most powerful ever recorded – the 'mega

View over Lake Taupo, looking south towards Tongariro National Park.

The Emerald Lakes below the summit of Mount Tongariro. Their waters are coloured by minerals leaching from the volcanic crater on the peak.

colossal' grade 8 (which occurred only once, on Indonesia, some 75,000 years ago). The effects of Taupo's eruption were even remarked upon by contemporary commentators as far away as Rome and China, who noted the appearance of ominous red skies around that time.

Today Taupo is considered dormant rather than extinct, and from the hills to its west plumes of white smoke often drift into the sky, above bubbling mud pools and hot springs, while to the northeast you can visit thermal caves and bathe in streams where hot and cold water mingle.

TAUHARA AND THE HERMETIC ORDER OF THE GOLDEN DAWN

On the northern shores of Taupo one of the most successful spiritual centres in the country, Tauhara, offers a fascinating example of the way an older European influence has acted as a catalyst for a new manifestation of spirituality in the unique environment of New Zealand.

The Hermetic Order of the Golden Dawn, which briefly flourished in Britain between 1888 and 1900, continued to function as a magical order in its farthest outpost of New Zealand's South Island until 1978. But already, by 1939, one of its leading lights, Harriet Felkin, had drawn up plans for a retreat centre that would promote organic agriculture, and had bought land near Taupo. Once the Order was closed, the Tauhara Centre rapidly evolved into a spiritual and educational centre that has attracted people from all over the world to attend conferences and retreats, and to meditate in its gardens overlooking the lake, with Tongariro on the horizon.

ZUVUYALAND – CREATING A NEW SACRED SITE

Across the road from the Tauhara Centre an even more recent sacred site has come into being. In 1991 Vivien Johnson felt inspired to create a magical garden that would be open to all, and which would be energetically linked to spiritual centres in England – particularly the Chalice Well Gardens, Glastonbury (see pages 122–125) and Silbury Hill (see pages 112–115). In a wonderful example of how we can create 'paradise on Earth' the Zuvuyaland project has transformed a small patch of a few acres of bare rock and pasture into a magical landscape filled with native trees and bushes.

A spiral labyrinth of large stones has been created on flat ground, and Vivien Johnson believes the rocks on the high point of the land connect us to the male principle, while the female energy of the land is held in the 'Chalice', a miniature wooded valley with a 'flow-form' sculpture that channels a small stream over bowls of water that represent the seven planets, each of which is individually shaped to allow the water to swirl in a slightly different pattern as it tumbles downward past the punga ferns, maples, camellias and rhododendrons.

Here at Zuvuyaland, as at Lake Taupo and Tongariro nearby, the powers of female and male, goddess and god, yin and yang, are brought into balance and harmony. Fire and water, the great symbols of these two principles, found in spiritual and magical traditions the world over, meet here in the heart of the North Island, in a spiritual marriage that long ago on the other side of the world was once called 'The Alchemical Wedding'.

There are those who maintain that the Earth has 'chakras' – centres of spiritual energy that are also found in the human body. If they are right, then surely a great heart chakra must exist around Lake Taupo and North Island's mighty volcanoes.

A Maori-inspired sculpted head on the shores of Lake Taupo. The tranquillity of the lake and its status as a Maori sacred place have attracted other spiritual seekers to the area.

"*Let it be to us a sacred mountain, a place of the spirit!" cried Tuwharétoa. 'In days to come it will be a tribal glory, it will add mana to our tribal name. Greetings, humble greetings to Tongariro!'*
'Greetings, humble greetings to Tongariro, to Sacred Tongariro!' chanted the warriors, as they held up their dripping paddles for a moment in willing tribute."

FRANK O.V. ACHESON, *PLUME OF THE ARAWAS* (1930)

ULURU AND KATA TJUTA

Uluru and Kata Tjuta are great sandstone rock formations in the central Australian desert, over 400 miles (650 km) from the sea south of the Nullabor Plain and 208 miles (335 km) southwest of the nearest large town of Alice Springs. Both sites are sacred to the Aboriginal people, who now own the land and manage it jointly with the National Parks and Wildlife Agency.

LIKE A GREAT ISLAND RISING OUT OF THE SEA OF THE CENTRAL AUSTRALIAN DESERT, Uluru – or Ayers Rock as it was once known – is one of the most sacred sites for the Aboriginal people of Australia. It rises 340 metres (1115 ft) out of the desert plain and is formed of sandstone that has been here for around 500 million years. Situated around the base of Uluru and among the 50 peaks of the nearby outcrop of Kata Tjuta are initiation and ceremonial sites connected by songlines that weave topography and mythology together through the medium of song, dance, ceremony and story.

According to the widely accepted 'Out of Africa' theory of human origins, the Aboriginal people came to Australia between 65 and 70 thousand years ago, migrating along the coastline of East Africa and India before voyaging across the sea from Timor – which was then only 100 miles (160 km) from Australia – to populate first the northwestern territories, then later the central and southern regions of this great continent.

The Aboriginal people who live in the central desert area refer to themselves as the Anangu ('people'). After decades of discrimination and dispossession by the White settlers who began arriving in Australia in the late 18th century, the Aborigines have in the last 20 years begun to regain land rights over their ancestral territories throughout the country. In line with this, both Uluru and Kata Tjuta are now in the hands of the Anangu once more. However, this arrangement is conditional upon the land being leased back to the state for 99 years.

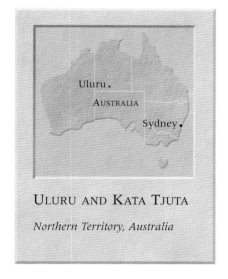

ULURU AND KATA TJUTA

Northern Territory, Australia

MEANING OF THE DREAMTIME

At the heart of Aboriginal culture lies the concept that has been translated as 'Dreamtime'. Although this term is now widely used, a spokesperson for the Anangu says in the official guide to the park that they prefer not to translate their word for this – Tjukurpa – since 'Dreamtime' evokes a sense of something imaginary or fleeting, when in reality Tjukurpa is a deep and complex term with a number of meanings, including traditional law and religious heritage, but also mythology and a particular way of understanding and relating to Time itself.

Translators need many words to 'unpack' the meaning of this central idea in Aboriginal culture. In *Wisdom from the Earth – The Living Legacy of the Aboriginal Dreamtime*, Anna Voigt and Nevill Drury suggest it means 'the quintessence of existence itself, which encompasses the land and the people'.

Quintessence suggests potential and potency, and in coming to Uluru you are faced not with a great lump of inert rock but with a vibrant, potent world animated with plants and creatures, and an extraordinary sense of presence and timelessness. If the Dreamtime represents the realms of past, present and future as coexistent in one reality, then Uluru seems a place where you can experience this perhaps more strongly than anywhere else on the planet.

Glowing red in the light of the evening sun, the sacred rock known as Uluru rises starkly out of the surrounding desert scrubland.

TIMELINE

550–530 m.y.a. The rocks of Uluru and Kata Tjuta are formed

400–300 m.y.a. The horizontal layers of sandstone are shifted to an almost vertical position

65–70,000 y.a. Likely time that the first inhabitants of Australia arrived via Timor

10,000 y.a. First archaeological finds in the region date to this era

AD 1872 The rock is first mapped when explorer Ernest Giles is the first non-indigenous person to sight the rock formation from a distance

1873 The surveyor William Gosse visits the rock and names it Ayers Rock after the Chief Secretary of South Australia, Sir Henry Ayers

1920 Part of the region is declared an Aboriginal reserve

1936 The first tourists arrive

1958 The Ayers Rock–Mount Olga National Park is established

1985 The Australian government returns ownership to the Anangu people, on condition that it is leased to the National Parks and Wildlife Agency for 99 years and is jointly managed with them

2002 The rock is officially renamed Uluru/Ayers Rock

A MAGICAL OTHERWORLD

Although around 400,000 people visit the park each year, it is still possible to find yourself alone here. Despite the advice of the custodians of this sacred rock not to climb it, thousands insist on doing so – either out of defiance or more likely out of thoughtlessness. To climb Uluru is foolish – not just because it is disrespectful and dangerous (35 people have died in the attempt) but also because in doing so you risk spoiling your relationship with something that is sacred. Rather than clambering on top of it, and running the risk of slipping to your death while following a trail of tourists, Uluru encourages a deeper experience by inviting you to walk round it – as if in a ritual circumambulation. The long journey taken to get here is then rewarded by the discovery that Uluru is not simply a rock but is actually an entire world.

As you walk the 5.8-mile (9.4-km) track around Uluru, you gaze up into valleys that you have chosen not to trespass into, and the land takes on a numinous power – that is, you are gazing into and walking through a magical 'Otherworld'. You pass male and female initiation sites, clearly distinguishable by their remarkable resemblance to phalluses and vulvas, and if you are able to treat this journey as a walking meditation, then perhaps you can touch the 'Dreamtime' of Tjukurpa and come to know – however fleetingly – the Aboriginal experience of 'walkabout'. This does not at all denote a kind of aimless wandering, but instead a spiritual odyssey through a landscape. Pilgrims renew their relationship with the ancestral past, while remaining totally focused on the present moment.

THE WALKABOUT AND THE SONGLINES

An anthropologist once said 'no one has ever met a lost Aborigine'. Despite the lack of apparent distinguishing features in the desert landscape, Aboriginal people grow up with a powerful awareness of the land and with a tradition of songlines or 'Dreaming tracks' that help them navigate across country, and which provide a strong sense of identity with the land. The songlines are physical paths that have legends and stories attached to them, which are often sung or danced at particular points along the way. They were created at the dawn of time and have been walked for tens of thousands of years. Like an invisible matrix, they criss-cross the land and can stretch for hundreds of miles, passing through the territories of different tribes, each of which possesses part of the knowledge of that particular track.

It is said that 'walkabout' mirrors the eternal movements of the sun, moon and stars, and that the original dreaming tracks were laid down by the ancestor spirits as they moved from sacred site to sacred site. Although the tracks have utilitarian purposes – linking water-holes and aiding navigation – they are used primarily for pilgrimage to sacred places to conduct ceremonies.

Many songlines converge on Uluru, which is considered a place of great power, where in Tjukurpa it was the scene of epic battles that marked the end of the Dreamtime creation period.

THE PLACE OF MANY HEADS

Situated 31 miles (50 kilometres) west of Uluru, the rock formation of Kata Tjuta is also considered very powerful and sacred and is made up of 50 domes of rock that soar up 600 metres (1968 ft) from the desert floor. Within this landscape are sacred sites and places of initiation. Kata Tjuta means 'The Place of Many Heads', and is the focus of numerous legends. The Rainbow Serpent Wanambi is said to live in a waterhole on the summit of the largest dome, and the Ancestral Women have their cave in one of the gorges. Camps of the Mice Women and the Curlew Man are found on the eastern side of Kata Tjuta, and Malu the Kangaroo Man can be seen – frozen in stone – dying in the arms of his Lizard Woman sister.

Here, as at Uluru, in the fierce heat of the day or in the gold and red light of sunset, time seems to stand still.

Kata Tjuta is the scene of a number of Aboriginal rites and ceremonies, many of which are conducted at night.

> **"** *That's a really important sacred thing that you are climbing … You shouldn't climb. It's not the real thing about this place. The real thing is listening to everything.* **"**

KUNMANARA – ANANGU TRADITIONAL OWNER OF ULURU

MOUNT FUJI

The highest mountain in Japan, Mount Fuji has been revered since ancient times. Today thousands of people climb to its summit every summer to view the sunrise and visit the many shrines and teahouses sited along the pilgrimage routes that thread their way to the crater of this dormant volcano, which last erupted in 1708.

To THE WEST OF TOKYO, JUST OFF THE SOUTHERN COAST OF JAPAN, Mount Fuji's perfect symmetry and snow-capped peak preside majestically over the surrounding landscape. Although there are a number of sacred mountains across the country, it is Fuji that has become the quintessential symbol of Japan. In the past, it inspired such reverence that cults grew up around a belief that it was a manifestation of a deity.

Magnetic anomalies distort compass readings in the forested foothills, and bears are sometimes spotted on the mountain. Fuji's serene presence has been immortalized in many haikus (17-syllable poems) by the 17th-century poet Matsuo Basho (*c.*1644–94), as well as in a famous series of woodblock prints (*Ukiyo-e*) by the artist Katsushika Hokusai (1760–1849).

Certain parts of the mountain have had a long association with military activity. In the 12th century, shogun warriors practised archery in its foothills, followed in later centuries by the samurai, who built a training camp on its slopes and ultimately a shrine to their dead comrades higher up the mountain. Today the warriors training in the Aokigahara forest at the base of Fuji are US marines and Japanese troops, who use an artillery range there.

Myths abound concerning the mountain: monsters, ghosts and goblins are said to haunt caves in one area on its slopes, which has also become the most popular site for suicides in Japan. But it is Fuji's role in the spiritual life of Japan that is most enduring and fascinating. An appreciation of this gives us an insight into how a striking natural feature can act as a catalyst and focus for devotions and intense spiritual experiences.

MOUNT FUJI

Near Tokyo, Honshu, Japan

Mount Fuji stands at 3776 metres (12,388 ft); pilgrims who climb the sacred mountain every summer take between three and eight hours to make their ascent.

" *This Mountain is born from between Heaven and Earth. It is the origin of yin and yang. It is the In-Breath and Out-Breath Source-of-All Sun and Moon. It is the Wondrous Sovereign Sengen. It is the original substance of all things. It becomes Person and all people are born from it. This Mountain is the yin-essence and yang-essence of the three luminaries: the Sun, the Moon, and the Shining Stars.* "

THE BOOK OF THE GREAT PRACTICE (18TH/19TH CENTURY)

TIMELINE

100,000 y.a. 'Old Fuji' is formed over a basalt layer several hundred thousand years older

8000 BC Mt Fuji assumes its present form ('New Fuji')

6th century AD Chinese culture and religious ideas enter Japan and influence religious use of mountains

c.700 The mythic first ascent by the wizard-sage En no Gyoja

c.1000 The process of mandal-ization begins through the interaction of Buddhism, Shintoism and the 'mountain practices' of *Sangaku shinko*

12th century Practice of pilgrimages to sacred mountains begins, including Fuji; devotional confraternities are founded to conduct group pilgrimages

15th century Fuji becomes increasingly popular as a pilgrimage destination

1541 Birth of ascetic Kakugyo

1644 Birth of the poet Basho, who wrote some of the most famous poetry inspired by Mt Fuji

1688 Jikigyo Miroku, a sage and Fuji confraternity member, makes a pilgrimage to the summit, where he experiences a revelation that the 'renewal of the world of Maitreya' is beginning

1707-8 Last eruptions of Fuji

1827 The first 36 famous pictures of Mt Fuji by the *Ukiyo-e* artist Katsushika Hokusai are published

1860 Sir Rutherford Alcock makes the first ascent by a foreigner

1868 Women are first permitted to scale the mountain

'THE GREATEST MOUNTAIN IN THE THREE LANDS'

From the very earliest of times Fuji was considered sacred, and the original inhabitants of the region, the Ainu, who are now only found on Japan's northernmost island of Hokkaido, believed it was the abode of the fire goddess Fuchi. Fuji became known as 'the greatest mountain in the three lands', meaning India, China and Japan, and became sacred to followers of Shinto, Buddhism and the Taoist cult of Koshin.

Originally reverence for the mountain grew out of a tradition of folk beliefs and religious and shamanic practice known as *Sangaku shinko* (literally 'mountain faith'). This form of ritual observance focused on the inspiration emanating from particular peaks. The tradition was based on the Shinto belief that many aspects of the natural world, such as trees, springs, lakes and mountains, were the abode of *kami* – spirits of place – and that humans needed to placate them through ritual and prayer to ensure their benign influence.

In common with many cultures worldwide, certain mountain peaks were seen as the abode of the dead. Here the spirits of the ancestors would undergo a process of purification before becoming *kami* themselves and influencing human affairs.

Even in its earliest phases, Shinto, and the mountain shamanism of *Sangaku shinko*, were influenced by Taoism and Confucianism. In the sixth century, the beliefs of Chinese Buddhism also began to pervade Japan. As a result, some people came to regard the *kami* as manifestations of Buddhist divinities, and Buddhist monks and wandering ascetics began to build hermitages on sacred mountains such as Fuji.

THE BODHISATTVA SENGEN DAINICHI AND THE FUJI MANDALA

Mount Fuji became known as the manifestation of the Bodhisattva Sengen Dainichi, and according to tradition, the first ascent to its summit was made either by an anonymous monk in AD 663 or by the wizard-sage En no Gyoja (b.634), sometimes referred to as the 'Japanese Merlin' in around 700.

By the tenth century the Yamabushi, a community of mountain ascetics, were living on the southwestern slope of Fuji. They supervised regular pilgrimages and combined Buddhist teachings with the practice of the *Shugendo* ('the path of training and testing') tradition of mountain asceticism that had evolved on virtually every sacred mountain in the country. *Shugendo* provided a heady mix of the pre-Buddhist folk traditions of *Sangaku shinko* and Shinto with Tantric Buddhism, Chinese yin-yang magic and Taoism.

The samurai warrior élite that dominated Japan from the 16th to the late 19th century developed strong associations with Mount Fuji. This work, created in 1855 by the printmaker Kunikazu, shows a samurai in a kabuki performance, with Fuji as a backcloth.

Mount Fuji offered the perfect environment for such an approach. The majestic, tranquil mountain, which exuded stability and calm, yet also contained transformative fire, came to be seen as a powerful source of yin and yang – the two forces, male and female, that uphold the universe.

At the same time, there arose a practice of designating whole areas of the countryside as sacred by visualizing them as domains of the Buddha, or Bodhisattvas. These domains were represented in mandalas – sacred paintings – which were used as aids to meditation, and as guides for both inner pilgrimages and outer journeys to the different areas represented in the mandala.

> ❝ *The Deity Fuji Sengen Dainichi, whom you will find westward from here in the province of Suruga, is the pillar of the world after the parting of Heaven and Earth. This Deity is the source of the Sun and Moon, of the Pure Lands, and of the human body.* ❞

THE BOOK OF THE GREAT PRACTICE

In the mandala centred on Fuji, the Bodhisattva Sengen Dainichi was seated at the centre of eight petals that radiated into the surrounding landscape. Conveniently, the crater of Fuji has eight peaks.

THE FUJI CONFRATERNITIES

In the 12th century, pilgrimages up Fuji became popular with peasant farmers and tradespeople, in addition to monks, ascetics and the nobility. Cults of mountain veneration arose, known as the Fuji confraternities, which organized group pilgrimages to the mountain to seek spiritual renewal. By the late 18th century many of these groups were flourishing in nearby Edo – present-day Tokyo. Some began to call for 'world renewal' and fearing the destabilizing effect of a reformist movement, the government tried unsuccessfully to ban them. However, 1000 years after their inception, Fuji confraternities still exist, and still organize visits to the mountain.

'THE BOOK OF THE GREAT PRACTICE'

The most important document of the confraternities recounts the life and teachings of the ascetic Kakugyo Tobutsu (1541–1646), who devoted his life to the worship of Mount Fuji and its deity. Known as *The Book of the Great Practice*, it first appeared in the 19th century, when the confraternities were at their height, and combined legendary and real events in a way that proved inspiring to its readers.

A first-century AD statue of Dainichi Nyorai, the 'Great Sun Buddha'. Although Mount Fuji had long been revered as a sacred site in Shinto, the native religion of Japan, the growing influence of Buddhism also imbued the peak with profound spiritual significance.

Kakugyo Tobutsu was born in Nagasaki in southern Japan. At the age of 18, he decided to seek enlightenment, and began to perform standing vigils. In a dream he was told to climb Mount Fuji. Having done so, a 'celestial child' then showed him a cave that he used for meditation. The deity Sengen Dainichi Bodhisattva then began to teach Kakugyo directly, beginning by stressing the need for harmony not only between Heaven and Earth, but also between rulers and subjects; so that interwoven with the spiritual teachings was a political message.

The deity then ordered him to practise standing vigils on a wooden block and taught him about the creation of Fuji: 'This Mountain is the pillar of the land [after] the parting of Heaven and Earth, and the source of all things. In the time when the cosmos was void, water congealed and this Mountain appeared. It did so because from each of the four directions, east, south, west, and north, there came a wave, and these waves collided.'

Kakugyo was then told to institute a practice that involved travelling to eight lakes around the mountain, to fast, pray and bathe in the waters for 100 days and 100 nights at each place. At every lake he was given 'Utterances' or spells by Sengen, such as 'The Utterance to Dispel Evil Influences', 'The Spell against Epilepsy' and 'The Utterance of the Stars'.

Having completed 'The Great Practice of the Eight Lakes' there was no time for rest. Kakugyo was told to begin 'The Practice of the Eight Outer Seas', travelling all over Japan to seas and lakes to engage in the ascetic disciplines he had been taught. The purpose of this practice was to bring the living presence of the Fuji deity to all of the country, deepening the 'harmony and obedience' of all its inhabitants.

Although Kakugyo only had two followers during his lifetime, together they performed many acts of healing, and a movement grew up inspired by the tales of the master's life and deeds. Over time, the Fuji cult grew immensely in popularity, with devotees making pilgrimages to the spots visited by their founder – caves, waterfalls and sacred springs, as well as the mountain itself. They also tried to emulate Kakugyo as best they could in the way they led their own lives.

Today most of the 200,000 or so tourists and pilgrims who visit the mountain each year make their ascent in July and August, when the snows have cleared and the weather is warmest. To catch the sunrise, many set out at night, and such is the throng along the path to the summit that progress can be painfully slow. So much environmental damage has now been caused to the mountain by refuse and the erosion of paths that it may be time to amend the local proverb: 'He who climbs Mount Fuji once is a wise man, he who climbs it twice is a fool'. Today the wise person might choose not to climb this sacred mountain even once, but instead decide to admire it from a distance or travel to its summit in their dreams.

> **" *clouds for roots,*
> *Mt Fuji's green foliage,*
> *the shape of a cedar.* "**
>
> BASHO

Under the Wave off Kanagawa (1827), from the series 'Thirty-Six Views of Mount Fuji' by Hokusai. This artist produced a series of ten further prints of the mountain in 1832.

LUANG PRABANG

Luang Prabang in northern Laos lies at the junction of the Mekong River and its tributary, the Nam Khan. For just over 200 years from the 14th century onwards, the city was a royal capital. Filled with dozens of exquisite temples and fine examples of French colonial architecture, it has been called 'the jewel of Indochina' and is now a World Heritage Site.

MOST LAOTIANS ARE BUDDHISTS OF THE THERAVADA SCHOOL, and at dawn as many as 1000 monks walk through the streets of this ancient city with their alms bowls to receive offerings, before going to work in schools, monasteries or *wats* (temples). The all-pervading sense of calm they radiate, combined with the lazily flowing Mekong and the year-round sunshine and warmth here make Luang Prabang one of the most relaxing places on Earth.

LAND OF BUDDHAS

Standing on Mount Phu Si ('Marvellous Mountain') in the centre of the town, you can steep yourself in the city's sacred atmosphere. This derives not just from its monks and its proliferation of temples but also from its natural surroundings; far in the distance, the lush green hills recall one of Luang Prabang's past glories – the Emerald Buddha.

Although the historical Buddha often stressed the illusory and transient nature of material things and taught a doctrine of non-attachment, a figurine of him just 66 centimetres (26 in) high, carved out of jade, has acted as a provocative talisman of political power in Southeast Asia ever since the 15th century.

❝Dawn trickled into Luang Prabang in cobalt blues and mauves flecked with gold and coddled in a cocoon of mist. Before 6 o'clock, thuds of drums echoed in the distance, and from my balcony I watched silent processions of saffron-swaddled monks, wooden bowls cradled in their palms, pad toward the town center on their morning alms round.❞

EDWARD GARGAN, *THE RIVER'S TALE: A YEAR ON THE MEKONG* (2002)

In legend, this small statue weaves together the histories of the region. Created in India, then kept in Sri Lanka, it was destined for Burma, but due to a shipwreck ended up in Cambodia before arriving in Thailand. The Emerald Buddha's story then enters recorded history; it was taken from Thailand to Laos in 1552, where it first resided in Luang Prabang for 12 years and thereafter Vientiane. In 1779 a Thai general captured Vientiane and returned the statue to his country – the kingdom of Siam.

Since 1784 it has been kept in a temple in Bangkok, and is Thailand's most sacred Buddha statue. Every year the king of Thailand dresses the Emerald Buddha in different golden clothes at a special ceremony at the onset of each of the three seasons. Meanwhile, across the Mekong some Laotians cling to the belief that the Emerald Buddha will one day return. Others maintain it never left its hiding place in Laos, and that the statue in Bangkok is a fake.

A lavishly decorated Buddhist temple in Luang Prabang – one of 32 such buildings within the ancient royal capital.

Though it may no longer host the Emerald Buddha, other depictions of the Buddha are ubiquitous in Laos, and the country is famed for its artistic tradition of exquisite sculpture in bronze, silver and gold. The museum in Luang Prabang contains many fine examples from the golden age of the Lao Buddha image of the 15th and 16th centuries. Yet the most poignant example of the Lao people's devotion to Buddhism are the Caves of a Thousand Buddhas.

The Mekong River at Luang Prabang in Laos. Its biodiversity is one of the greatest in the world, but it is under threat from human activity.

A two-hour boat journey up the Mekong takes you to a series of limestone caverns at Pak Ou, where for centuries local people have brought their Buddha images when they wished to replace them. Rather than discarding them, they have reverently placed them in nooks and on shelves cut into the walls so that today there are estimated to be over 4000 statues in the two main caverns.

THE MOTHER OF ALL RIVERS

The Mekong River flowing past the mouth of the Pak Ou caves is another key factor in both the everyday and spiritual lives of the Lao people. From its source high on the Tibetan Plateau, the Mekong flows through China, Myanmar (Burma), Thailand, Laos, Cambodia and Vietnam before emptying into the South China Sea through a delta south of Ho Chi Minh City. Laos is landlocked between Thailand to the west and Vietnam to the east. China and Myanmar share its northern border, while Cambodia lies on its southern frontier.

In Lao folk tradition the Mekong was formed by *nagas* – water serpents – and Luang Prabang has 15 guardian *nagas*. Locals believe it is these creatures that are responsible for the 'Naga fireballs' – strange egg-sized balls of glowing red light that rise up from the river at certain times, sometimes in their thousands.

The Mekong is known in Laos as *Maè Nam Khong* ('Mother of all Rivers'), and like a parent providing for her children, the river brings life to all the countries she flows through. It supports one of the world's most diverse fisheries, second only to the Amazon, but sadly its abundant fish stocks and its unique species of Mekong dolphin and manatee are likely to be among the first casualties of China's plan to build eight dams along its stretch of the river. None of the countries downstream have been consulted, and three barrages have already been constructed. Cambodia, which is almost totally dependent on the river for its food supply, fears mass starvation and Laos would suffer severely too if the river's flow was significantly reduced – the country is already one of the poorest in Southeast Asia and can ill afford further economic hardship.

A PERILOUS SITE – THE PLAIN OF JARS

The sufferings of Laos are not confined to poverty; a substantial number of adults and children are killed or maimed there every month. This is the dreadful legacy of the 'secret war' that America waged against Laos as part of the long-running conflict in neighbouring Vietnam. The operation was designed to prevent resupply of Vietcong forces from North Vietnam along the Ho Chi Minh Trail, which partly ran through Laos. For ten years, between 1964 and 1973, the US Air Force flew 580,000 missions over the region, dropping more than 2 million tons of bombs – double the amount that fell on Nazi Germany. As a result, Laos has an unenviable reputation as the most heavily bombed nation in the history of warfare. In today's terms, the United States spent $9 million a day on its bombing campaign, but has to date contributed only $1 million towards clearing the unexploded cluster bombs that litter the countryside.

The greatest concentration of ordnance occurs at one of the world's most fascinating archaeological sites – the Plain of Jars. Here, 80 miles (128 km) southeast of Luang Prabang on a plateau surrounded by mountains, 250 huge sandstone jars lie scattered about. Quarried a few miles away between 1500 and 2500 years ago, they are thought to be Bronze Age burial urns. The vessels are so massive – up to 2.6 metres (9 ft) tall – that legends tell of a race of giants who made them. Like Luang Prabang itself, the Plain of Jars is a hallowed place where you can sense eternity but, like other sacred sites around the world that have been in war zones, it has become a place of great suffering as well as peace.

Visitors to Laos are struck by the fact that its inhabitants, for all the terrible hardship they have endured, remain among the most charming and easy-going people in the world. It is only by appreciating the centrality of Buddhist spirituality in the Lao way of life – in particular the Four Noble Truths, which explain the way of release from suffering – that we can begin to comprehend their remarkable composure and endurance.

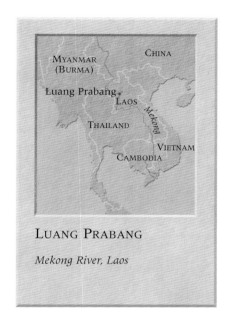

LUANG PRABANG

Mekong River, Laos

The Plain of Jars in Xieng Khuang province in central Laos.

ANGKOR

Before the modern age, the largest city in the world was Angkor, the capital of the Khmer empire in what is now Cambodia. Here, for 300 years from the ninth century onwards, the Khmers built magnificent buildings and temples, which were at first dedicated to the Hindu gods, then to Buddhism, then once more to Hinduism, before finally – in the 14th century – reverting to Buddhist use.

THE MOST CELEBRATED TEMPLE AT ANGKOR IS KNOWN AS ANGKOR WAT, which has remained in use as a Buddhist shrine for over 500 years. Angkor was first brought to the attention of the Western world in the 19th century, but it was never a 'lost city'. Even so, Angkor Wat was the only temple that was kept free of the jungle that gradually engulfed the other buildings once the city's heyday ended in the 15th century.

Much of the magic of Angkor in its current condition comes from the way in which great roots of trees have grown over the stones of the temples, so that we find ourselves looking at an eerie and evocative meeting of the forces of nature with the power of human effort. Sometimes the combination seems creative, as the elegance of the silkwood and strangler fig trees and their roots enhances the beauty of the buildings and sculptures. At other times, the juxtaposition seems sinister, reminding us of our mortality as the trees relentlessly destroy the symbols of a once-proud monarchy.

AN ANCIENT METROPOLIS

The sheer size of the temple at Angkor Wat staggers the imagination. An outer wall surrounded by a moat encloses an area of 93 hectares (230 acres) – in the centre of which stands the temple building, with its great towers and magnificent bas-reliefs and sculptures. Among these carvings are images of human beings with birds' heads. This motif can be found at several other ancient sites the world over. In Ancient Egypt, India, Indonesia, Peru and Rapa Nui (Easter Island),

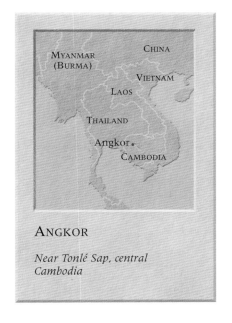

ANGKOR

Near Tonlé Sap, central Cambodia

The temple at Angkor Wat in Cambodia. Its five central towers are said to represent the five peaks of Mount Meru, the home of the gods in Hindu cosmology.

TIMELINE

5–10,000 y.a. Animist ancestors of the Khmers settle in the region

1st century AD Hinduism arrives from India

802 Construction of the stone temples of Angkor begins

1113–50 Angkor Wat is built

1181 King Jayavarman VII is crowned and begins building Buddhist temples

1243 Start of the Hindu Restoration; statues of the Buddha are replaced with lingams

1296 The Chinese diplomat Zhou Daguan visits the city and provides an invaluable written account of life in Angkor, noting both Hindu and Buddhist worship

14th century The temples are dedicated to Theravada Buddhism and remain so to the present day

1431 The city is sacked and looted by the Thais

1432 Nearly all of Angkor is abandoned except for Angkor Wat

16th–19th century Pilgrims visit the site from all over Asia and inscribe their 'vows of truth' on the walls of Angkor Wat

1860 The French explorer Henri Mouhot discovers the site

1907–70 Under French direction the site is cleared of forest and restoration is carried out

1989 Buddhism becomes the state religion of Cambodia once more

1992 Angkor designated a World Heritage Site

our ancestors carved figures of creatures that were half-bird, half-human. These may represent supernatural beings, but may also be images of the universal figure of the shaman, who can leave his body in 'spirit flight' to soar above the Earth.

Satellite photography confirms the extent of the site of Angkor. It occupied an area about the size of Los Angeles, and was the largest city in the pre-industrial world – covering some 1150 square miles (2978 sq km). Today over half a million people a year come to visit the ruins which have been designated a World Heritage Site, and which once stood at the heart of the Khmer empire that flourished between the ninth and 15th centuries. So closely has Angkor Wat become identified with Cambodian nationhood that it appears on the centre of the country's flag.

AN EPIC IN STONE

In AD 802 the Khmer King Jayavarman II (r. 802–50) proclaimed the independence of Cambodia from Java and established his capital at Angkor, just north of the great lake of Tonlé Sap. Jayavarman declared himself a universal monarch and god-king, and over the next 300 years dozens of monumental stone temples and buildings were constructed as each new king either extended the territory of the city, or moved the centre of his capital to a new site.

Relief carving of the Khmer army from the capital city of Angkor Thom, established by the monarch Jayavarman VII (r. 1181–1215).

Angkor Wat was built in the first half of the 12th century by King Suryavarman II (r. 1113–50) as both a temple and a new capital city. Surrounded by a moat, its towers were designed to look like lotus buds and were once covered in gilded stucco. It is indeed, as the British historian Arnold J. Toynbee (1889–1975) once memorably put it, an 'epic poem' in stone, not only thanks to its size and complexity, but also because an actual epic poem of 550 stanzas is inscribed upon its walls.

Known simply as 'The Poem of Angkor Wat', this epic is the earliest original literary work in Khmer, and probably emerged out of oral tradition to be carved on the walls of the temple in the 16th century. When Cambodia gained independence in 1953, after almost a century of French colonial rule, the poem was a key text used to promote Khmer culture and national identity.

VOWS OF TRUTH AND THE CHURNING OF THE SEA OF MILK

The great city of Angkor was abandoned after being sacked by Thai forces in 1431, and the Khmer kings moved their capital to the region around Phnom Penh. Yet Angkor Wat continued to function as a Buddhist temple over the following centuries, attracting pilgrims from all over Southeast Asia. This fact is attested by the so-called 'vows of truth', inscriptions left by pilgrims who visited the temple between the 17th and 19th centuries.

Lush tropical vegetation, such as this strangler fig tree, is in the process of reclaiming many of the buildings on the extensive Angkor site.

The bas-relief known as the 'Churning of the Sea of Milk' portrays the Hindu deity Vishnu (centre), while to the left and right asuras *and* devas *vie to win supremacy.*

When the French explorer Henri Mouhot (1826–61) came across the site in 1860, Angkor was already widely known about in Asia, and had been visited by Europeans in the 16th century.

The temple itself was designed as a symbolic representation of Mount Meru, the abode of the gods in Hindu mythology. The writer Graham Hancock (b.1950) has suggested that its placement, alongside other temples in the complex, mirrors the stars in the constellation of Draco at the time of the spring equinox in 10,500 BC. However, a more convincing theory on hidden meanings encoded in the temple is provided by Eleanor Mannika, whose book *Angkor Wat: Time, Space, and Kingship* analyzes the numerological relationships found at the site.

By looking at the units of measurement used by the Khmer builders, the proportions of the temple, and the images depicted on the great bas-relief known as the 'Churning of the Sea of Milk', Mannika believes that a number of cosmological meanings can be discerned, which in combination were designed to affirm the king's divine mandate to rule. The 'Churning of the Sea of Milk' depicts the Hindu creation myth, in which the divine ambrosia of 'amrita', together with other treasures and a poison, is released from the Sea of Milk, the Ocean of Immortality, after it has been churned by a great stick that has been pulled back and forth for a thousand years. The stick is the giant serpent Vasuki, who is used like a rope in a tug-of-war with 91 *asuras* (demons) pulling one way while 88 *devas* (gods) pull in the other direction.

Mannika maintains that this bas-relief acted as a solstice calculator, with the demons depicted on it representing the 91 days between the winter solstice and spring equinox, and the gods symbolizing the 88 days between the equinox and the summer solstice.

The Churning of the Sea of Milk is a profound and complex myth that speaks of the way in which life emerges out of tension and conflict. Powerful forces of creation and destruction whirl together in this story to produce the 'thirteen precious things', which include the elixir of life.

STABILITY IN A SEA OF CONFLICT

Angkor is awesome and beautiful in part because we see in it the struggle between the forces of time and timelessness. The great monuments cry out to remain eternal in their grandeur and yet they grapple with the forces of decay, as the jungle vegetation wraps its roots around them and attempts to crush them in its deadly embrace.

Cambodia and its surrounding countries have seen untold destruction and suffering. The Khmers were often at war – fighting the Vietnamese, the Thais and the Chinese – and their great monuments may well have been built by captured slaves. In more recent times, occupation by France and Japan was followed by intensive bombardment by the United States in 1969–70, which killed as many as 800,000 people and made a further 2 million refugees. Shortly thereafter, the Khmer Rouge dictator Pol Pot (1925–98) came to power; his genocidal regime was responsible for the deaths of up to 1.7 million Cambodians.

In many ways, the myth of the Churning Sea encapsulates the history both of Angkor and of the wider region. Cambodia, and Southeast Asia in general have played host to so much conflict and the ghosts of the past continue to haunt the countryside. Nevertheless, life remains vibrant and strong here. Little wonder, then, that Buddhism – a path that teaches liberation from suffering – became the most widely practised religion in Cambodia.

> *" Angkor is not orchestral; it is monumental. It is an epic poem which makes its effect, like the* Odyssey *and like* Paradise Lost, *by the grandeur of its structure as well as by the beauty of the details. Angkor is an epic in rectangular forms imposed upon the Cambodian jungle. "*
>
> ARNOLD TOYNBEE, *EAST TO WEST* (1958)

THE SACRED MOUNTAINS OF CHINA

Gazing up at mountains induces awe in all of us. In their presence we feel closer to the spirit. In China there is a long tradition of reverence for mountains, dating back to more than 4000 years ago. Indeed, the idea of mountain visits providing essential spiritual sustenance is so central to Chinese culture that their term for 'pilgrimage' translates literally as 'paying one's respect to a mountain'.

FROM THE VERY EARLIEST TIMES IN CHINA, local traditions of shamanism revered sacred mountains. Evocative legends arose of peak-dwelling hermits known as 'the immortals', who had discovered the secrets of longevity. These sages were reputed to sustain themselves on elixirs that were part physical – extracted from mountain herbs – and part spiritual, drawing on the life-force that emanates so strongly from mountains. Some were said to live for between 400 and 800 years.

With the advent of Taosim and Buddhism in the Far East, from around the third century BC, remote mountain monasteries were built, which over time became major centres of culture and learning. These institutions endured for well over two millennia until, in the Maoist Cultural Revolution of the 1960s, many were dissolved and their treasures destroyed. Recent years, though, have seen a resurgence of interest and pride in Chinese culture, and many of these sites are undergoing renovation.

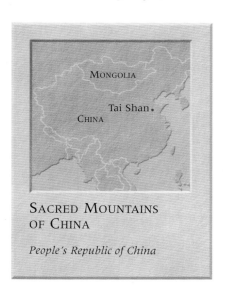

SACRED MOUNTAINS OF CHINA

People's Republic of China

TAOIST AND BUDDHIST SACRED PEAKS

Many peaks all over China were, and still are, venerated as sacred, and to elevate one over another is in many ways artificial. Nevertheless, three in particular have played an important role in Taoism: Mao Shan (in the far eastern province of Jiangsu), Lung-hu Shan (in the southeastern province of Jiangxi), and Ko-tsao Shan (also in Jiangxi) which evolved as centres of the Shang-ch'ing, Cheng-i, and Ling-pao sects of Taoism respectively. But over time, nine other mountains have come to be seen as the most senior sacred mountains of China: five of them Taoist and four Buddhist.

New religious centres are springing up in China; this is the Tagong Buddhist Centre (founded 1988) in the shadow of the Zhare Lhatse sacred mountain in Sichuan.

"*From time immemorial the mountains have been the dwelling place of great sages; wise men and sages have all made the mountains their own chambers, their own body and mind.*"

13TH-CENTURY BUDDHIST TEACHER DOGEN

TIMELINE

22nd century BC The emperor Shun makes a pilgrimage to Tai Shan every five years during his 50-year reign

219 BC Emperor Shih-huang makes a pilgrimage to the mountain

AD 1987 Tai Shan listed as World Heritage Site

2005 The structures at Tai Shan receive a US$2 million 'facelift' that includes destroying buildings that spoil the view

2007 Mining is banned at Wu Tai Shan after protests by monks

The five Taoist mountains in China are distributed in the five sacred directions of Taoism, which are the centre and the four cardinal points. Tai Shan stands in the east (Shandong province), Heng Shan Nan in the south (Hunan province), Hua Shan in the west (Shaanxi province), Heng Shan Bei in the north (Shanxi province) and Song Shan in the centre (Henan province).

The four Buddhist mountains are also related to the four cardinal directions and are dedicated to different Buddhist deities. Pu Tuo Shan stands in the east (Zhejiang province), and is sacred to Bodhisattva Kuan-Yin. Jiu Hua Shan in the south (Anhui province) is sacred to Bodhisattva Kshitigarbha. Emei Shan in the west (Sichuan province) is sacred to Bodhisattva Samantabhadra, and Wu Tai Shan in the north (Shanxi province) is sacred to Bodhisattva Manjushri.

THE SON OF THE EMPEROR OF HEAVEN

The eastern Taoist peak of Tai Shan, which stands at 1545 metres (5069 ft), is the most famous of all the mountains, and is known as the 'Son of the Emperor of Heaven'. It has been revered for millennia: the emperor Shun, who ruled for 50 years in the 22nd century BC (at the time of Egypt's Old Kingdom) made a pilgrimage every five years to the four mountains that defined the limits of his realm, one of which was Tai Shan.

An inscription carved into the rocks of Tai Shan indicates that Emperor Shih-huang (r. 221–210 BC), under whose reign construction of the Great Wall began, made a pilgrimage here in 219 BC. Confucius (551–479 BC) may also have visited Tai Shan, and communist leader Mao Zedong (1893–1976) certainly came here.

More than 7000 steps lead up the 'Stairway to Heaven' to the mountain's summit. The route is lined with shrines, temples and carved stones that record the poems and tributes of previous pilgrims. At the peak stands the Temple of the Jade Emperor, and the Temple of the Princess of the Azure Clouds, his daughter. The Temple of the Princess has become the foremost place of pilgrimage for Chinese women. Tai Shan is now a World Heritage Site and receives so many visitors that in 2005 nearly 15 million yuan (US$2 million) were spent on renovations.

UNDER GROWING THREAT

Ironically, the very revival of interest in China's sacred mountains, combined with the country's rising prosperity, poses a new threat to these sites. To cater for the rapidly growing numbers of visitors, cable cars have been built up some of the mountains to make access to the peaks easier. The tourist influx not only compromises the sacred atmosphere of these places, but also endangers the many rare species of plants, birds and animals found there. Illegal logging of the forested foothills and burgeoning mining interests further contribute to the steady degradation of the environment.

The Alliance of Religions and Conservation is now engaged in a major effort with Chinese Buddhist and Taoist groups to promote conservation of the sacred mountains of China, by training the monks to be guardians of the environment. This worldwide organization, which has a web presence, offers an inspiring example of the way in which diverse peoples can co-operate to preserve the natural world and sacred sites.

In ancient times, mountains were seen as the abode of the gods – sacrosanct areas only to be visited rarely, if at all. A pilgrimage to a peak, if it was carried out, was perhaps a once-in-a-lifetime event for all but mountain hermits or monks who made their homes in caves on the mountainside or in monasteries that were either built on peaks, or clung precariously to the side of a cliff, like the 'Flying Temple' of Heng Shan Bei.

Perhaps it is time to explore the virtue of not visiting a site, and of learning instead to embody its qualities in our being. Reverence expressed in restraint is not familiar to many of us, but it brings its own reward. The mountain teaches stillness and the contentment that comes from simply being.

Heng Shan Bei, the northernmost of the Five Sacred Mountains of Taoism, is home to the remarkable Hanging (or Flying) Temple, built in around the sixth century AD, during the reign of the Northern Wei dynasty.

> **"** *On top of Cold Mountain the lone round moon*
> *Lights the whole clear cloudless sky.*
> *Honour this priceless natural treasure*
> *Concealed in five shadows, sunk deep in the flesh.* **"**

HERMIT HANSHAN, NINTH CENTURY AD

THE GANGES

The mighty River Ganges flows for a total of 1557 miles (2510 km) from its source in the Himalayas to the Bay of Bengal in Bangladesh. Along the way, its waters bring life to millions of people who look upon it as sacred and revere it as the goddess – or mother – Ganga. Yet in the very act of bringing mortal life into being, a mother also ensures that it will die; accordingly, the dead are returned to Ganga, most commonly from the ghats (steps) at the holy city of Varanasi.

FOUR OF THE WORLD'S LARGEST RIVER SYSTEMS begin their life in the Himalayas – the Indus, which flows through Pakistan and gives India (Hindustan) its name; the Yangtze, which flows through China and is the longest river in Asia; the Mekong, which traverses Southeast Asia; and the Ganges, sometimes known in India as Atula, 'the Peerless', or Savitri, 'the Stimulator'.

More commonly, however, the Ganges is known in India as Mother Ganga, who is personified as the goddess 'Ganga devi', the daughter of Meru, the god of the Himalayas. Every daughter has a mother, and for Ganga devi it is the Gangotri glacier high up in the Himalayas, who feeds her daughter with icy meltwater at the river's source.

The holy city of Varanasi on the Ganges. Many of the sets of shallow steps (ghats) leading down to the river here are used for cremation. Varanasi is sacred to Hindus, Buddhists and Jains alike.

" *The Ganga, especially, is the river of India, beloved of her people,
round which are intertwined her memories, her hopes and fears, her songs
of triumph, her victories and her defeats. She has been a symbol of India's
age-long culture and civilization, ever changing, ever flowing,
and yet ever the same Ganga.* "

JAWAHARLAL NEHRU, FIRST PRIME MINISTER OF INDIA

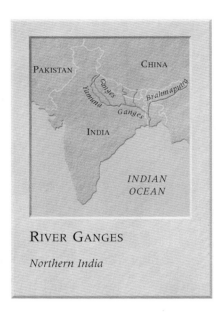

RIVER GANGES

Northern India

Tragically the mother is running out of nourishment. Gangotri is a place of pilgrimage – holy men bathe in its icy waters – but the sheer number of visitors and pilgrims has resulted in environmental damage as hotels are built and forests cut down in an area that was once a haven. Moreover, as a result of global warming, the glacier has begun to recede at an alarming rate, and in 2007 the World Wildlife Fund issued a warning, based on UN research, that the Ganges could start to dry up by 2030, with dire consequences for the 500 million people who depend on it for their drinking water and agriculture.

Standing on the banks of this great river at Varanasi (Benares) in Uttar Pradesh, one of the holiest cities in India, you might find it hard to imagine the Ganges ever drying up. Here the living and the dying come to the banks of the river in search of liberation and blessing. For Hindus, it is deemed auspicious to die beside the Ganges, which will then carry you home. Many of India's leaders have been cremated beside the Ganges or its tributaries. After Prime Minister Indira Gandhi (1917–84) was assassinated, she was cremated on the banks of the River Yamuna in Delhi, and her ashes were then scattered by an Indian Air Force plane over the Gangotri glacier.

Millions of Hindus flock to the banks of the Ganges during the Kumbh Mela *pilgrimage. Pictured below is the 1974 gathering at Haridwar.*

HEALING WATERS

It is also considered good to drink Ganga's water just before you take your last breath – it will help to take you to heaven – and if you cannot get to the river relatives are likely to bring you some to sip.

The living bathe in the Ganges and drink it too, believing that the water has healing powers and can wash away sins. A Hindu scripture states: 'When the body is afflicted with senility and diseases, the holy water of Mother Ganga is the medicine', and although the river water is often laden with impurities from raw sewage and chemical effluents, a scientific explanation has now been found to support the miraculous cures that have been reported anecdotally since ancient times. Bacteriophages have been found in Ganges water – these are virus-like agents that kill bacteria in a more accurate and powerful way than antibiotics, and with no known side-effects. Although bacteriophage research and therapy has been undertaken in Russia for over 60 years, the Western medical establishment has only just begun to explore their potential.

THE *KUMBH MELA*

Such is the magnetic power of the Holy Ganges that many festivals are held on its banks. In the Hindu creation myth, the 'Churning of the Sea of Milk' (see pages 212–213), a pot (*kumbh*) splashes drops of nectar on four locations in India. To commemorate this event a great festival (*Mela*) is held every three years at each of these locations in turn. Two are on the Ganges, at Allahabad (Prayag) and Haridwar.

The first *Kumbh Mela* festival of the new millennium, held at Allahabad in 2001, attracted record crowds of 70 million people, making it the largest pilgrimage gathering on Earth and in history. Thousands of itinerant monks pitched camp for six weeks alongside pilgrims and tourists. To gain spiritual merit, as many as ten million devotees at a time converged on the Ganges like a human river attempting to merge with the divine Ganga devi.

TIMELINE

*c.*1700–1100 BC The Ganga is mentioned in the Rig-Veda, the earliest of the Hindu scriptures

*c.*900 BC The Ganges is mentioned again in the Hindu epic, the *Mahabharata*

*c.*500 BC River mentioned once more in the *Ramayana*

AD 1896 Ernest Hanbury Hankin reported that something in the waters of the Ganges and Jumna rivers in India had marked antibacterial action against cholera and could pass through a very fine porcelain filter

1984 The Indian government draws up the Ganga Action Plan to address the problem of raw sewage and partially burnt and unburnt corpses polluting the river

1996 The Ganges river dolphin is listed as an endangered species

2001 Largest ever *Kumbh Mela* held at Allahabad

2007 The Ganges is named as one of the world's ten rivers at most risk in a WWF report suggesting that by 2030 it may lose its source of glacial water and become seasonally dependent on monsoon rains only

"*Oh Mother Ganga, cleanse us of our sins and bring peace to our souls. Help our dreams come true and give us long lives. We salute you, oh Mother Ganga and bestow upon you this gift of flowers.*"

HINDU PRAYER

THE ELLORA CAVES

Wherever you go in India, an extraordinary and vibrant connection with the ancestors seems to emerge from the very land itself. Nowhere do you feel this more potently than at Ellora, 186 miles (300 km) northeast of Mumbai (Bombay) where adherents of three of Asia's great faiths – Buddhism, Hinduism and Jainism – carved a complex of 34 caves containing temples, shrines and monks' cells out of the basalt hillside.

SCULPTED CAVES WITH CARVINGS AND SOMETIMES PAINTINGS OCCUR at a number of sites throughout India, but particularly in the western state of Maharashtra. For example, at Ajanta, near Ellora, there is a group of 29 Buddhist caves with exquisite murals. The earliest of the Ajanta caves date from the second century BC, and they are thought to have been abandoned by AD 650. The same region contains the Jogeshwari cave temple dedicated to Shiva; the Elephanta cave on an island in Mumbai harbour (one of the city's most popular tourist attractions); and the Mandapeshwar and Jogeshwari caves, which are tucked into a slum and suburb respectively of Mumbai and are hardly known.

A MONUMENTAL ACHIEVEMENT

Work at Ellora began between the fifth and sixth centuries AD, when Buddhist monks – possibly refugees from Ajanta – began tunnelling into the hill. They created a network of 12 caves containing meeting halls and monasteries. Some of these caverns were on several storeys; the great hall known as the 'Carpenter's Cave' boasts a tall, seated Buddha and an arched roof sculpted to simulate wooden beams.

Subsequently, between the ninth and tenth centuries, Jain monks dug a further five caves here, painting fine murals on their ceilings. However, it is the Hindu contribution to Ellora that has come to be seen as the jewel in the crown of Indian cave temples.

Hindus arrived at Ellora around the beginning of the seventh century. In addition to hewing 16 elaborately decorated caves from the rock, they also embarked upon their *pièce de résistance* – the Kailasa temple. This monumental architectural feat remains the largest excavated rock structure in the world; so colossal is it that you have continually to remind yourself that it is all

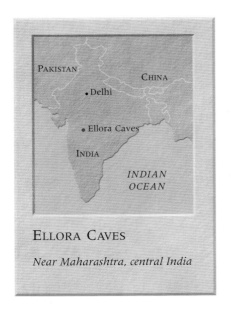

ELLORA CAVES

Near Maharashtra, central India

The magnificent Kailasa temple at Ellora. Unlike the other caves at the site, this edifice is surrounded by a huge courtyard open to the sky.

TIMELINE

between 200 BC and AD 650
Ajanta caves created using rudimentary hand tools

5th–7th centuries Buddhist caves at Ellora were constructed

7th century Ajanta caves abandoned; monks may have relocated to Ellora

7th–9th centuries The Hindu caves are constructed

8th century Work on the Kailasa temple is started by Krishna I (757–773) of the Rashtrakuta dynasty

800–1000 The Jain caves are created

1819 John Smith, a British Army officer, finds the Ajanta caves while on a hunting expedition

1895 James Fergusson and James Burgess of the Archaeological Survey of India, publish a study of cave art at Arjanta and Ellora and other sites

1983 Cave systems at Ellora and Ajanta are designated World Heritage Sites

fashioned from a single, solid mass of stone. The huge pyramidal structure was designed as a symbolic representation of Lord Shiva's Himalayan abode – the sacred Mount Kailash in Tibet (see pages 242–245). Construction of the temple began under the direction of the Rashtrakuta king Krishna I (r. 757–773)

It is estimated that the Kailasa temple took some 7000 labourers a century and a half to complete and involved the removal of 200,000 tons of stone. Covering an area double the size of the Parthenon in Athens, the building is on two storeys, with a third storey of galleries. Inner and outer rooms and gathering halls, complete with pillars and windows, encircle the heart of the temple, where an enormous *lingam* – an altar representing Shiva – is surrounded with images of deities and erotic figures carved in bas-relief on the walls.

THE POWER OF LIGHT, SOUND AND THE LAND

A inescapable sense of magic pervades the cave temple complex at Ellora. But what exactly is its source? At least three factors combine to lend this sacred site its numinous power. Visit the caves at a festival time or when a group of worshippers is chanting and you will instantly notice one of these: namely, how strongly the caves resonate with the sound of the human voice. The ribbed ceiling of the Buddhist 'Carpenter's Cave' in particular produces a deep echo, suggesting that the caves' acoustic properties may well have been used to induce or deepen meditative or trance-like states in the worshippers who gathered here.

The most famous of the Buddhist caves at Ellora is cave ten, popularly known as the 'Carpenter's Cave', with its extravagant vaulting and statue of a Buddha at prayer.

Alice Boner (1889–1981), a Swiss artist who lived in India for over 40 years, discovered another factor that is harder to discern until you have the key. She spent months at Ellora, drawing the temple reliefs, until one day in 1941 she had an epiphany that allowed her to decode the geometrical pattern used to create them. Boner later described her experience: 'all of a sudden one of the images…began to resolve … into a kind of geometrical pattern woven in rhythms of abstract lines'. Just as the use of enhanced sound for spiritual purposes is found the world over, so is the use of sacred geometry, and Boner's findings confirmed that part of the magic we experience at the caves comes from the visual effect these reliefs have on us.

The third factor resides in the location of these places of worship. As you meditate or sing in them you are literally inside the Earth. In his book *Facing the World with Soul*, spiritual psychologist Robert Sardello provides the clue: '[The Magical tradition's] third gateway gives passage into the soul substance of the land.' This sense of enclosure is especially strong in the rainy season, when a waterfall cascades down the hillside, blessing the complex, while worshippers remain dry and ensconced in the galleried caves beneath.

The Ellora caves are a glorious display of the tolerance and diversity of faith found in India. When the Italian film-maker Simonetta Gatto travelled to the Subcontinent in 2004 to compile a documentary about pilgrims at Ellora, she was immediately struck by the way in which Hindus, Buddhists and Jains continued to visit the site and carry out practices that have been passed down in an unbroken chain since the earliest of times: 'I found there a mystical world of colours, people and age-old traditions kept alive to this day with continuous devotion, manifesting the deep spiritual link India has with its own past.'

The elephants carved on the plinth of the Kailasa temple are just one example of the exquisitely beautiful sculpture that was carried out here.

❝*The ancient civilization of India differs from those of Egypt, Mesopotamia and Greece, in that its traditions have been preserved without a break down to the present day.*❞

A. L. BASHAM, *THE WONDER THAT WAS INDIA* (1954)

BODH GAYA

There are many Buddhist sites of pilgrimage, but the most sacred of all is in northeast India, at Bodh Gaya. Here, in the forest of Uruvela, a young man who had been a prince and an ascetic sat under a fig tree and remained in meditation until he reached enlightenment, which is known as bodhi *in Pali and Sanskrit. His name was Siddhartha Gautama, but from that moment on he became the Buddha, while the tree that sheltered him was henceforth known as the Bodhi tree.*

THE ORIGINAL BODHI TREE, OF COURSE, IS NO LONGER THERE – it has been reborn many times since then – but such is the atmosphere at Bodh Gaya, the tree that is now there seems easily to transcend its own mortality and connect pilgrims directly to the moment when Siddhartha Gautama sat beneath its ancestor's branches. Around this spot temples, shrines, monasteries and retreat houses have grown up. A red sandstone slab marks the spot where the Buddha meditated, and the 'Jewelled Walk' follows the path he took as he paced up and down, deep in thought, after he had gained enlightenment. The Mahabodhi Temple, the first to be constructed, encloses both a statue of the Buddha and a Hindu *shiva-lingam* (an altar to the god Shiva) and has been designated a World Heritage Site.

GAUTAMA'S ENLIGHTENMENT

Siddhartha Gautama was born in the fifth or sixth century BC in the grove of Lumbini (today a small village in Nepal, near the border with India). He married, but shortly afterwards left his wife and child, and spent six years sitting at the feet of various teachers in search of enlightenment. Presently, he was drawn to another grove, at Uruvela, where sacred fig trees grew beside a river. He is later said to have told a disciple:

> 'There I saw a beautiful stretch of countryside, a beautiful grove, a clear flowing river, a lovely ford and a village nearby for support. And I thought to myself; "Indeed, this is a good place for a young man set on striving".'

A villager gave him freshly cut grass to use as a cushion, and a young woman, Sujata, gave him a bowl of milk, rice and honey. Seating himself beneath one of the sacred

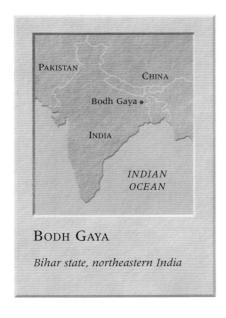

BODH GAYA

Bihar state, northeastern India

The Mahabodhi temple complex. After the decline of Buddhism in Mughal India, the site was restored to its former glory in the late 19th century.

TIMELINE

566 BC Traditional date of Siddhartha Gautama's birth

*c.*531 BC Gautama reaches enlightenment beneath the Bodhi tree and becomes the Buddha

*c.*265–238 BC Reign of Ashoka, who promotes Buddhism

AD 100–400 The Mahabodhi temple is constructed; the tree is probably moved back from its previous position

400–800 Many monuments and monasteries now occupy the site; the Mahabodhi temple assumes its present form

800–1200 Bodh Gaya is a major Buddhist centre, patronized by the Pala Dynasty of Bengal

1200–1800 As the area comes under the rulership of the Islamic Delhi sultanate, state patronage of Bodh Gaya ceases – the temples and monasteries fall into decay; Shaivite (Hindu) ascetics found a monastery there

1880s A Burmese mission, and later the British Archaeological Survey of India, begins to repair the temple

1891 Bodh Gaya again becomes a Buddhist pilgrimage site; Anagarika Dharmapala, a Buddhist leader from Ceylon, founds the Mahabodhi Society and begins a long campaign to take the management of the temple into Buddhist hands

1953 Control of the Mahabodhi temple is transferred from Hindu abbots to a management committee, but with a statutory majority of Hindus; renovations are carried out

1990s Buddhists gain control of the management committee

2002 Mahabodhi temple complex becomes a World Heritage Site

Ficus religiosa trees, commonly called a pipal or bo tree, he resolved to remain in meditation until he gained enlightenment. He achieved his goal and became the Buddha, which means 'Enlightened One'. Some say that this took 49 days of meditation, others three days and three nights, and yet others just one day and one night.

Historians disagree about the exact date of this momentous event, which signalled the start of one of the world's major religions, but the broad consensus is that it occurred about half a millennium before the proposed date of Jesus' birth.

SITES OF BUDDHIST DEVOTION

Following the pattern of other religions, there soon arose a variety of different interpretations of the Buddha's teachings, which he never wrote down, and by 100 BC there were 18 different sects of Buddhism. By this time the site of the Buddha's illumination was already a place of pilgrimage; the village there was no longer called Uruvela but was known as Sambodhi, Mahabodhi and later Bodh Gaya.

Other sites became places of pilgrimage too: Lumbini Grove; Sarnath, where he preached his first sermon seven weeks after gaining enlightenment, and Kushinagar, where he died at the age of 80, after 45 years of teaching.

In addition to these four major sites, hundreds of other places attracted pilgrims as, like other world religions, Buddhism began to assimilate sites that were sacred to other traditions, such as the Bön in Tibet and the Taoists in China. Relics also became important foci for shrines and temples. The Buddha's cremation ashes were at first separated and, according to legend, buried in ten different locations in reliquary cairns called stupas. Some of these were subsequently opened by the Emperor Ashoka (r. *c.*265–238 BC), who divided the relics into 84,000 portions – a symbolic rather than actual number. These were distributed to the many temples and monasteries he built in his empire.

THE PARADOX OF PILGRIMAGE

Relics assumed such importance as objects of devotion that a trade in false ones grew up – just as it did for Christian relics in medieval Europe and the Holy Land. Today many Buddhists still regard relics as powerful aids to devotion, and they form a key component in a contemporary project that was due to be sited at Bodh Gaya, but which is now planned for Kushinagar.

There, where the Buddha achieved parinirvana (the state beyond the illumination of nirvana), a Tibetan Buddhist group based in the USA plans to build the largest statue in the world, surrounded by a monastery, nunnery, library, school and

> **"***Illumined with all wisdom sat the Buddha, the Perfected One, having at last attained, and the light strengthened and grew in rapture. And about him the world lay calm and bright and a soft breeze lifted the leaves.***"**

L. ADAMS BECK, *THE LIFE OF THE BUDDHA* (1957)

hospital. Made of bronze and 50 storeys high, the Maitreya Project will cost US$150 million and is planned to house a million relics. A selection of these relics have already gone on tour to help raise funds for the project, but some Buddhists feel the project is unnecessarily lavish – arguing that there is such poverty in the region it would be better to alleviate this rather than create a monument which might deplete the region's already scarce natural resources.

Whether or not the great Buddha statue is ever built, Bodh Gaya is likely to remain as the most important site of pilgrimage for Buddhists, because it is here that their founder gained a state of grace and clarity of mind that enabled him to see beyond the spell cast by the world of form. Although he then devoted the rest of his life to teaching how to go beyond this world of form, personality, ego and the body, the image of the Buddha is still deeply revered.

Some may see this as ironic, but for others the truth is clothed in paradox, and the form of the Buddha represents not a single historical man, but an archetypal being who is every one of us in essence, if we are to believe those Buddhist teachers who say that each of us has the potential to awaken to our essential Buddha-nature.

The paradox of using form to go beyond form expresses perfectly the inherent contradiction in humanity's reverence for sacred sites and the urge to go on pilgrimage. If we are too attached to the act of pilgrimage or to the site itself we become lost in the outer world – in illusion. And yet, and yet ... as the Japanese poet Basho, much influenced by Zen Buddhism, once wrote.

The deer park at Sarnath (now in Uttar Pradesh state) is where the Buddha first revealed the Eightfold Path leading to nirvana. Pictured here is the Dhamekh stupa at the site, built c.500 AD.

SHATRUNJAYA

The most significant sites of pilgrimage in the Jain religion are the temple-covered hills of Mount Abu, Mount Parshavanth, Girnar and Shatrunjaya. Of these four, Shatrunjaya in Gujarat is considered the most holy, and today its nine hill tops are crowned with hundreds of finely carved white buildings that welcome thousands of pilgrims and tourists every year.

I{N THE STATE OF GUJARAT, IN THE NORTHWESTERN CORNER OF INDIA}, the city of Palitana and the nine summits of the Shatrunjaya hills are considered the most sacred of all Jain holy places. Every Jain is urged to make a pilgrimage here at least once in their lifetime to help them attain spiritual illumination.

A DAZZLING HOLY CITY

Jains are masters in the art of seeing both sides of an argument. It is they who follow more assiduously than Buddhists or Hindus the doctrine of *ahimsa*, harmlessness, which so influenced the civil rights leader Mohandas ('Mahatma') Gandhi (1869–1948). You can only preach a doctrine of non-conflict if you believe in the relativity of existence – that somewhere beyond opposition lies reconciliation and union. And in their holiest place of pilgrimage at Shatrunjaya, the Jains have managed to resolve the age-old conflict between a belief that the summits of holy mountains are sanctuaries of the highest forms of spiritual energy and should not be visited, and a desire to attain these heights to benefit from their atmosphere.

Because Shatrunjaya was built as an abode for divine beings, everyone must

The mystical spires of countless temples and shrines fill the view of the Shatrunjaya hills, the most sacred place of pilgrimage for Jains.

leave the summit of the holy hill by dusk. At night no human presence is permitted among the Camelot-like white spires and temples of this exquisite sanctuary.

During the day hundreds, often thousands, of pilgrims make the ascent up the 3000 and more steps that lead to the summit. If they are elderly or unwell they climb aboard a small platform that is suspended on ropes like a swing from a pole, and are carried up by porters.

When they arrive they are confronted by a city of such beauty and complexity that when writers attempt to count the number of temples they become dazzled and confused. Some people claim that you will find 863, others 1250, and yet others 3500. A more sober estimate suggests that there are 108 large temples, 872 small shrines and about 7000 images within Shatrunjaya.

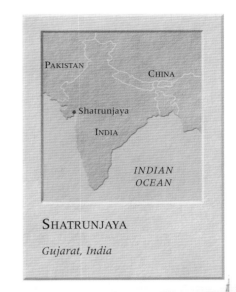

SHATRUNJAYA

Gujarat, India

MOKSHA — LIBERATION

The reason for this huge proliferation of temples on the mountain at Shatrunjaya is that it was here, according to tradition, that nearly all of the 24 revered sages of the Jain religion attained *moksha* – liberation from the cycle of death and rebirth and from the limitations of worldly existence. These sages are known as Tirthankaras, which means teachers who 'make a ford' – in other words, those who cross over the river of birth and death and show the way towards an enlightened state of existence.

Jains believe that we are all capable of attaining *moksha*, and consequently that the Tirthankaras should be respected as role models, rather than worshipped as divinities. In common with Buddhism, Taoism and Shinto the concept of God is not used in Jainism. Instead each individual soul is seen as eternal and capable of achieving the divine state of liberation in a universe that is beyond time.

Marble statues of the Tirthankaras adorn the temples as objects of inspiration rather than worship, and these figures are naked to symbolize not only their perfection but also because they embody the doctrine of *ahimsa* – since clothes have to be washed, wearing them results in the harming of creatures. One sect of Jain monks renounces both clothes and bathing for this simple reason.

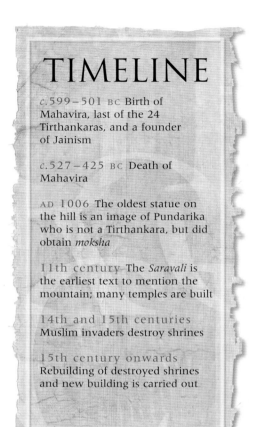

TIMELINE

*c.*599–501 BC Birth of Mahavira, last of the 24 Tirthankaras, and a founder of Jainism

*c.*527–425 BC Death of Mahavira

AD 1006 The oldest statue on the hill is an image of Pundarika who is not a Tirthankara, but did obtain *moksha*

11th century The *Saravali* is the earliest text to mention the mountain; many temples are built

14th and 15th centuries Muslim invaders destroy shrines

15th century onwards Rebuilding of destroyed shrines and new building is carried out

Although such ascetic practices may seem excessive, they are the result of a distinctive and highly sophisticated understanding of the nature of karma, which sees it as a fine type of matter that is attracted to each soul to create the circumstances of its experience. Even though most Jains are not ascetics, they adhere to a strict moral code, a vegetarian diet, the practice of *ahimsa* and pilgrimage to holy places, such as Shatrunjaya.

A SHRINE BUILT BY THE WHOLE OF INDIA

We can be sure that there have been temples in Shatrunjaya for over a thousand years, since a statue at the site has been definitively dated to 1006. Several of the temples were originally built in the 11th century. However, in the 14th and 15th centuries invading armies from the Delhi sultanate and other Muslim states destroyed many of Shatrunjaya's buildings. Major

> ❝ *I grant forgiveness to all living beings. May all living beings grant me forgiveness. My friendship is with all living beings. My enmity is totally nonexistent.* ❞

JAIN UNIVERSAL FORGIVENESS PRAYER

Shatrunjaya means 'The Place of Victory'. It is here that nearly all of the great sages of the Jain tradition achieved victory over the cycle of birth and death and gained liberation.

reconstruction took place in the latter half of the 15th century. In the city of Palitana, below the hill, there are hundreds of temples too – and unlike those on the holy hill they can be visited after dusk. Every year there is a great pilgrimage festival on the full moon of each Karttika – a time in October or November. Thousands of pilgrims walk through the streets of the town and up to Shatrunjaya, carrying huge pictures of the holy hill.

Jains have long been associated with trading activities on the Indian Subcontinent. Many generations of devotees have donated the wealth they accrued from their profession to enhance the glory of Shatrunjaya. It is often said that there is hardly a city the length and breadth of India that has not at some time contributed to the magnificent edifices at Shatrunjaya.

THE GOLDEN TEMPLE AT AMRITSAR

The Golden Temple at Amritsar in the Punjab is the holiest site of the Sikh religion, which developed in the 16th century as a conscious fusion of Hindu and Islamic teachings. Between 1499 and 1708 ten gurus taught a path that stresses devotion to the One God – chanting or using His name, usually given as 'Waheguru', as a mantra. The tenth guru declared that the written teachings would become the next guru, and a sacred book – the Guru Granth Sahib – now takes pride of place in the Golden Temple.

THE GOLDEN TEMPLE STANDS IN A STRIKING LOCATION, in the centre of a lake fed by an underground spring – the Pool of the Nectar of Immortality, or *Amritsar*, which gave its name to the city that grew up around it. On its shores, great dormitories welcome visitors from all over the world. In a radical departure from Buddhism, Hinduism and Jainism, Sikhism rejects the concept of *ahimsa* – harmlessness – and places great emphasis on fighting social injustice. Thus, all are welcome at the Golden Temple (officially called the Harimandir Sahib, or 'Abode of God') and every day free meals are dispensed to as many as 40,000 people.

THE GENESIS OF SIKHISM

Amritsar lies just east of the border with Pakistan, with Kashmir to the north. The Punjab region has seen much unrest, especially in the 20th century, but the Golden Temple, one of the world's most beautiful sacred sites, has weathered this turbulent and often tragic history.

The Sikh religion is relatively young – beginning only at the end of the 15th century – and is notable for the way in which it consciously fuses elements of Hinduism with inspiration from Islam. These two great streams of religious thought can be found both in Sikh teachings and in the very architecture of the Golden Temple itself.

Before the temple was built, the site was a small lake in the forest, visited by wandering sages and close to a major trade route connecting the lands that are now India and Asia to the east, with Afghanistan and the Middle East to the west. Legends recount that the great Hindu epic, the *Ramayana,* was written beside the pool, and that here a jug of the divine nectar of immortality 'Amrita' descended from heaven to restore the soldiers of Lord Rama to life.

The founder of Sikhism, Guru Nanak (1469–1539), began teaching the new faith in 1499, and over the following two centuries, a further nine gurus developed the tradition. Sikhism now ranks as the world's fifth largest religion, and its adherents are dispersed across many continents, largely as a result of the migration of indentured labour within the British empire.

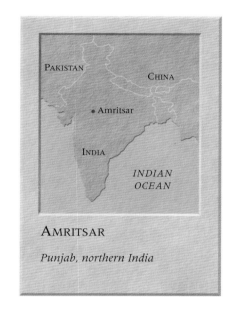

AMRITSAR

Punjab, northern India

The Golden Temple complex at Amritsar. From early morning to past sunset, hymns are chanted to musical accompaniment from the temple.

The palanquin holding the Guru Granth Sahib *is paraded during a festival marking the birth of the fourth guru.*

GURU RAM DAS AND THE FIRST TEMPLE

Amritsar only began to develop as a site dedicated to the Sikh faith when in 1574, the fourth guru, Ram Das (1534–81), made his home beside the lake, which by now had a reputation as a source of healing. Three years later he purchased it and the surrounding land from its owners. Guru Ram Das enlarged the lake and paved its sides, and followers began to build houses nearby, creating a small town that would in time become the city of Amritsar.

> " *I do not go to see sacred shrines of pilgrimage, or bathe in the sacred waters; I do not bother any beings or creatures. The Guru has shown me the sixty-eight places of pilgrimage within my own heart, where I now take my cleansing bath.* "

SIKH HOLY TEXT, THE *GURU GRANTH SAHIB*

In 1588 the fifth guru, Arjan Dev (1563–1606) began the building of the first temple and invited an Islamic mystic to lay the foundation stone. Sixteen years later, the first edition of the *Guru Granth Sahib* (or *Adi Granth*) was installed in the temple and a caretaker, or granthi, entrusted with its safekeeping. The first granthi was a devoted disciple of Guru Nanak called Baba Buddha (1506–1631).

DESTRUCTION AND CREATION

Although the teachings of Sikhism are focused on devotion to God, and reject the need for pilgrimage and acts such as ritual bathing, there seems to be an innate human desire to pay homage to certain places, and over the years the temple became a much-visited shrine, and some devotees now ritually bathe in the lake.

In the middle of the 18th century the city was invaded by the Afghanis, the temple was destroyed and the lake desecrated – some say with the bodies of slaughtered horses, tragically prefiguring the massacre by British troops that occurred nearby over a century and a half later, when many bodies were recovered from a well.

At the end of the 18th century a Sikh kingdom was established and in the early years of the following century the temple began to assume the form it takes today. Muslim architects and craftsmen worked on the buildings, and the Harimandir was decorated with marble, with much of the exterior plated in gold – giving rise to the name 'The Golden Temple'. The walls were decorated with gypsum and gold frescoes encrusted with gemstones: lapis lazuli, red cornelian, onyx and mother-of-pearl.

Unrest threatened the serenity of the temple in the 1980s, when twice the Indian army stormed the sanctuary in pursuit of Sikh militants. In retaliation, the Indian prime minister Indira Gandhi (1917–84) was assassinated by two Sikh members of her bodyguard. Thousands of Sikhs were killed in subsequent rioting.

Since then, the damage has been repaired and peace has returned to the Golden Temple. Every morning the sacred scripture is carried out before dawn on a gold and silver palanquin that has been sprinkled with rose water. As drums beat, the assembled worshippers shower rose petals on the procession, which travels across the causeway to the Abode of God. Inside the book is laid on cushions beneath a velvet canopy and the head priest begins reading a message for the day from the text. All through the day and into the evening texts are read and hymns from the *Adi Granth* are chanted to the accompaniment of flutes, drums and stringed instruments.

In a region that has witnessed such intense conflict, the Golden Temple – which welcomes, lodges and feeds members of all faiths – acts as a shining example of the potential for harmony that exists between human beings.

TIMELINE

1499 Guru Nanak begins teaching the new Sikh faith

1574 The fourth Guru, Ram Das, settles by the Amritsar pool

1581 The lake is paved on all four sides as the shrine becomes popular as a place of pilgrimage

*c.*1588–1601 The first temple is built. Muslim leader, Mian Mir of Lahore, is invited by the fifth guru to lay the foundation stone

1604 The first edition of the Sikh Holy Book – the *Guru Granth Sahib* – is placed in the temple

1740 The ruler of Amritsar desecrates the temple by using it as a dancing hall; he is killed by Mahtab Singh

1757 Ahmad Shah Durrani from Afghanistan destroys the temple

1799 Formation of the Sikh Kingdom

1803 The Maharaja Ranjit begins the refurbishment of the temple, much of which is carried out by skilled Muslim craftsmen

1830 Gold plating of the temple is carried out

1919 General Dyer initiates the Amritsar Massacre, in which 3000 people are killed or injured

1940 In London a Sikh wounded at the massacre assassinates Sir Michael O'Dwyer, who, as Lieutenant-Governor of the Punjab, approved Dyer's action

1984 'Operation Blue Star': 575 people die when the Indian army storms the temple

1986 In 'Operation Black Thunder II', Indian army commandos storm the temple; the Chief of the Indian Army is assassinated by Sikh militants

POTALA PALACE AND LUKHANG

In the centre of the Lhasa Valley in Tibet, the mighty and imposing Potala Palace is the most sacred of all sites for Tibetan Buddhists. Pilgrims from all over the country will walk for great distances to visit the temples of Lhasa, to perform prostrations before the Buddha statues there, and to pay homage to the shrines of the eight Dalai Lamas who are entombed within the palace.

AS A SYMBOL OF SPIRITUAL AUTHORITY AND ANCIENT TRADITION, few buildings can rival the Potala Palace, which stands on a rocky hill known as Marpa Ri or 'Red Mountain' in the centre of the Tibetan capital of Lhasa. Since the 17th century the Potala has been the holiest site in Tibetan Buddhism and the chief residence of the Dalai Lama, although the 14th Dalai Lama was obliged to flee the palace in 1959 after a failed uprising against the Chinese communists who invaded the country in 1950.

According to legend, there was a sacred cave on the Red Mountain that was used for meditation by the first emperor of a unified Tibet, Songtsen Gampo (*c.*605–649), who is credited with having introduced Buddhism to the country in the seventh century. After his successful military campaign against China, peace was forged between the two regions when he married a Chinese princess and built a fort on the hill to receive his bride.

Nearly a thousand years later, in 1645, at the site of the Red Fort, which had burnt to the ground during a war, the fifth Dalai Lama began construction on the Potala Palace, which took almost 43 years to complete. The complex of buildings, which rises in some places to 13 storeys, acted as the residence of the Dalai Lama and the seat of Tibetan government. The Dalai Lama lived in the White Palace, which also housed a seminary and printing press. The larger Red Palace, which contains many chapels

MONGOLIA

CHINA

TIBET

•Lhasa

POTALA PALACE AND LUKHANG

Lhasa Valley, Tibet

Before the Chinese invasion of 1950, thousands of monks lived, worked and prayed in the Potala Palace. Today, just a handful act as caretakers and await the return of the Dalai Lama.

> " *Peacocks from eastern India,*
> *Parrots from the depths of Kogbo,*
> *Though born in different countries,*
> *Come together at last in the holy city of Lhasa.* "
>
> SIXTH DALAI LAMA TSANGYANG GYATSO, 'THE OCEAN OF PURE MELODY'

TIMELINE

637 Emperor Songtsen Gampo builds the Red Fort to greet his bride, Princess Wen Cheng of the Tang Dynasty of China

1645 The construction of the present palace begins under the fifth Dalai Lama, Lozang Gyatso

1648 The Potrang Karpo (White Palace) is completed

1692 The Potrang Marpo (Red Palace) is completed

1700 The sixth Dalai Lama builds the Dzonggyab Lukhang, meaning literally 'Water Spirit Temple behind the Fort'

1791 The eighth Dalai Lama enlarges the temple

1801 The Eighth Dalai Lama and the Panchen Lama perform a 'Lu vase realization ritual' in propitiation of the deities at the temple to attract rain

1933 The tomb of the 13th Dalai Lama is built in the Red Palace. The giant stupa contains priceless jewels and one ton of solid gold

1950 Communist China invades Tibet

1959 The 14th Dalai Lama flees the palace after a failed uprising against the Chinese

1984 Major restoration of the Lukhang temple is carried out

1994 The Potala is recognized as a World Heritage Site

filled with treasures of Buddhist art, was used for state ceremonies and contains eight stupas which hold the bodies of previous Dalai Lamas.

Around 2 miles (3 km) to the west, Norbulingka Palace was built in the late 18th century for the Dalai Lama as a summer residence, but it is to the north, behind the Potala and the Red Mountain, that you must travel if you wish to discover the Dalai Lama's secret temple.

THE WHISPERED LINEAGE AND A HIDDEN JEWEL OF TIBETAN CIVILIZATION

As he was building the Potala, the fifth Dalai Lama was visited in meditation by a Lu – a female water spirit – who complained of the disturbance being caused to the ground behind the Red Mountain. Builders were excavating earth for the palace, and the oblong pit they had made was starting to fill with water from underground springs. The Dalai Lama promised to build a temple to the disturbed spirits at the site, but died before this could be done.

His successor, a poet and lover of both drink and women, became the only Dalai Lama to renounce his monkhood. In around 1700, on an island in the lake, he built the temple his predecessor had promised to the Lu – Dzonggyab Lukhang, the 'Water Spirit Temple behind the Fort'. According to legend, the sixth Dalai Lama used the pavilion he had built as a place to meet his lovers, and it was not until 1791 that the eighth Dalai Lama completed the four-storey mandala structure seen today.

On the top floor a secret room 6 metres (20 ft) square, reached by a ladder and trap-door, was reserved for the private meditations and retreats of the Dalai Lama. The walls were decorated with a series of extraordinary paintings that represent a 'whispered lineage' of secret teachings. The mural on the eastern wall depicts the 84 Mahasiddhas – Tantric masters who lived in India over a thousand years ago. The murals on the northern and western walls depict the path to

Behind the palace, on an island in an artificial lake, the Lukhang Temple contains a treasure of Tibetan art and religion.

enlightenment via the esoteric practices of the Tibetan Dzogchen tradition, which combines elements of Buddhism with the pre-Buddhist Bön tradition and Tantra. Inscriptions that accompany many of these images come from a 15th-century work entitled *Kunsang Gongdu, The Realization of Vast Beneficence*, which is a compendium of Dzogchen teachings revealed by the Terton, or 'treasure revealer', Pema Lingpa.

In the past the temple island was reached only by boat. Today members of the public can cross over a footbridge to the willow-fringed island and climb to the meditation room to contemplate the paintings, which the Dalai Lama describes as 'one of the hidden jewels of Tibetan civilization'.

As hallowed secrets of Tibetan spirituality become public knowledge, and the Chinese occupation continues to raise concerns over human rights violations, the landscape of the Tibetan plateau is changing before our eyes. Global warming is proceeding at double the world average here. The glaciers and permafrost are melting, and grassland is turning into desert as lakes and rivers run out of water.

Norbulingka Palace was once the Dalai Lama's summer residence. Its gardens are now a popular venue for theatre, dancing and festivals.

❝ *Wherever I live, I shall feel homesick for Tibet.
I often think I can still hear the wild cries of geese and cranes and the
beating of their wings as they fly over Lhasa in the clear cold moonlight.* **❞**

HEINRICH HARRER, *SEVEN YEARS IN TIBET* (1953)

MOUNT KAILASH

Like a great natural pyramid soaring to 6705 metres (22,000 feet) and covered with ice and snow, Kailash reflects the light of the sun and moon with such beauty that it is known in Tibetan as Kang Rinpoche – 'Jewel of the Snows'. Just as the Great Pyramid of Khufu is oriented with each side facing a cardinal direction, so the four faces of Kailash point to each of the four directions, as if ritually placed by the gods at the centre of the world.

APART FROM A SMALL STREAM OF CURIOUS AND INTREPID TOURISTS who have been able to visit the region since 1984, the only visitors to Mount Kailash in Tibet are the followers of four religions who make one of the most arduous pilgrimages in the world to this remote landscape.

For Hindus, Mount Kailash is Mount Meru, the abode of Shiva, the centre of the universe. For Buddhists, it is the home of the Buddha Demchok. For Jains, Kailash, or a mountain nearby, is 'Ashtapada', where the first of their 24 founding teachers gained enlightenment, and for the Bönpo, who follow the ancient pre-Buddhist Bön religion of Tibet, this land is the home of their founder.

Like a great pyramid, the four sides of Kailash face the cardinal directions, and four of the largest rivers in Asia begin within a 62-mile (100-km) radius of the mountain: the Indus, the Brahmaputra, the Sutlej and the Karnali, which leads to the Ganges.

Pilgrims traditionally make circuits, first of Lake Manasarovar, which lies south of Kailash, then of the mountain itself, sometimes 13 times, before travelling to the hot springs of Tirthapuri, sacred to Padmasambhava and his consort Yeshe Tsogyel.

MONGOLIA

CHINA

•Mount Kailash
TIBET

MOUNT KAILASH

Gangdisê Mountains, Tibet

For the pilgrim, Kailash represents the most pristine and spiritually powerful place on Earth. *The Way of the White Clouds* by Lama Anagarika Govinda (1898–1985), one of the greatest accounts of pilgrimage of the 20th century, reveals what a journey to the mountain means to such a traveller. In 1948, the German-born Lama and his Parsi wife Li Gotami, trekked into Tibet and made their pilgrimage to Kailash. In the book he later wrote about their journey – *The Way of the White Clouds* – Anagarika Govinda recounts that:

Hidden high in remote southwestern Tibet, just north of the border with Nepal, Mount Kailash is the holiest spot on Earth for Buddhists, Hindus, Jains and Bönpo.

There is no mountain like Himachal, for in it are Kailash and Mansarovar. As the dew is dried up by the morning sun, so are the sins of the world dried up at this sight of Himachal.

The *Ramayana*

'On our way to the sacred mountain Li Gotami and I felt ourselves merely as a link in the eternal chain of pilgrims who since time immemorial travelled the lonely and perilous paths of an untamed mountain world and the limitless spaces of the Tibetan highland'.

Anagarika Govinda and Li Gotami found there 'a glorious vision of the sacred land' and 'received an initiation of the most profound nature'.

A Pilgrimage of Liberation

To reach the Jewel of the Snows involves a long and arduous journey, braving freezing temperatures and altitude sickness. Even so, some Tibetan, Nepalese and Indian pilgrims walk from their homes to this isolated spot, and there are some who have made numerous pilgrimages.

The founder of the Bön religion, Tönpa Shenrab Miwoche, is said to have lived some 18,000 years ago in the region of Kailash, and some say he came to Earth from the mountain-top. Bönpo pilgrims walk anticlockwise along the 32-mile (56-km) route that encircles the mountain. Jains, Hindus and Buddhists make the journey clockwise. Tibetans used to living at such altitudes can make a full circuit of the mountain in a day, although a few choose to undertake the journey by prostration: lying flat on the ground, they then stand up and prostrate themselves again at the point reached by their outstretched hands. With this method a circuit can take up to a month.

For most people, though, the ritual circumambulation takes two or three days. The reward is said to be freedom from many of the bonds that accumulate during a lifetime – some say a circuit purifies you of the negative consequences of a lifetime's actions, and that 108 circuits enable you to achieve nirvana.

THE MAGICIANS' BATTLE AND THE LAKES OF THE SUN AND MOON

Climbing the mountain is forbidden – and no-one has dared commit this sacrilege. But there was a legendary battle between two magicians that did involve scaling the mountain.

At sunrise, the Tantric Buddhist Milarepa sat meditating while the champion of the Bön religion, Naro-Bönchung, soared up the mountainside upon his magic drum. At the last moment, Milarepa stood and rode the rays of the sun to the top of the mountain in an instant, claiming victory for the Buddhists. In his surprise, Bönchung fell from his drum, which dropped down the mountain, gouging a large crevice in its south face that can still be seen today.

A few miles to the south lie the lakes of Manasarovar and Rakshastal. The salt-water Rakshastal is considered the lake of demons and is not visited – a strange atmosphere haunts the place. The fresh water in Manasarovar is considered healing and pilgrims traditionally perform circuits around its shore before approaching Kailash, sometimes staying in one of the five monasteries around the lake.

Lama Anagarika Govinda explains that the crescent-shaped Rakshastal, reminiscent of the moon, represents the hidden forces of night, while Manasarovar, shaped like the sun, represents the forces of light. Both are necessary to life and act as reservoirs of spiritual force connected to the great 'temple' of Mount Kailash in the north.

Whether we journey to this sacred and pristine land physically, on the wings of our imagination, or in the depths of our soul, Kailash has the power to transform our lives by offering us an experience of paradise – of a landscape of the greatest radiance and clarity.

TIMELINE

1040 Birth of Milarepa, who undertook a legendary race to the summit with a Bön priest

1715 Jesuit missionaries Ippolito Desideri and Emanoel Freyre are the first Westerners to see Kailash

1812 The first Briton sees Kailash – William Moorcroft

1900 A Japanese monk, Ekai Kawagucji, disguises himself as a lama and makes a pilgrimage to the mountain

1907 Swedish explorer Sven Hedin may be the first Westerner to perform a pilgrimage around Kailash

1950 The Chinese occupation of Tibet begins, and travel is highly restricted

1984 Travel restrictions are lifted and pilgrims from India and abroad are able to visit the area

> 66 *Who can put into words the immensity of space? Who can put into words a landscape that breathes this immensity? – where vast blue lakes, set in emerald-green pastures and golden foothills, are seen against a distant range of snow mountains, in the centre of which rises the dazzling dome of Kailash, the 'Jewel of the Snows', as the Tibetans call the holy mountain.* 99

LAMA ANAGARIKA GOVINDA, *THE WAY OF THE WHITE CLOUDS* (1966)

245

INDEX

Page numbers in **bold** type indicate main references to the various topics; those in *italic* refer to illustrations

FURTHER RESOURCES

Many sacred sites are under pressure from the volume of visitors they now receive. You can help the sites, the environment and your pocket by only visiting them when you feel a deep urge to make a visit or pilgrimage. At other times try to 'think globally and act locally' by travelling to sites far away using books and the internet, your imagination and meditation, and visit instead a sacred site near to you. Consider creating a new sacred place where you live or with others in your community. Take a pilgrimage in your own landscape and support one of the organizations that protect sacred sites and their local inhabitants listed below. More information and practical suggestions on how you can work with these ideas can be found at www.sacredplaces.info

GENERAL BOOKS

Cousineau, Phil *The Art of Pilgrimage – The Seeker's Guide to Making Travel Sacred* (Conari, 1998)

Devereux, Paul, *Secrets of Ancient and Sacred Places* (Blandford, 1992)

Devereux, Paul *Places of Power: Measuring the Secret Energy of Ancient Sites* (Blandford, 1999)

Gray, Martin *Sacred Earth - Places of Peace and Power* (Sterling, 2007)

Harpur, James *The Atlas of Sacred Places – Meeting Points of Heaven and Earth* (BCA, 1994)

Harpur, James & Westwood, Jennifer, *The Traveller's Atlas of Sacred & Historical Places* (Apple, 2003)

Hind, Rebecca *Sacred Places - Sites of Spirituality & Faith* (Carlton, 2007)

James, Sean & O'Reilly, Tim, *The Road Within – True Stories of Transformation and the Soul* (Travelers' Tales, 2002)

Lehrman, Fredric *The Sacred Landscape* (Celestial Arts, 1988)

McLuhan, T.C. *Cathedrals of the Spirit – The Message of Sacred Places* (Thorsons, 1996)

Molyneaux, Brian Leigh *The Sacred Earth* (Macmillan, 1995)

Paine, Crispin *Sacred Places* (National Trust, 2004)

Swan, James A. *Sacred Places – How the Living Earth Seeks Our Friendship* (Bear & Co., 1990)

Wilson, Colin *The Atlas of Holy Places & Sacred Sites* (Dorling Kindersley, 1996)

York, Sarah *Pilgrim Heart – The Inner Journey Home* (Jossey-Bass, 2001)

GENERAL WEBSITES

witcombe.sbc.edu/sacredplaces/sacredplacesintro.html Art History Professor Christopher L. C. E. Witcombe's site on sacred places.

www.acoracle.org Promotes individual pilgrimages.

www.earth.google.com Sacred places from the air.

www.gatekeeper.org.uk - Explores personal and planetary healing through pilgrimage.

www.pauldevereux.co.uk The site of Paul Devereux, veteran researcher and author on sacred places.

www.sacredplaces.info The website for this book. Includes more material.

www.sacredsites.com Author of *Sacred Earth*, Martin Gray's comprehensive site.

www.sacred-destinations.com A guide to over a thousand sacred sites, holy places, religious buildings, religious artefacts, and pilgrimage destinations.

www.whc.unesco.org Information on the UNESCO World Heritage Sites.

www.world-heritage-tour.org - 360 degree photo tours of World Heritage sites.

WEBSITES OF ORGANIZATIONS THAT RESEARCH AND PROTECT SACRED PLACES

www.arcworld.org The Alliance of Religions & Conservation helps the major religions of the world develop their own environmental programmes, based on their own teachings, beliefs and practices. Their Sacred Land project helps to revive sacred sites and create new ones.

www.landmarksfoundation.org The Landmarks Foundation works to conserve sacred sites and landscapes around the world, and directs funding and technical expertise to local groups that cannot protect their sacred cultural heritage without assistance.

www.mountain.org The Mountain Institute's Sacred Mountains Program works globally to promote the protection of sacred sites around the world, and to include the spiritual and cultural significance of mountains in environmental and sustainable use policies.

www.sacredland.org Protecting the Earth's sacred places by deepening public understanding of sacred places, indigenous cultures and environmental justice.

www.sacred-sites.org Advocates the preservation of natural and built sacred places, believing that protecting sacred sites is key to preserving traditional cultures and time-honoured values of respecting the Earth.

www.wmf.org The World Monuments Fund acts like the World Wildlife Fund to protect endangered monuments, including those at sacred sites.

BOOKS AND WEBSITES RELATED TO THE SACRED PLACES FEATURED IN THIS BOOK

MOUNT KILIMANJARO

Ridgeway, Rick *The Shadow of Kilimanjaro* (Holt, 1999)

Ondaatje, Sir Christopher, Kilimanjaro: Genius in an African Dawn, *The Independent*, 2001 at: www.independent.co.uk/travel/africa/kilimanjaro-genius-in-an-african-dawn-616725.html

BANDIAGARA

Hind, Rebecca *Sacred Places - Sites of Spirituality & Faith* (Carlton 2007, pp.132-5)

THE SOURCE OF THE BLUE NILE

Bredin, Miles *The Pale Abyssinian: The Life of James Bruce* (Flamingo 2001)

LAKE FUNDUZI

http://thulamela.limpopo.gov.za/welcome/introduction/history.htm

The Initiation Cycle: Vhusha, Tshikanda, and Domba:

http://www.era.anthropology.ac.uk/Era_Resources/Era/
VendaGirls/Introduction/I_GIS_Text.html

THE PYRAMIDS AND THE SPHINX
Lehner, Mark *The Complete Pyramids: Solving the Ancient
Mysteries* (Thames & Hudson, 2008)

PIR-E-SABZ
www.sacredsites.com/middle_east/iran/
zoroastrian.htm

THE CHURCH OF THE HOLY SEPULCHRE
Biddle, Martin *et al. The Church of the Holy Sepulchre* (Rizzoli,
2000)

DOME OF THE ROCK AND TEMPLE MOUNT
Andrews, Richard *Blood on the Mountain: A History of the Temple
Mount from the Ark to the Third Millennium* (Weidenfeld &
Nicholson, 1999)
Landay, J.M. *Dome Of The Rock; Three Faiths Of Jerusalem*
(Reader's Digest Books, 1972)

MECCA
Muhammad, Asad *Road to Mecca* (Fons Vitae, 2000)
www.themuslimwoman.com/myjourneytohajj/
tawafzumzum.htm

THE BAHÁ'Í SHRINES AT ACRE AND HAIFA
Ruhe, David *Door of Hope: The Bahá'í Faith in the Holy Land*
(George Ronald, 1983)
https://bahai.bwc.org/pilgrimage

THE TEMPLES OF MALTA
Zammit, T. *The Prehistoric Temples of Malta and Gozo*
(Karl Mayrhofer, 1997)
web.infinito.it/utenti/m/malta_mega_temples

THE ORACLE AT DELPHI
Fontenrose, Joseph *The Delphic Oracle* (Berkeley: University of
California Press, 1978)
www.delphic-oracle.info

PERPERIKON
Ovcharov, Prof. Nikolay *Perperikon A Civilization of the Rock
People* (Borina 2003)
www.perperikon.bg

THE TAROT GARDEN
Restany, Pierre, Niki De Saint Phalle *The Tarot Garden*
(Charta 1998)
www.nikidesaintphalle.com

THE TEMPLES OF HUMANKIND
Buffagni, Sylvia *Damanhur: Temples of Humankind*
(Cosm Press/North Atlantic Books, 2006)
www.thetemples.org

EL CAMINO DE SANTIAGO (THE WAY OF ST JAMES)
Coelho, Paulo *The Pilgrimage* (Thorsons, 1999)
Sewell, Brian, The Naked Pilgrim – Road to Santiago, DVD,
Wag TV 2004

CHAUVET CAVE
Clottes, Jean *Return to Chauvet Cave: Excavating the Birthplace of
Art - The First Full Report* (Thames & Hudson, 2003)
www.culture.gouv.fr/culture/arcnat/chauvet/fr/
www.bradshawfoundation.com/chauvet/index.php

THE GULF OF MORBIHAN
Mohen, Jean-Pierre *The World of Megaliths* (Cassell 1989)
www.ecm.culture.gouv.fr/culture/arcnat/megalithes/en/
index_en.html

CHARTRES CATHEDRAL
Markale, Jean *Cathedral of the Black Madonna: The Druids and
the Mysteries of Chartres* (Inner Traditions Bear and Company,
2005)
www.sacred-destinations.com/france/chartres-cathedral.htm

RENNES LE CHÂTEAU
Putnam, Bill & Wood, John Edwin *The Treasure of Rennes-Le-
Château: A Mystery Solved* (The History Press, 2005)
R.F.Dietrich 'The Rennes le Chateau Theme Park' at
http://chuma.cas.usf.edu/~dietrich/rennes-summary.html

THE EXTERNSTEINE
Coster, Will & Spicer, Andrew (eds) *Sacred Space in Early
Modern Europe* (Cambridge University Press, 2005)
Pepper, Elizabeth, & Wilcock, John *Magical and Mystical Sites:
Europe and the British Isles* (Phanes, 1992)

STONEHENGE
Chippindale, Christopher *Stonehenge Complete* (Thames &
Hudson, 1994)
Worthington, Andy *Stonehenge – Celebration & Subversion*
(Alternative Albion 2004)

CERNE ABBAS GIANT
Newman, Paul *The Lost Gods of Albion – The Chalk Hill-figures of
Britain* (Sutton, 1997)
www.stone-circles.org.uk/stone/cerne.htm

GLASTONBURY
Howard-Gordon, Frances *Glastonbury – Maker of Myths*
(Gothic Image, 1982)
www.chalicewell.org.uk

NEWGRANGE
Stout, Geraldine *Newgrange and the Bend of the Boyne*
(Cork University Press, 2003)
www.philipcoppens.com/newgrange.html

IONA
Bardsley, Warren *Against the Tide, The Story of Adomnán of Iona*
(Wild Goose, 2007)
www.isle-of-iona.com

WALDEN POND
Robinson, David M. *Natural Life – Thoreau's Worldly
Transcendentalism* (Cornell University Press 2004)
www.thoreausociety.org and www.walden.org

DENALI
Sherwonit, Bill.(ed.) *Denali: A Literary Anthology* (The

Mountaineers Books, 2001)
www.nps.gov/dena/details.htm

MATO PAHA (BEAR BUTTE)
Gulliford, Andrew *Sacred Objects and Sacred Places: Preserving Tribal Traditions*, (University Press of Colorado, 2000)
www.defendbearbutte.org

YOSEMITE
Neill, William & Palmer, Tim *Yosemite: The Promise of Wildness* (Yosemite Association 1996)
www.yosemite.org

CHACO CANYON
www.traditionsofthesun.org
www.solsticeproject.org

PALENQUE
Freidel, David, & Schele, Linda *A Forest of Kings: The Untold Story of the Ancient Maya* (Harper Perennial, 1992)

WIRIKUTA
Fikes, Jay Courtney *Carlos Castaneda, Academic Opportunism and the Psychedelic Sixties* (Millennia Press 1993)
www.arcworld.org/news.asp?pageID=141

SIERRA NEVADA DE SANTA MARTA
Ereira, Alan *The Heart of the World* (Jonathan Cape 1990)
Ereira, Alan *The Elder Brothers* (Vintage 1993)
www.nationalgeographic.com - search for Kogi
The Tairona Heritage Trust at www.taironatrust.org

MACHU PICCHU
Cumes, Carol *Journey to Machu Picchu: Spiritual Wisdom from the Andes* (Llewellyn Publications 1999)
www.sacredland.org/world_sites_pages/M_Picchu.html
www.mp360.com

SILLUSTANI
Bandelier, Adolph *The Aboriginal Ruins at Sillustani, Peru* (American Anthropologist, 1905)

RAPA NUI
Fischer, Steven Roger *Island at the End of the World - The Turbulent History of Easter Island* (Reaktion Books, 2006)
Diamond, Jared *Collapse – How Societies Choose to Fail or Survive* (Penguin 2006)
www.birdmancult.com

HALEAKALA AND KAHO'OLAWE
Morrell, Rima *The Sacred Power of Huna: Spirituality and Shamanism in Hawaii* (Inner Traditions, 2005)
www.kahoolawe.org

TONGARIRO AND TAUPO
Potton, Craig *Tongariro: A Sacred Gift* (Lansdowne Press, 1987)
www.sacredland.org/world_sites_pages/Tongariro.html
www.tauharacentre.org.nz

ULURU AND KATA TJUTA
Breeden, Stanley *Uluru: Looking After Uluru-Kata Tjuta – The Anangu Way* (Simon and Schuster, 1995)
www.dreamtime.net.au

MOUNT FUJI
Schattschneider, Ellen *Immortal Wishes: Labor and Transcendence on a Japanese Sacred Mountain* (Duke University Press, 2003)

LUANG PRABANG
Heywood, Denise *Ancient Luang Prabang* (River Books, 2006)
Berger, Hans Geor, *Het Bun Dai Bun: Laos - Sacred Rituals of Luang Prabang* (Westzone Publishing, 2000)
360 degree photo tour of the city at www.world-heritage-tour.org/asia/la/luangPrabang/map.html

ANGKOR
Mannikka, Eleanor *Angkor Wat: Time, Space, and Kingship* (University of Hawaii Press, 1996)
www.smithsonianmag.com/travel/angkor.html

THE SACRED MOUNTAINS OF CHINA
Naquin, Susan & Chun-fang Yu *Pilgrims and Sacred Sites in China* (University of California Press, Berkeley, 1992)
www.arcworld.org

THE GANGES
Nicholson, Jon *Ganges* (BBC Books, 2007)
Gods, Gurus and the Ganges by Karl Grobl at www.karlgrobl.com/km/index.htm
www.africanwater.org/ganges.htm

THE ELLORA CAVES
Boner, Alice *Principles of Composition in Hindu Sculpture* (South Asia Books, 1990)
www.world-mysteries.com/mpl_11.htm
www.archaeology.org/0705/abstracts/cave.html

BODH GAYA
Trevithick, Alan *Revival of Buddhist Pilgrimage at Bodh Gaya, 1811-1949* (Motilal, 2007)
www.bodhgayanews.net

SHATRUNJAYA
Gray, Martin *Sacred Earth* (Sterling 2007 pp.149-151)
Singhvi, L. M. *Jain Temples in India and Around the World* (Himalayan Publishers, 2003)
www.herenow4u.de

THE GOLDEN TEMPLE AT AMRITSAR
Harpur, James *The Atlas of Sacred Places* (BCA, 1994)
www.sikhiwiki.org

POTALA PALACE AND LUKHANG
Baker, Ian A., Tenzin Gyatso & Thomas Laird *The Dalai Lama's Secret Temple: Tantric Wall Paintings from Tibet* (Thames & Hudson, 2000)
The Tibetan and Himalayan Digital Library at www.thdl.org
www.dalailama.com

MOUNT KAILASH
Huber, Toni *The Cult of Pure Crystal Mountain: Popular Pilgrimage and Visionary Landscape in Southeast Tibet* (Oxford University Press, 1999)
Lama Anagarika Govinda *The Way of the White Clouds* (Shambhala, 1988)
www.drsethufoundation.org/page20.html

PICTURE CREDITS

Author's Acknowledgements

This book is dedicated with love to Joshie, James, Joey, Jemma, and Timothy

With grateful thanks for the valuable comments and support of Tony Morris, Danny Gill, Roger Webster, Ziauddin Sardar, Richard Heygate, Ronald Hutton, Esperide Ananas, Sarah Fuhro, Ed McGaa, Alan Ereira, Karen Ehrenfeldt, Bill Mistele, Rima Morrell, Pamela Meekings-Stewart, and Paul Hastie.

First published in Great Britain in 2008 by

Quercus
21 Bloomsbury Square
London
WC1A 2NS

A CIP catalogue record for this book is available from the British Library

Cloth case edition: ISBN-978 1 84724 421 5

Printed case edition: ISBN-978 1 84724 240 2

Printed and bound in China

10 9 8 7 6 5 4 3 2 1

Designed and edited by BCS Publishing Limited, Oxford.